Resurgence
in Jane Urquhart's Œuvre

P.I.E. Peter Lang

Bruxelles · Bern · Berlin · Frankfurt am Main · New York · Oxford · Wien

Canadian Studies

The series Canadian Studies examines the many facets of Canadian reality from a multidisciplinary perspective. Contributions from both the humanities and the social sciences are invited. The editor wel-comes manuscripts whose primary object is "Canada" in the widest possible sense of the term. The series therefore covers a variety of fields such as literature, history, sociology, politics, economics, geog-raphy, law, media, museology, etc. as well as comparative studies.

One of the most innovative features of this series is its focus on the latest research conducted outside Canada. It therefore illuminates vari-ous aspects of the country in a new and significant manner and encour-ages a constant and innovative dialogue between Canadian scholars and the community of Canadian studies specialists world-wide.

Series editor: **Serge JAUMAIN**
Centre d'études nord-américaines
Université libre de Bruxelles (Belgium)

Héliane DAZIRON-VENTURA & Marta DVOŘÁK (eds.)

Resurgence
in Jane Urquhart's Œuvre

Canadian Studies

n° 21

This volume was inspired by the 48th Conference of Professors of English at the University of Orléans (May 16-18, 2008).

© P.I.E. PETER LANG s.a.
Éditions scientifiques internationales
Brussels, 2010
1 avenue Maurice, B-1050 Bruxelles, Belgique
www.peterlang.com ; info@peterlang.com
Printed in Germany

ISSN 1781-3867
ISBN 978-90-5201-634-4
D/2010/5678/43

Library of Congress Cataloging-in-Publication Data
Resurgence in Jane Urquhart's oeuvre / Héliane Daziron-Ventura & Marta Dvořák (eds.).
p. cm. — (Canadian studies ; no. 21) «This volume was inspired by the 48th Conference of Professors of English at the University of Orléans (May 16-18, 2008).» Includes bibliographical references. Includes contributions mainly in English and one in French. ISBN 978-90-5201-634-4
1. Urquhart, Jane—Criticism and interpretation. 2. Return in literature. 3. Landscapes in literature. 4. Place (Philosophy) in literature. 5. Memory in literature. 6. Continuity in literature. 7. Setting (Literature) I. Ventura, Héliane. II. Dvorak, Marta. III. Conference of Professors of English (48th : 2008 : Université d'Orléans) IV. Title: Jane Urquhart's oeuvre.
PR9199.3.U7Z86 2010   813'.54—dc22   2010026792

CIP also available from the British Library, GB

"Die Deutsche Nationalbibliothek" lists this publication in the "Deutsche Nationalbibliografie"; detailed bibliographic data is available on the Internet at <http://dnb.d-nb.de>.

Contents

Acknowledgments

The editors would like to thank the authors for their contribution to this volume and the following institutions and learned societies for their kind support:

- Société des Anglicistes de l'Enseignement Supérieur
- Société d'Études des Pays du Commonwealth
- Jawaharlal Nehru Institute of Advanced Study, New Delhi (for the support provided to M. Dvořák as Visiting Fellow during the editing process, 2009-10)
- Université d'Orléans
- Équipe d'Accueil « Meta »
- Conseil Scientifique de l'Université d'Orléans
- Faculté des Lettres Langues et Sciences Humaines de l'Université d'Orléans
- Ville d'Orléans
- Conseil régional : Région Centre
- Conseil général du Loiret

We are especially indebted to Jane and Tony Urquhart.

INTRODUCTION

Resurgence

Héliane DAZIRON-VENTURA & Marta DVOŘÁK

This collection of essays on Jane Urquhart's prose and poetry, which opens with a previously unpublished address by Urquhart herself, was inspired by a conference entitled "Resurgence," held on 16-18 May 2008, in France, at the University of Orléans. It provided the conceptual framework for the investigation of Urquhart's works by French academics, before it was supplemented with a selection of international contributions, mainly from Canada and Spain.

The conference was the 48th annual conference of the Association of University Professors of English and Jane Urquhart was the invited key speaker. The theme of resurgence upon which it was based directly tied in with the special location of the university, where the Loiret River, a tributary of the Loire, resurges in a Floral Park. The significance of location was meant to enhance a process which is simultaneously a natural phenomenon and a cultural practice: the process of reappearance or return, and the various shapes and configurations it may assume. Co extensive with this process are the tensions between rupture and continuity, depth and surface, but also resistance and reinscription, latency and manifestation.

Literally speaking, the concept implies the possibility of being buried and of resurfacing. More metaphorically, it derives from polarities that are antithetic, if they are considered simultaneously, but which can be reconciled if they are contemplated successively. The spatial discontinuity that is evidenced in the phenomenon of resurgence cannot be dissociated from temporal discontinuity since resurgence is a process that hinges on loss and restitution. It is necessarily inscribed in a territory: it conjugates the themes of memory and oblivion, of the visible and the invisible, of suppression and persistence. It has affinities with the unsaid and the half-said, resting on the implicit and its subtle manifestations. It opens up infinite sources of virtualities, buried in a dynamic diachrony, in meandering speech acts, convoluted detours, and the dormant possibilities of language.

These possibilities are remarkably exemplified in Jane Urquhart's works and, strikingly enough, in her very name, so much so that it seems only appropriate to begin with the homonymy and homography of her married name. In the world of letters, Jane Urquhart has had an illustrious predecessor who happens to be her husband's ancestor: Urquhart of Cromarty (1611-1660), a Scottish writer who, in his spare time, most often in the Tower of London or at Windsor where he was incarcerated, produced books with such titles as *Trissotetras, Panto-chronochanon, Exkubalauron* and *Logopandecteison*. Sir Thomas's linguistic exuberance gave rise to "tremendous outpouring of words in catalogues, abusive epithets, and erudite technicalities," which, as demonstrated by Northrop Frye, are "the mainstay of satire in the age of Burton, Nashe, and Marston, and have also found their way into North American culture" through the tall talk of the Folklore boaster, the catalogues of Whitman, or the spouting forth in *Moby Dick* (Frye 236).

Unlike Urquhart of Cromarty, Jane Urquhart is less a satirist than a romanticist. She is very often introduced as a neo-Victorian writer, for she has often revised the canon, or recycled some of its latent structures in literary journeys that take the reader from Niagara Falls to Brontë country, from Ireland to the city of Pompeii, or from Lake Superior to Vimy Ridge and back to Lake Ontario.

In the opening Address of this volume, Jane Urquhart sets the foundation for engaging with resurgence in her work, by concentrating on the significance of landscape. Starting with the Flemish painter Joachim Patinir (*c.* 1485-1524) and his world-landscapes in which the figure of Saint Jerome seems subordinated to the vastness of his surroundings, she moves on to the landscape where she was born in northern, northern, Ontario, some two hundred miles north west of the top of Lake Superior and to the other landscape which is meaningful in her childhood: rural Northumberland and Prince Edward country. She also provides us with a view of the other two landscapes that have acquired a special significance for her: that of a Burgundy village where she lived for a year and that of a remote Ghaeltacht (Irish speaking) region in the west of Ireland where, for some years, she has owned a small cottage.

By telling us that "[W]ithout a place you do not have a story. Sometimes you do not even have feeling," Jane Urquhart provides us with an aesthetic manifesto which is also a deeply humanistic way of envisaging landscape and its resurgence in writing. This pronouncement about the significance of human presence in landscape goes against the grain of such postcolonial criticism which emphasizes "ethnoscapes, technoscapes, finanscapes, mediascapes and ideoscapes" (Appadurai). It risks being taken for a Eurocentric, conservative, even reactionary attachment to forms of continuity. Such a hasty reading would fail to recognize the diverse manifestations of rupture from tradition and the deeply anti-imperialist stand that are entailed in Jane Urquhart's prose and poetry. The inhabited landscapes that resurge in her writing constitute a major break from male visual configurations proposed by the Group of Seven in the 1920s. They also signal a rupture from more recent visual aesthetics such as Richard Long's empty landscapes, or Michael Snow's relentless record of a piece of wilderness in a three-hour film, *La Région Centrale*, which takes place in north-eastern Canada, and which Malcolm Andrews analyses in the conclusion to his essay on *Landscape and Western Art* (Andrews 223).

Urquhart's romantic, humanistic aesthetics, her significant recourse to the visual in prose and poetry, testify to her resistance to and reactivation of symbolic forms, which render possible a comparison with a 19th century female writer, George Sand, who is particularly noted for her visual allegories. A very famous one, which deserves to be quoted *in extenso*, is ekphrastically inserted in the opening page of *La Mare au Diable/The Devil's Pool*, when the authorial voice addresses the reader directly to define the processes of her fiction. Sand invokes and describes a woodcut by Holbein:

> The engraving represents a ploughman driving his plough through a field. A vast expanse of country stretches away in the distance, with some poor cabins here and there; the sun is setting behind the hill. It is the close of a hard day's work. The peasant is a short, thick-set man, old, and clothed in rags. The four horses that he urges forward are thin and gaunt; the ploughshare is buried in rough, unyielding soil. A single figure is joyous and alert in that scene of sweat and toil. It is a fantastic personage, a skeleton armed with a whip, who runs in the furrow beside the terrified horses and belabours them, thus serving the old husbandman as ploughboy. This spectre, which Holbein has introduced allegorically in the succession of philosophical and religious subjects, at once lugubrious and burlesque, entitled the *Dance of Death*, is Death itself. (Sand, "The Author to the Reader")

The ploughman tilling a stony and ungrateful soil, and goaded by the skeleton of Death is an emblematic figure of the *roman du terroir* (or novel of the land) in early Canadian literature, which Jane Urquhart, a graduate in English and Art History, has revised under many guises (the moor-edger, the painter, the stonecarver, the wanderer) in her strikingly visual prose and poetry.

This volume of critical essays revolving around the concept of resurgence has set out to map the modes of conservation, transformation, and invention of the literary, visual, and cultural expression which

Urquhart's singular voice has brought about on the Canadian but also international scene.

The volume comprises three parts extending from the analysis of her first published novel: *The Whirlpool* (1986), to the latest to date: *A Map of Glass* (2005), while including essays dedicated to her poetry: *False Shuffles* (1982), *Some Other Garden* (2000), to her short stories: *Storm Glass* (1987), and to *The Penguin Anthology of Canadian Short Stories* (2007) she edited. Special emphasis has been given to *A Map of Glass*, with the third chapter entirely dedicated to its specific or comparative examination, but the other five novels, notably, *The Whirlpool*, *Changing Heaven* (1990), *Away* (1993), *The Underpainter* (1997), *The Stonecarvers* (2001) have also garnered single or comparative critical attention from the present contributors. Thus, the volume provides a complete survey of her works (excluding only her biography of Lucy Maud Montgomery) at the point in time when the volume was in press.

In their study of the modalities of resurgence in Urquhart's prose and poetry, a significant number of contributors have emphasized the emergence of the intertext. Catherine Lanone and Claire Omhovère envisage the return of a romantic aesthetics in *The Whirlpool*, while George Letissier stresses the link with the Brontës in *Changing Heaven* and Pilar Cuder accounts for the romantic return of mutability and mourning in Urquhart's sixth novel.

On another plane, Marta Dvořák focuses on the return of the extra-textual and the metatextual in Urquhart's novelistic production, investigating in close textual readings which go on to privilege *The Stone Carvers*, the reconfigured correspondences the writer posits between continents and cultures, as she relocates and reinscribes axiologies and agencies. Ian Rae stresses the return of the intra-textual as well as the extra-textual, drawing connections between Urquhart's early poetry and her first novel as well as between Urquhart's and Margaret Avison's poetry.

Georgiana Colvile addresses the return of the repressed in *A Map of Glass* while Christine Lorre investigates how objects re-emerge to weave the texture of the past. Similarly, Neta Gordon engages with Urquhart's representations of the archival artist: the artist recovering "dispersed traces of the past." Barbara Bruce theorizes the link between the resurfacing of objects in collections and Canadian nationalism.

Marlene Goldman argues that *Away* provides readers with a very useful opportunity to explore the uncanny return and reactivation of the 19th century tensions between the Irish and British discourses of romantic nationalism that were carried across the ocean to the New World. Héliane Daziron-Ventura addresses another type of the uncanny based on the return of the visual and the vocal within the verbal: she hypothesizes the synaesthesic mode as a distinct stylistic feature in the works of Urquhart who makes us see a scream which emerges as an image in "Italian Postcards."

Karis Shearer's essay is a case study of the critical discourse surrounding the publication of *The Penguin Anthology of Canadian Short Stories*, edited by Urquhart. It examines the critical response to the anthology, identifying and questioning a series of problematic assumptions in the reception – namely that literary value is inherent and stable, rather than constructed, and that the literary and the popular are mutually exclusive.

Given the conceptual framework of this collection of essays which begins with an opening address by Urquhart herself, it seems only appropriate that the closing words should favour the resurgence of the author's voice. Thus, the conclusion takes the shape of a discussion with Jane Urquhart which took place during the conference in a special Urquhart session slotted within the framework of the New Literatures panel organized by Marta Dvořák and Christine Lorre. The discussion particularly engages with the persistence of facts in the creative process through which her novels are elaborated.

Taking resurgence as the informing principle of investigation, the volume as a whole focuses on the rewriting and reconstruction of the past, on the modalities of its resurfacing or of its erasure. It raises questions about the explicit or implicit ideological repercussions of such concealment and disclosure, such rupture and resilience. Through the prism of this concept, through surveys, close textual scrutiny and comparative analyses, the book explores Urquhart's discursive practices, the way they hinge on intertextuality or citation, at the same time as upon intratextuality or self-citation. It brings to the fore the extratextual and metatextual quality of her writing together with the transmediality, the transcoding or intersemioticity which characterize the interaction between literature and the visual arts in her fictional and poetic works.

As early as 1986 Geoff Hancock said of her writing that it high-lighted "that conflict between order and chaos, that split between the old world and the new that is in the Canadian psyche" (Hancock 23). The contributors to this volume have attempted to demonstrate that Urquhart's writing bridges the split between the old order and the new: rewriting the canon, neither in satirical nor reverential fashion, but through the recycling of latent structures which take us to Ireland, to France or Italy, her process of revision is transformative. It uses fiction to transform fiction, but it also uses reality to transform literature and literature to transform reality. As Clara, the narrator of the short story entitled "Italian Postcards" realizes in a revealing metalepsis, the boundaries between reality and art may be effaced:

And the colours in the postcards were real after all – they spill out from red walls into the vegetable displays on the street. (Urquhart 116)

From the whiteness of the Arctic to the ambiguous opacity of storm glass, through the red walls of Assisi or Pompeii, the uncanny array of Urquhart's resurgent colours makes us see "through the power of the written word" that there is a genuine mystery in art and a real place for wonder. It is the resurgence of such innermost forces, in the creative and critical landscapes of contemporaneity that the present collection aims at bringing forth.

References

ANDREWS, M. (1999), *Landscape and Western Art*, Oxford, Oxford University Press.

APPADURAI, A. (1996), *Modernity at large. Cultural Dimension of Globalisation*, Minneapolis, University of Minnesota Press.

FRYE, N. (1957), *Anatomy of Criticism*, Princeton, Princeton University Press.

HANCOCK, G. (1986), "An Interview with Jane Urquhart," *Canadian Fiction Magazine* 55: 23-40.

SAND, G. [1894] (2004), *La mare au diable*, Paris, Larousse. (1901), *The Devil's Pool*, Trans. George B. Ives, Philadelphia, George Barrie & Sons. Project Gutenberg Ebook 12816.

URQUHART, J. (1982), *False Shuffles*, Victoria, BC, Porcépic.

– (1986), *The Whirlpool*, Toronto, McClelland & Stewart.

– (1987), *Storm Glass*, Erin, The Porcupine's Quill.

– (1990), *Changing Heaven*, Toronto, McClelland & Stewart.

– (1993), *Away*, Toronto, McClelland & Stewart.

– (1997), *The Underpainter*, Toronto, McClelland & Stewart.

– (2000), *Some Other Garden*, Toronto, McClelland & Stewart.

– [2001] (2003), *The Stone Carvers*, Harmondsworth, Penguin.

– (2005), *A Map of Glass*, Toronto, McClelland & Stewart.

– (2007), "Introduction," *The Penguin Book of Canadian Short Stories*, J. Urquhart, Ed., Toronto, Penguin, ix-xv.

1

An Address

Jane URQUHART

If I were forced to select just one landscape from the entire history of art, that landscape might very likely be one of 15th century Flemish painter Joachim Patinir's "St Jeromes"; "The Penitence of Saint Jerome," also called "Saint Jerome in the Desert," or "Saint Jerome in a Landscape." Patinir's Saint Jeromes are always placed in landscapes, landscapes so rich in detail, so gorgeously filled with vibrant colour, and so spatially interesting – with rivers meandering off into the distance, and tiny hill towns gracing the tops of intriguing mountains – one might think that Saint Jerome need not be in the scene at all. But this is not at all the case because, although from a visual point of view any one of Patinir's landscapes is a ravishing painted tapestry, there is something else going on in the work, and that "something else" is the telling of a story. Arguably any figure in any landscape hints at the telling of a story, but the Patinir that I am thinking of, "Saint Jerome in a Landscape," let's say, tells many stories at the same time and on the same canvas. In one part of the painting, near a cave, we see Saint Jerome removing the thorn from the lion's paw. In another, near the river, the lion chases wolves away from sheep. In still another spot in the painting, the lion seems to be chatting with a gathering of people in front of the gate of a town miles and miles away. So there it is, almost everything I would want to say about multi-layered, interwoven plot lines and how they are connected to the perceived world, the "environment." Simply put, without the richly detailed landscape the stories would have no place to unfold. Alternatively, looked at from the perspective of making a work of art, without the stories, the landscape itself might never have existed.

As a child I was ferociously romantic about landscape. I was born in northern, northern, Ontario some two hundred miles north west of the top of Lake Superior and, as I have said many times since, northern, northern Ontario should never be confused with northern Ontario. Northern Ontario is where families utterly unlike my own had their summer cottages. Northern Ontario was Huntsville, Gravenhurst, North Bay, Barrie, towns my family drove through in order to get to our summer place which was situated at the eastern end of Lake Ontario. (We were the only people I knew about who actually went south in the summer.) Northern, northern Ontario had no summer cottages at the time; instead it was graced with a scattering of not very attractive mines and the settlements attached to them, interspersed with the odd lumber camp. The rest was pure wilderness, a blanket of similar fir trees, now and then a lake. Even the natural world was visually uninteresting, (with the exception of the gorgeous northern shore of Lake Superior,) mostly because of the flatness of the terrain and the monotony of the trees. Still, I was very attached to this landscape and very romantic about it. It has taken me a long time to understand why I felt this sentimental attachment but now I think I know. Not only was this my first world, the one I was born into and, as a result, the one I would imprint forever, but it was also a world I would leave behind at the age of five or six. It would become, therefore, a lost landscape, and there is nothing like loss to encourage romanticism. But there was something else.

Because my young parents had come into this territory at a time when there were no roads, no schools, no stores, they, and those who came with them were true pioneers inventing the physical and social order that would be in place by the time I, their last child, was born almost twenty years later. The stories connected to this period of development would be recounted for years afterwards around city dinner tables. The time that the whores at Coffee Annie's (so called because the Madame did not approve of drinking and therefore ran a dry house) were sitting outside on their porch with their feet on the railing and no underwear on and the RCMP, when alerted by the priest, agreed to keep the house "under strict surveillance." The time that my father, Nugget Nick Carter and my Godfather, the Irishman and prospector Danny Henry went out with a bottle of Jameson's whiskey to stake claims in winter. Not realizing – after several drinks – that they were travelling in a circle, they were enraged to discover by evidence of staked claims and footprints that "someone else" had already staked the territory they thought was theirs. The magnificent forest fires that all the men in the district were obliged to fight 24 hours a day, while in the middle of the lake, the women sat in row boats chatting and drinking beer from good china teacups. I could go on and on: my father and Godfather certainly did. Pipe Fitter Slim, Backwoods Bessie, Pump House Harry, Nugget Nick of the North. The characters came into being. The narratives followed suit. But without the place, without the head-frame of the mine, the bunk house for the unmarried miners, and the mysterious underworld labyrinth of the mine itself, without the log houses of the settlement, the dog teams, the bush planes coming and going, the forty below temperatures in the winter and the black flies in the summer, without the sea of trees stretching off in all directions from the shores of a not very distinguished small lake, neither the narratives nor the characters could have fully taken shape. This is what I learned at a very early age. Without a place you do not have a story. Sometimes you do not even have feeling.

There are the places that we lose; those that change and are lost while we remain, and those we walk away from. And, then, there are the places, not many anymore it is true, but there are still some that stay the same, and are lost to us only when we die. Concerning the latter, I am put in mind of the Nobel address given by the wonderful Portuguese writer Jose Saramago. Speaking of his childhood, he recalled the night time stories told to him by his grandfather while they both lay looking at stars shining through the branches of a fig tree in the garden of the family farmstead, and he remembered his grandmother as well, gazing at those same stars years after his grandfather's death. "At the time," he told the people gathered in Sweden to honour him;

> I thought, though my grandmother was a very wise woman, she couldn't rise to the heights grandfather could, a man who, lying under a fig tree having at his side Jose, his grandson, could set the universe in motion just with a couple of words. It was only many years after, when my grandfather had departed from the world and I was a grown man, I finally came to realize that my grandmother, after all, also believed in dreams. There could have been no other reason why, sitting one evening at the door of her cottage where she now lived alone, staring at the biggest and the smallest stars overhead, she said these words. "The world is so beautiful and it is such a pity that I have to die." She didn't say that she was afraid of dying, but that it was a pity to die, as if her hard life of unrelenting work was, in that almost final moment, receiving the grace of a supreme and final farewell, the consolation of a beauty revealed. She was sitting at the door of a house like none other that I can imagine in all the world, because in it lived people who could sleep with piglets as if they were their own children, people who were sorry to leave life just because the world was beautiful; and this Jeronimo, my grandfather, swineherd and story-teller, feeling death about to arrive and take him, went and said good-bye to the trees in the yard, one by one, embracing them and crying because he knew he would not see them again.

The critic, poet, and novelist John Berger also makes reference to this love of place, to this notion of being emplaced, in his laments for the disappearing European *paysannerie*, (or as we would put it in English, the peasantry, or the people of the land,). These particular people, he suggests, are beginning to disappear. They are becoming extinct after thousands of years of working on the land, thousands of years creating what we recognize as the European landscape. With them everything they are and everything they know will disappear as well, never to return. Berger has lived for years now in a French village in the

Alps, and his writing in "Into Their Labours" represents a kind of homage to the agricultural village people with whom he has lived and from whom he has learned so much. One of the things he has learned is that story is central to the experience of a long, multi-generational relationship with place.

"All villages tell stories," he comments in an early part of *Pig Earth*, a chapter called "An Explanation":

> Stories of the past, even the distant past. Once I was walking in the mountains with a friend of seventy. As we walked along the foot of a high cliff, he told me how a young girl had fallen to her death there, whilst haymaking in the alpage above. Was that before the war? I asked. In 1833, he said. And equally, stories of the very same day. Most of what happens during a day is recounted by somebody before the day ends.

About his companion Berger says,

> He remembered the date and the day of the week of every disaster. He remembered the month of every marriage of which he had a story to tell. He could trace the family relations of his protagonists back to their second cousins by marriage.

And attached to all of this would have been a place, a place with which the storyteller would have been so intimate that there would be scarcely a stone on the hillside that would not be connected, in some way or another, with narrative. Geographical intimacy, I think, is the essential component in the development of narrative, and by association, in the development of a collection of stories or of a novel. The world that Berger describes is one in which the protagonists and their forebears have lived all their lives and yet, we cannot help but note, that the writer describing this world is essentially a foreigner and a newcomer and would have to be, in some ways, always a stranger to it. And yet, none of the stories in *Pig Earth* could possibly have come to light, or to life, had Berger just been passing through on his way to somewhere else. It was necessary, I think, for him to become intimate with the terrain, in a visual as well as a social sense, before he could write about it. And, in reference to "just passing through," it is important to remember that even the picaresque moves at a slow and stately pace, and its narratives illuminate a closely observed landscape or series of landscapes, a closely observed world.

I, myself, have been fortunate in that two resonant landscapes illuminated the world of my childhood and filled that childhood with enough material for a lifetime of writing. The first was the northern terrain I have already described, and the second was rural Northumberland and Prince Edward country, home of my maternal and paternal extended families, respectively. What I remembered about the north, and what I was told about it while sitting at one of those city dinner tables, would be the driving force behind the writing of my novel *The Underpainter*. The bucolic agricultural world of southern Ontario's Northumberland County, home of my mother's Irish family, entered that novel as well, but it was more fully behind the writing of the novel *Away*, my own attempt to decipher how a family might be able to be attached to both the abandoned homeland (in this case Ireland) while, at the same time becoming emplaced in the new world. *A Map of Glass*, my most recent novel, is partly set in Prince Edward County and, though I am at the moment far too close to it to know for certain, I think it deals with what happens if one is emplaced for too long, on the one hand, or when one forgets one's place altogether on the other.

As an author, and as a human being, I have been doubly blessed in that I have been able to add to the landscapes of my childhood two further much loved places. In 1979, just at the time when I was beginning to dare to take myself seriously as a writer, my husband and I spent a full year in an agricultural hilltop village in the heart of Burgundy, one that, with the exception of the installation of electricity and plumbing, and the arrival of motorized vehicles, had not changed much over the course of several hundred years. There were no televisions in the village and the only telephone resided in the post office. There was an 18th century convent at one end of the village, and a monastery with a Carolingian crypt at the other, and three gates in the walls that surrounded the village; one from the 16th century, another from the seventeenth, and the third, and most impressive, was Romanesque. Each morning the village farmers drove herds of animals down into the valley to pasture, and each evening the farmers brought the same animals back up the hill, through the gate and inside the walls of the village to stone barns that were connected to their houses. Like Berger's *paysans*, these people loved to tell stories; stories that related to the daily life of the village, or stories from the past. I remember one old man pointing to a number carved into the stone of the gate and telling us that the English had made that mark the last time they were there. Like John Berger, I was confused by the reference. You mean the Second World War, I said. No, he replied, we did not see the English in our village then. I am speaking of the 14th century, the Hundred Years War. He looked out over the ravishingly beautiful valley. The meadows were dark with English soldiers, he told me, as if he had witnessed their approach and, in some ways, genetically, and through his intimate knowledge of both landscape and narrative, he had. I also recall that, shortly after our arrival in the village, I foolishly asked a common North American question of our nearest neighbours. When did your family come to this place? The bewildered expression on their faces gave me the answer. It had never occurred to them that their forbears had ever been anywhere but here.

This reminds me of something I recently read in Geoffrey Heinricks' *A Fool and Forty Acres*, a book that is about both wine making and the power of place. In it Heinricks makes reference to the French term *terroir*, a word that, as he says, is difficult to translate into English, one that is used by vintners to describe a wine that carries the taste of its native soil in its flavour. Looking up this term in my French/English dictionary I was delighted to discover that the French also use the word to describe language. The phrase *mots du terroir*, for example, means words with a rural flavour, and a *poète du terroir* refers to a poet of the land. My neighbours who were so puzzled by my question carried the taste of their native landscape in their blood in the same way that the flavour of that landscape's soil entered the grapes in their vineyard.

The second landscape that I have been privileged to come to know as an adult is that of a remote Ghaeltacht (Irish speaking) region in the west of Ireland where, for some years now, my husband and I have owned a small cottage. Here one is quite literally able to read the marks on the landscape, a landscape where place names are exactly that; the names of places – an unusual geological form, perhaps, a natural phenomenon, or a spot where something significant happened. With the exception of the stone walls, which are everywhere, the architectural structures in the area are so scattered, and so often in ruins, they remain unnamed, as if the certain knowledge of their transience made the naming of them not worth the trouble. Not so the land itself, however. And so it is that on the one two mile long road where our cottage is, there are four important named locations, locations that figure in local lore and appear in the folk songs of the area, and are fixed in the collective psyche to such an extent that they determine the postal address of anyone who lives near them. At the beginning of the road is Croissharta, the place where two tracks cross, a sacred spot in that a grotto has been built there to house a statue of the Virgin. The second, the one nearest to our cottage is Coshcummeragh and refers to the fact that access to the little Cummeragh River is easy there. The third, another half mile down the road, is called Cappanagrown meaning a height of land, a place from which one can look deep into the distance, and the last, Cloonaghlin means "meadow of the horses." Here, a long, long time ago, a herd of magical wild horses is said to have grazed. The post office is on another, lonely road nearby, and is situated at the end of a river valley that channels the gales sweeping in from the Atlantic. The place, therefore, is called Mastergeehy, or King of the Winds. After ten years I am still astonished by the fact that, in a terrain where there is neither village nor town for ten miles in any direction, a letter posted in

Dublin, addressed to Jane Urquhart, Coshcummeragh, Mastergeehy, County Kerry will arrive at my door a mere twenty four hours later. The postman who drives the little green truck is, of course, from a family who has been in the district for hundreds of years, and could, I suppose, as a result be called *un facteur du terroir*.

What is it about landscape that holds us? And why is it that when the landscapes that we love and are intimate with change, or when we are forced to abandon them, the resulting sense of loss is so pervasive and so powerful that it causes men to go to war or, as in the case of many indigenous people, our own native people included, results in entire races experiencing a loss of hope? These are extreme situations, collective tragedies caused by political forces and the arrogance of imperialism. But there are the smaller tragedies as well associated with loss of a known landscape. I am thinking now about the feelings of alienation experienced by a friend of mine when he went back to visit his family farm on the outskirts of Toronto only to discover that that farm, its barns and fields, even the creek he remembered playing near as a boy had vanished utterly, swallowed up by miles of industrial buildings, paved over, in effect. I am thinking also about the Anglo Irish writer Elizabeth Bowen returning to her family demesne, Bowen's Court, to find a sub division where once the Georgian House and its gardens had stood. I am also thinking about my Uncle Cliff, the one son who remained to work my grandfather's farm, feeling despondent, when upon retirement he sold the land where, as he said, all the horses he had loved were buried. I think of my Grandmother who, like Berger's companion, could point to a hill, or a pond, or a house within half a mile of where she lived and tell me such a profound story that I would never forget it, and who, when taken for a drive through the countryside late in her life, would experience such distress when an orchard or a barn or a meadow she had known as a younger woman was, for one reason or another no longer there. I think of my Grandfather, the rural school board trustee who, when the small country schoolhouses were, one by one, being closed, insisted that the desks, the books, the maps, the chalk on the ledge beneath the blackboard should remain in place because, as he told my mother, "they'll come to understand that they were wrong to abandon these schools, and they'll need all the supplies to be in place when the students come back." The sense of loss, I believe is related to a knowledge, perhaps unconscious, of a loss of narrative.

And yet, in some cases, riding alongside this sense of loss, comes the desire to recreate, to re-establish a landscape through the making of literature. I knew a very old man in Ireland during the last decade of his life. His name was Michael Kirby and he died just a few months ago at the age of ninety-nine after a life spent primarily as a fisherman, but also as a poet, a naturalist, and a painter in a place called Ballinskelligs on the most western tip of Ireland's Iveragh Peninsula. Like Saramago's grandfather, when Michael Kirby knew he was near the end of his life, he wanted to embrace all that remained and all that had vanished from the landscape he knew so intimately. He claimed he had three hundred and thirty-three different kinds of skies in his memory, skies that, as a fisherman, he had needed to be able to read for survival purposes. Near the end of his life he began to paint those skies on board, and to write about them in his books. He also began a series of farewell poems; one to his house, one to the ruined cluster of cottages known as Cill Rialaig out on Bolus Head, one to the boat in which he had fished all his life. At the age of 96 he began to write a book, (which was published when he was 98 by Lilliput Press) a book in which he lovingly recorded the details of all of the marine life, fish, birds, seals, plants, lichen, rocks, caves, he had become so intimate with over ten decades spent on and near the sea around the Iveragh peninsula. And in this book he also put down all the old myths associated with these creatures, as well as the various names they were called in Irish Gaelic.

The question I ask myself now that he is gone is twofold: Who would Michael Kirby have been without that landscape, that seascape? And what would that landscape, that seascape have been for me, and for many others, without Michael Kirby in it?

PART I

A ROMANTIC AESTHETICS

2

Mourning/Mocking Browning

The Resurgence of a Romantic Aesthetics
in Jane Urquhart's *The Whirlpool*

Catherine LANONE & Claire OMHOVÈRE

Université de Toulouse 2 & Université de Montpellier 3

In a special issue of *Cercles* devoted to the remanence of Romanticism in contemporary poetry, Joanny Moulin elaborates on the distinction between "high" Romanticism and the "downstream, post-romantic rumination" best exemplified in the later works of Tennyson and Browning (Moulin 3).[1] The affinity of Romanticism with water imagery is indeed so persuasive that figurative language frequently seeps into critical accounts, introducing some of its fluidity into the categories of literary history. Given the prominence of water in Jane Urquhart's *The Whirlpool*,[2] a work in which the Niagara River serves less as setting than as *primum mobile*, the notion of resurgence offers another suggestive analogy to apprehend the complex intertextual dynamics, the intermittent yet persistent process, through which the novel taps into the fund of British Romanticism. In a postcolonial context, however, issues of literary transmission are often fraught with more than an anxiety of influence. Since Edward Said's pioneering work in the late 1970s, links between Romanticism, the constitution of orientalism, and the cultural sway of British imperialism have been thoroughly analysed. So, when Jane Urquhart has a group of characters realize that they are "never going to find Wordsworth's daffodils [t]here" while gazing at a wall of "unvaried spruce, up to their hips in

---

[1] See T.S. Eliot's quip in his 1921 essay on "The Metaphysical Poets": "Keats and Shelley died, and Tennyson and Browning ruminated," (qtd in Moulin 8). In the same line of thought, Roger Gallet considers the label "post-romanticism" preferable to "Victorianism," the conflictual continuation implicit in the prefix "post-" being historically more accurate than the fresh start the latter term suggests (Gallet 21).

[2] Hitherto otherwise unspecified page references refer to *The Whirlpool*.

snow" (69), one has little trouble recognizing in the anecdote a rather customary dig at a legacy which, for many postcolonial writers, has thwarted the emergence of a Canadian sense of place.[3] In this respect, Marlene Goldman's article "Translating the Sublime" is typical of the initial response met by a novel primarily viewed as a reflection on the experience of postcolonial dislocation and the challenge of translating an imported aesthetics into local terms.

Yet Urquhart, who began her career as a poet, introduces a subtle shift as she negotiates cultural heritage; she only deals with the sublime, as it were, at one remove. In fact, not only does she refuse to actually depict the arch-famous Niagara Falls – or the spectacular but broken suspension bridge – but she chooses not to summon the authority of the flamboyant Romantic rebels, though her characters do quote Wordsworth and Shelley. Instead, the novel's main narrative is contained within the narrow compass of a prelude and an epilogue devoted to the last days of Robert Browning. Thus the novel opens in December 1889 in Venice, loops back in time to June 1889 in Canada, and returns to December and death in Venice, turning the frame into a fluid circle which holds the novel in its magnetic pull. The author's choice of Browning – a Victorian late-comer, little more than a follower by T.S. Eliot's standards – is an intriguing one.

The individual storylines combined in the novel's main section rarely stray from the third person. Except in the excerpts from Fleda's diary, the narrative does not lapse into the first person, and neither does it tend towards anything comparable with Browning's dramatic monologues. With each short chapter involving a change in focalization, *The Whirlpool* relies on a kaleidoscopic vision for its effect much more than on a plurality of voices. The novel's spatial unity is dislocated into several perspectives envisioning Niagara Falls as borderland, destination, home and, finally and most problematically, as landscape. The juxtaposition of diverging, sometimes incompatible, points of view is a well-known characteristic of the historiographical fiction of the 1980s, when Canadian postmodernists engaged in a rewriting of master-narratives that led to a twofold reassessment of the past and its relevance to the present. In *The Whirlpool*, however, Jane Urquhart's reworking of the romantic intertext is rather more ambivalent than the counter-discursive attacks of her postmodern contemporaries.

---

[3]   W. H. New notes that "the Caribbean antipathy to 'Daffodils' is practically endemic," and goes on to cite an impressive list of works going back to V. S. Naipaul's *Miguel Street* (1960) (New 88). Similar colonial resentment can be found in Canadian letters, from Isabella Valency Crawford's *Malcolm's Katie* (Bentley 178) to the long list of absences informing Robert Kroetsch's "Seed Catalogue."

The prelude's description of the squalid, putrid city where Browning wanders aimlessly, voices from his past intruding into his unravelling mind, is a case in point, suggesting the dialogic but problematic force of literary influences. It is only in the epilogue, with visions of Shelley's drowned body resurging into his consciousness, that the dying Browning finally grasps the impact of his predecessor's art over his own writing:

> And now Browning understood. It was Shelley's absence he had carried with him all these years until it had passed beyond his understanding. *Soft star.* Shelley's emotions so absent from the old poet's life, his work, leaving him unanswered, speaking through the mouths of others, until he had to turn away from Shelley altogether in anger and disgust. The drowned spirit had outdistanced him wherever he sought it. *Lone and sunny idleness of heaven.* The anger, the disgust, the evaporation. *Suntreader, soft star.* The formless form he never possessed and was never possessed by. (236)

Urquhart's recreation of the scene displaces Harold Bloom's agonistic model of literary influence into an anxiety of dereliction – not a reactive defence against predecessors but a creative response to abandonment, a searching for direction.[4] In this respect, it is significant that the legal acceptation *dereliction* should refer to "an accretion of dry land gained by the gradual receding of the sea or a by a river changing its course."[5] The term may therefore be applied to the geological history of the Niagara River and the subsequent formation of the whirlpool. As David McDougal, the novel's historian, informs his rapt audience:

> 'There used to be another river here, you see [...] then the ice age came along and filled it up with rocks and soil.'

> 'So there used to be a fork in the river here, then, am I right? And now some of the water still wants to go that route. But, of course, it can't because there is nowhere to go so it turns back on itself.' (103)

The coincidence between the novel's topography and the ornate literary frame in which it is set is so boldly artificial that it calls for critical attention. Carefully tracing the influence of Browning's poetry on Urquhart's novel would, of course, be perfectly valid for scholars interested in the remanence of 19th century poetry. In this case, the emphasis would be placed on the rhetoric of creation, and interpretation would be author-oriented. But for those concerned with the resurgence of a Romantic aesthetics, the investigation veers towards a poetics of

---

[4] Bloom's analysis of the emulation between Shelley and Browning, and more generally his theory of influence, are informed by a clearly Oedipal model: "Poetic strength comes only from a triumphant wrestling with the greatest of the dead, and from an even more triumphant solipsism" (Bloom 9).

[5] *The Collins Dictionary of the English Language*, 1986.

29

reception reorienting interpretation towards the reader. That is the reason why this paper will not address the figure of Browning in *The Whirlpool* in terms of stylistic emulation, but rather analyze its inscription as a way of articulating both a post-romantic and a post-colonial ethos.

Outside: A Contextual Frame

The eponymous whirlpool thus becomes a metaphor for intertextuality. For Browning specialist Bernard Brugière, Urquhart's recreation of Browning's end is entirely convincing, full of accurate, moving echoes[6] – but also, we might add, tongue-in-cheek echoes. For Browning's last days in Venice are indeed portrayed in decidedly bathetic terms: "How had it all happened? He had placed himself in the centre of some of the world's most exotic scenery and had then lived his life with the regularity of a copy clerk" (10-11). The same mildly ironic tone is sustained throughout the opening. Browning wearing a prosaic night-cap longs for Shelleyan impulse and sympathy.

A dreary, droning Italian duke in period costume forces the door to the old poet's memory in a scene which doubly alludes to Browning's invention of the dramatic monologue and to his four-volume masterpiece, *The Ring and the Book* (1868-1869), set in 17th century Italy (W 12). The depiction of the city is equally self-conscious in the numerous indications that point to the artificiality of the composition:

> Empty Gothic and Renaissance palaces floated on either side of him *like* soiled pink dreams. *Like* sunsets with dirty faces, he mused, and then, pleased with the phrase, he reached into his jacket for his notebook, ink pot and pen. [...] the light, too, harsh and metallic, not at all like the golden Venice of summer. There was something broken about all of it, torn. The sky, for instance, was *like* a damaged canvas. Pleased again by his own metaphorical thoughts, Browning considered reaching for the notebook. But the cold forced him to reject the idea before it had fully formed in his mind. (8, emphases added)

Even more than the contrived contrasts between "soiled" and "pink," "sunset" and "dirty," the recurring painterly similes make the structural function of the prelude rather explicit. Venice is seen as a mouldy monument to a heritage which, in Browning's own *fin de siècle*, already referred to a past splendour preserved for the enjoyment of rich and idle tourists.[7] The realistic view is troubled by its ironic diffraction into a set

---

[6] We are grateful for the insights about Browning's work which Bernard Brugière kindly gave us (private letter, 29 January 2008).

[7] Or course, both Urquhart and her readers necessarily read Browning's Venice through the additional filter of Thomas Mann's *Death in Venice* (1913).

of imperfect copies. It is not so much a city that is on display as an aesthetics which should create spontaneous delight but merely prompts postures of mimicry. Such an elaborately-wrought frame signals to the readers that they are being ushered into a field of representation informed by tensions between what is seen and ways of seeing it.

The prelude thus signals Urquhart's awareness of, and shift from, not simply Romantic but Victorian obsessive motifs. From Ophelia to mermaids, 19th century British literature and painting were haunted by hybrid figures of dangerous femininity, associating women with water in lethal fluidity. Urquhart chooses to provocatively replace the stereotype of the drowned female body, an icon of self-destructive fallen femininity, with a male drowned body, first Shelley's body which swims round the whirlpool of Browning's memory, in the eerily flooded, Titanic-like palaces of Venice – "He wavered for a few minutes near its crenellated peak before moving in a slow spiral along its edges to its base" (W 237) – then the beautiful but useless body of Patrick, the would-be Shelleyan poet and Canadian artist: "The young man was beautiful [...]. The drowning had hardly affected him" (232).

Patrick is a poet and authentic copy clerk from Ottawa, who came to his uncle's farm in Niagara County to recover from pneumonia. The reader is not told whether Patrick caught his chest infection looking for daffodils in snow banks. But the poet's obsession with landscape and his efforts to adjust the diction of the British Romantics to the geography of the Gatineau Hills recall similar endeavours in the production of the Confederation poets, for instance Charles G. D. Roberts or Archibald Lampman.[8] Although none of Patrick's poems is cited *verbatim*, we know from Major David McDougal that they feature a liberal quantity of pine trees, a staple of Confederation poetry (119). The Major admires Patrick's verse for its national sentiment, an allegiance he wishes he could stimulate in his wife, Fleda. But the young woman is still very much attached to the old country's tradition: "No English poet," she protests, "would spend a lot of time worrying about pine trees" (119). *She* does, however, during the pensive hours she spends at the desk her husband constructed on the acre where the couple's new house will soon be erected, on the plateau overlooking the

---

[8] "[Patrick] hated the cold, but clung to the concept of landscape and so he stubbornly persisted. With numb fingers he recorded his observations in his notebooks waiting sometimes months until he moulded them into poems. Some of them had been published in one small magazine or another south of the border, and finally in a slim collection he had paid for himself" (69). Mentioning the notebook and the numbing cold creates an explicit convergence between Patrick's attitude and Browning's in Venice. A good selection of Confederation poetry is available on the website of the University of Toronto Library <http:// rpo.library.utoronto.ca/poem/1191.html>.

whirlpool: "It is wonderful to sit there and read Browning ... feeling as close to him as if he were a friend about to drop in for tea," Fleda muses (35). The young woman's response to the local vegetation similarly jumbles places and distances in her aspiration to connect the acre with the Mediterranean settings the Romantic poets have taught her to value:

> I feel sometimes that my own special group of cedars is trying desperately to become cosmopolitan, to resemble their Italian cousin, the cyprus, and it makes me glad since I believe it to be unlikely that I would ever be fortunate enough to travel to that enchanted land. Perhaps I should speak to the Scotch pines about umbrella pines in hopes they might take the suggestion. The Haunted Poplars, on the other hand, look strange with their new leaves just beginning. They seem much less haunted at this stage and do not produce, yet, the curious sound of a long dead court lady's skirts moving across a parquet floor. (35)

Fleda's characterization, her determination to adapt her cultural baggage to her exotic circumstances and the incongruities that cannot fail to result, create a second convergence between frame and main narrative. Like Browning searching for the perfect destination in Asolo and Venice, she is engaged in the process of adapting to a place that will let her in. Adaptation suggests an organic process, a growing and shrinking to fit in, but also a willingness to be affected by one's surroundings, both of which require more malleability from the dweller than from the tourist whose integrity is rarely permanently challenged.

This may account for the ironic textual mirror effects. Fleda reads Browning's long poem *The Ring and the Book*, a title which connotes romance, but which actually tells the tale of the trial of a husband who murdered his wife for money. It is hard to understand why David puts his wife's exhilarating longing for lines of flight down to too much Browning, and no wonder that he should ascribe to Browning the angel with beating wings, an expression which, as Fleda points out, actually refers to Shelley. But romantic idealism is deceptive. Patrick, for instance, is lost in the Romantic fallacy; his whirlpool remains abstract, an obsession, a "vacuum," a "neutrality" (222). He loves the female figure in his landscape, but hates her voice, her flesh, her actuality: "I don't *want* to be this close, Fleda. I want the distance" (181). To borrow the terms used by Browning in his essay on Shelley, he is a "subjective" poet, all landscape, and not an "objective" poet, putting people in the foreground (Browning 448). The sublime merely means sexual sublimation. Denying the woman's flesh, Patrick's relationship to the whirlpool he wishes to swim and penetrate is ultimately colonial: "Why do you always have to conquer something because it's there," wonders Fleda (118). Browning's taste for the grotesque may therefore be more suitable to the *reality* of landscape, his irony may be a method which has to be transposed, appropriated, but which may well be more rewarding, in the end, than sublime subjectivity.

Inside: Intertext as a Haunting

Urquhart's text draws the reader's attention to echoes, especially in the dialogue between Patrick and Maud's autistic son, where they laugh and play and dwindle dialogue to gerunds, a sing-song of "talking," "walking," "stalking," "gawking," "shocking," "blocking," "knocking" (187-188), not quite a Deleuzian stutter, the becoming other of language, but a way of articulating the inarticulate, the resurgence of the flotsam and jetsam of lives and language, of experience and cultural inheritance, not as a significant whole, but as a whirlpool of sound. One might add to the list the implicit shift from "drowning" to "Browning" – a significant case of paronomasia, which corresponds to the partial breakthrough of characters like Fleda and Maud, as opposed to Patrick's suicidal quest.

Like Urquhart's Browning or Fleda, the character of Maud raises the question of intertext as a haunting. The return of echoes might lead the reader to expect spectral, or even Gothic resurgence, but just as she strays from Romantic intertextuality, Urquhart carefully and humorously distances herself from the Gothic. Maud's husband Charles is a Victorian entomologist with a vengeance, collecting spiders but also letting them roam freely in his own house, so that the upper story is a cave of webs (no wonder that Dickens's *Great Expectations* should stand on a shelf). The text is less spectral than gendered: Maud is a latter-day Lady-of-Shalott, trapped in a spider's web.[9] But when she dares kill a daddy-long-legs, she becomes pregnant, as if like a certain kind of female spider, she had managed to overcome her mate's domination.

Charles' death by disease forces Maud to become a female undertaker, to take the business of death into her own hands. Neither a visitor nor a newcomer, Maud Grady thus deals with permanence in ways that conjoin the literal with the figurative. She spends her two years of mourning attending to her customers' sorrows, taking orders for funerals, dressing the deceased before the wake and the burial. In addition, the town has entrusted the young widow with the care of the bodies that find their way across the Niagara rapids into the whirlpool after an accidental drowning or, more often than not, a suicide. Maud's

---

[9] Maud weaves the chronicle of death; she writes in her notebook and sorts out relics, much like the unknown woman who sewed the quilt depicting death and tombs, a quilt which Fleda sees in the museum (173). Her burial of angelic children, like dolls, also recalls the Victorian fascination for photographs of dead children (see for instance Julia Margaret Cameron's 1872 photograph, *Deathbed Study*).

ledger is the ultimate destination of the anonymous "floaters" whose physical description and material possessions the book ultimately records in entries that read like poems. The lists balance words and line-breaks in accounts that capture the stark appeal of the found object and the still life to which they are metonymically, though enigmatically, related (95).[10]

Thus Maud's life is ambivalent. Her husband's death empowers her, but she is also trapped in a whirlpool of passivity, chronicling and collecting the relics of the dead. She is caught in her widow's garb, the stiff armour which almost precludes walking and seeing ("It encased the female body, instead, in a suit of crumpled armour, tarnished to a dull black" [21-22]). The repetition of the adjective "black" – black parasol, underwear, stockings ribbons, bonnet, veil, stationery – hammers home the sense of constriction. Rain makes the colour black bleed onto the skin, writing the female body with almost indelible ink, turning skin into a parchment dedicated to mourning. Throughout the novel Maud scrapes her skin but cannot prevent the resurgence of blackish or greyish stains, merely "turning her upper torso from mottled black to spotty grey" (28). Maud's mourning is institutional rather than emotional – manuscripts show how Urquhart worked on the opening lines of the novel to emphasize the commercial and colonial function of a ritual imposed upon women, creating a powerful ternary rhythm through the repetition of the adjective "secret": "At Halstead in England, during the last half of the 19th century, employees at Courtauld Limited wove secret cloth on secret looms in secret factories" (21). Crape is unique, because it is so stiff and so secret, embalming the woman's body as if she should not be allowed to quite survive her husband. But it is also a tradition which is imposed upon women all over the Commonwealth, ensuring the wealth of British weavers: "the whole empire could have been wrapped; a depressing parcel with a black sheen" (21). The image, a dismal inversion of Christo's Land Art, turns England into a gigantic spider secretly weaving cloth in order to wrap the female body (and colonial land) in its gloomy net.

The representation of mourning, which stands in part for colonial domination, thus calls for fresh, healthy laughter, for liberation rather than nostalgia. And it is with some deviousness, the elegiac and the ironical blending into a disquieting combination, that the narrator intimates how the bereaved may recover from a fatal separation:

---

[10] Maud's character is clearly related to Tony Urquhart's grandmother, who inspired the section entitled "The Undertaker's Bride" in Jane Urquhart's early collection of poems, *False Shuffles* (1982).

After two or three months of widowhood and strange dreams, Maud decided to have an elaborate brooch made out of a lock of her husband's *hair*, his dead *hair*; an oval frame of gold would surround two *desolate hairy willows* which would, in turn, flank a *hairy tombstone* with his initials on it. All of this was to be placed under a bubble of thin glass; a sort of transparent barrier between that *tiny hairy world* of graves and weeping and the one that Maud walked around in everyday. A barrier, but one that was easy enough to see through nonetheless. (23, emphases added)

The shading of mourning into mocking results from the distance the narrator introduces between the facts and their account. Within the novel's diegesis, Maud's brooch indexes the penetration of the Victorian taste for hair jewellery into the far reaches of the Empire. But the realism of the description is undermined by the word "hair" that ceases to be descriptive with its first recurrence, and becomes decidedly grotesque in its adjectival combination with various emotions and objects. In terms of reception, the artefact is likely to arouse mixed feelings. At once hilarious – in its vague semblance to Poussin's *Et in Arcadia Ego*[11] – and equally repulsive – in its insistently material corporeality – Maud's spidery brooch leaves the reader rather uncertain as to how to value the loss it symbolizes. Such ironic reverberations entice the reader to look into the metafictional recesses of the literal anecdote. Beyond its referential function as part of a widow's mourning garb, the jewel may well point to a *mise-en-abyme* of the compositional devices through which containment and mastery over the remains of the dead may be achieved.

Aside: Mimicry

Straying from the "ironic compromise" Homi Bhabha calls "mimicry" (Bhabha 86), Urquhart drastically chooses to cut and warp her material. The replica inside the glass bubble is perhaps the most complete and self-contained landscape to be found in *The Whirlpool*. Everywhere else, the narrator's cropping of the visual field draws attention to the limits constraining the characters' vision. Just like the American factories across the river, the Falls are confined to the periphery of narrative. They are alluded to through incidental comments on the "garish tourist attractions" surrounding their booming fame (46, but also 108, 164, 195, 221). As early as the first chapter, their magnitude is drastically scaled down in the depiction of "a very young

---

[11] Admittedly, there are no willows in Poussin's masterpiece, which additionally counts a group of three shepherds. But with its two trees framing an inscribed tombstone, Maud's brooch mimics the basic composition of the painter's comment on the transience of all things human.

couple [...] giggling over a photograph of themselves in front of a very bad reproduction of the waterfall" (31) The cheap print stands in implicit contrast with the life-size landscape that fascinates the characters. The Niagara whirlpool lies at the bottom of the river gorge just below "Whirlpool Heights," the property the McDougals purchased on the plateau. Although nothing in the novel's topography would forbid the frontal prospect or commanding view one usually associates with picturesque sceneries, very little is done to satisfy the reader's expectations. Instead, the narrator insistently points out the presence of circumstances hindering the characters' visual perception. What with the weepers that hang from her bonnet and are blown across her opaque veil, Maud endures a "partial blindness" during most of her mourning (28). As for Fleda, indications abound – a cloud of cigar smoke (32), exuberant spring foliage (34, 144), or even the "mesh of netting" (129) covering her tent's window – suggesting that, no matter how closely she wishes to approach the landscape, impalpable but persistent barriers keep her away from it.

The effect is reinforced through frequent references to the texts which screen external space even as they mediate its appreciation as landscape. Fleda seeks solace in her compulsive reading during the uneventful days she spends on the acre, waiting for her husband to return from his study. The character's emotional dependence on books evokes a form of colonial bovarysm manifest upon her first appearance in the novel:

> Under her arm, near her heart, she cradled a copy of Swinburne's *Poems and Ballads*, *The Ring and the Book* by Robert Browning, and Patmore's *Angel in the House*. She had brought the books along in order to read them in a suitable setting; a setting that she hoped was about to cause the spiritual marriage of romance and domesticity in her life. (30)

Although she strives to escape from her husband's wish to turn her into both the Angel in the House and a fetishist surrogate of Laura Secord, Fleda's choice of Whirlpool Heights for her afternoon reading is not a Deleuzian line of flight but reminiscent of the trick the Claude-glass performed for the art amateurs of the previous century.[12] In the present case, the contrivance through which aesthetic emotion is aroused is rather more elaborate because not one but several intertextual frames are imbricated in the distancing that turns indifferent space into a "suitable setting" (Roger 27). In this respect, Fleda's book selection points to the cultural *mise-en-abyme* which causes actual space to recede infinitely

---

[12] "A small, portable mirror backed with dark foil, it was named for the French painter who most perfectly harmonized classical architecture, leafy groves, and distant water. If the view in the mirror approximated to this Claudian ideal, it was judged sufficiently 'picturesque' to be appreciated or even drawn" (Schama 12).

through the successive framing that fashions a clump of cedars into a bucolic grove, a romantic bower and a post-Romantic shrine to Nature's feminine profusion. Cutting her hair in a gesture of defiance which merely feeds Patrick's fetishism, Fleda's double exposure to the proper texts and right setting – the romantic *élan* slowing into post-romantic pose stiffening into colonial conformity[13] – produces nothing but more of the same conventions. No sooner does Patrick chance upon the pastoral scene than he becomes infatuated with the composition itself. The predictable love affair between the nymph and the bird-watcher peters out when Fleda realizes that both the conventions of romance and the poet's expectations force her into a rather uncomfortable space: "She looked out at her acre now from behind *the walls of a bubble of glass* that had grown around her" (159, emphasis added). It is significant that identical terms should relate Fleda's confinement within convention to the miniature landscape of loss encapsulated inside Maud's brooch.[14] Although the two women live in the same location, they do not inhabit place in the same way. Nowhere is the contrast sharper than in their relation to the whirlpool.

As David McDougal pointedly remarks about his wife: "[W]hen I explain [the site's geology] to my wife she perceives it as a metaphor or some such thing. Talks about interrupted journeys. As if the river were Ulysses or something." For the focalizer Patrick, another idea of the woman begins to take shape:

> She was a dreamer, living in the open, perceiving whirlpools as metaphors. How easy the landscape seemed to be for her. Awake, she watched and lived inside it. Asleep she dreamed it. Perhaps the woman *was* the landscape. Patrick was attracted to this idea of her. He wanted to become a part of the impression. (103)

In McDougal's positivist view, his wife's partiality for metaphor is both endearing and slightly silly. But beyond the Major's condescension, the reference to Ulysses as the figure of displacement *par excellence* impresses on readers that as long as Fleda stays there, she cannot see the whirlpool for what it is on account of everything it stands for. The same holds for Patrick who, like Browning in Venice, is falling for an alluring image much more than for the woman it refers to. In either case, the imperfect metaphors – the river *qua* Ulysses or the woman *qua*

---

[13] Urquhart's views on the evolution of Romanticism towards an increasingly formal, almost rigid aesthetics during the Victorian period is implicit in the novel's epilogue when Browning slips into unconsciousness dreaming of a siren-like Shelley. Narratorial focus then abruptly shifts and stops on the gondola waiting to take the poet's remains to San Michele cemetery: "All that cool white marble in exchange for the shifting sands of Lerici" (237).

[14] The hair motif also connects them.

landscape – index a crisis in a poetic language which strives but fails to configure anew the romantic encounter between man and nature.[15]

Nowhere is this more visible than in descriptions of the whirlpool. The geological amphitheatre is primarily a site of representation where avatars of the romantic encounter circulate endlessly:

> And even though the June foliage had thickened in earnest, she could see it clearly: the giant whirlpool – a cumbersome, magnificent merry-go-round on which *a few large logs were seemingly permanent passengers*. The awkward, ceaseless motion of going nowhere, the peace of it seen from above. (32)

Echoing the noisy attractions upriver, the metaphor of the "merry-go-round" unfurls into a simile connecting the human with the non-human. Yet the conceit's festive connotations do not quite balance the disquieting overtones attached to the troping of nature into a machinery, the circular motion of the current being translated into an absurd, endless repetition. Metaphoric displacement introduces further slippage between semantic categories, encouraging the grotesque association of the senseless logs with inert bodies. The evocation unexpectedly becomes real when the river stunts resume their seasonal *danse macabre* with the rapids (48). The depiction of the mangled corpses is another occasion to test the shifting limit between the ghastly and the ludicrous. Far too demure to join in the carnival, Fleda refuses to go and "watch a man who killed animals kill himself inside an animal" (119). Yet a subtle mirth tinges the phrasing, the bouncing syntax mimicking through its redundancies the looping trajectory that takes the Mighty Moose, not towards the intensity of some kind of becoming-animal, as he'd hoped, but down the rapids, round the whirlpool and into the undertaker's "meat wagon" (47).

All the novel's characters, much like Fleda, live "with a whirlpool on [their] mind" (31, 174). As a result the fantasmatic Romantic communion with nature goes through a wide spectrum of generic modulations. The aesthetic covenants that regulate the valuation of geographical space as landscape lack firmness; their adequacy is constantly questioned through bathos, or undermined by the grotesque excesses that Niagara has never ceased to inspire in fiction as well as in real life. When Patrick drowns in an attempt to swim the whirlpool, what comes to the fore is not a Shelleyan fusion with the elements but a repetition of the regressive *topos* of death by landscape famously identified by Margaret Atwood, stressed by the way the line fishing the body is

---

[15] Considered in strictly stylistic terms, no conflagration of meaning occurs, as tenor and vehicle do not fuse but remain quite distinct.

hooked to his belt buckle, like an umbilical cord (226).[16] But Urquhart does not follow the Canadian formula to the letter. Her poet's body does not disappear but ultimately drifts to float along with Fleda's birch bark reproductions in the same (literary) current:

> Little white vessels departing from the shore, set adrift on a long tour of the whirlpool. Like people, just like people. A complete revolution would be a long, long life. Not many are able to go the distance. Those that do I am unsure of. Have they moved around the full circumference or have they doubled back somehow on an unknown current? [...] I have begun to mark my boats in some way, making each one different from the others. And I have begun to give them names, like real ships. "Adonais," "Dreamhouse," "Warrior," "Angel." [...] Then I launch my small craft from the shore and pick up Browning in order to read while I wait for them to return. (60)

Urquhart's choice of "Adonais" is a clear nod to the elegy Shelley wrote after Keats's death while the other names evoke other favourites of Fleda's, from Swinburne to Patmore. The launching therefore encourages the reader to reconsider the cultural ruptures that supposedly occurred with each fresh departure to the New World, the journey taking them along more unpredictable currents, causing more unforeseen forms of resurgence than the staunch supporters of Canadian nationalism were ready to acknowledge, either among the novel's characters, or in the literary climate that prevailed when *The Whirlpool* was first published. The old River Man puts Fleda's occupation in perspective when he thoughtfully considers: "But you never really lost anything in the whirlpool forever. Eventually it came back around again. All it took was time, patience and a new hook," (226) or, one feels tempted to add, a new book.[17]

Thus the whirlpool may be seen as a metatextual emblem of post-colonial literature, not flowing straight ahead but breaking conformity and continuity, circling around, with its "floaters," the floating signifiers of cultural inheritance, and seeking a way out, a new direction, its own direction sideways. Browning's musing, as he heads home at the end of the prelude, expresses postcolonial disorientation, and attempt to find its own way: "'All the way back across the city', he murmured, 'Where have you been, where have you been, where did you go?'" (18) The

---

16 Atwood analysed the significance of this motif in Canadian culture in *Survival* before elaborating several versions of it in her own fiction, particularly in "Death by Landscape."

17 Both *Away* and *The Underpainter* develop on a wider scale the reflection on the artialisation of landscape initiated in *The Whirlpool*, an aspect that receives further attention in "The Artialisation of Landscape in Jane Urquhart's *The Whirlpool*", an essay by Claire Omhovère forthcoming in *Crosstalk: Canadian and Global Imaginaries in Dialogue* (eds. Diana Brydon and Marta Dvořák).

ending of the novel puts an end to mourning, whether it be the ritual imposed upon women by colonial England or postcolonial cultural nostalgia. No longer enticed by landscape and poetry, Fleda simply walks away, offstage, standing on her own two feet, taking her Browning with her, leaving no note for her husband, ignoring the dead body of Patrick, whom she will never see and never mourn. Just as Maud had dragged her child out of his cave of silence, forcing him to face the sun by pushing his eyelids open, forcing him to speak – or scream – "sawn" (i.e. sun/son), she too is forced to undergo the Platonic process of leaving the realm of shadows and illusion to enter the painful but benevolent light of truth. In the end, the child destroys his mother's carefully preserved relics, by re-allocating a random place to each of them, according to a configuration he has mysteriously devised. He picks up all the objects of the dead men which she had carefully preserved and labelled, and redistributes them spontaneously. Instead of Kant's sublime – the infinite accumulation of relics referring both to the magnetic pull of the sublime attempt to transcend death by water and to its degraded correlation, Niagara Falls and the society of spectacle, what Jenny Iles calls "Thanatourism,"[18] the child points to mathematical infinity (a random accumulation of relics), so that things, whether they be buttons, watches, collars, teeth, rings or shoelaces, simply dwindle into what they really are, mere objects, nothing more. After being silenced, uttering a few words, parroting and repeating entire conversations (just as Browning in the prelude was haunted by Shelley to the point of total recall), the weird child demystifies rituals of repetition and breaks the logic of mourning. He becomes creative in his own way, turning objects into exhilarating arrangements, still lifes.[19] In a way, like postcolonial literature, he may have come of age, found self-expression. When Patrick's corpse is brought in,[20] the child utters his epitaph, "man," "swim," but Maud, wearing a bright yellow, sunny dress, pulls him towards her, choosing life, not death. On this side of the Atlantic, far away from Browning's island of the dead, lies, not a Shelleyan Suntreader, not a boat coffin, but the postcolonial chrysalis.

Nota Bene: an earlier variant of this essay was published in *Commonwealth Essays and Studies*, 31.1, autumn 2008: 8-21.

---

[18] Jenny Iles in the context of First World War calls "thanatourism" a fascination with "the ever-present detritus of death" (Iles 236 & 242 respectively).

[19] The autistic child descends in a way from the Wordsworthian myth of the child as seer, like the Idiot Boy in *Lyrical Ballads*.

[20] His mistaken idealism also recalls Conrad's flawed idealist in *Lord Jim*, and Stein's advice to follow the dream *usque ad finem* and immerse oneself into the destructive element.

References

ATWOOD, M. (1972), *Survival: A Thematic Guide to Canadian Fiction*, Toronto, Anansi.

– (1991), "Death by Landscape," *Wilderness Tips*, Toronto, McClelland & Stewart, 109-129.

BENTLEY, D. M. R. (1992), *The Gay Grey Moose. Essays on the Ecologies and Mythologies of Canadian Poetry 1690-1990*, Ottawa, University of Ottawa Press.

BHABHA, H. (1994), *The Location of Culture*, London, New York, Routledge.

BLOOM, H. (1980), *A Map of Misreading*, New York, OUP.

BROWNING, R. (1979), *Robert Browning's Poetry*, Ed. J.F. LOUCKS, Norton Critical Edition, New York, Norton.

CONRAD, J. [1900] (1996), *Lord Jim*, Ed. T. C. MOSER, Norton Critical Edition, New York, Norton.

GALLET, R. (2005), "Romanticism and Post-romanticism: From Wordsworth to Pater," *Cercles* 12: 18-25.

GOLDMAN, M. (Autumn 1996), "Translating the Sublime: Jane Urqhuart's *The Whirlpool*," *Canadian Literature* 150: 23-42.

ILES, J. (2003), "Death, Leisure and Landscape: British Tourism to the Western Front," Eds. M. DORRIAN, and R. GILLIAN, *Deterritorialisations... Revisioning: Landscape and Politics*, London, Black Dog Publishing, 234-243.

KROETSCH, R. (1989), "*Seed Catalogue*," *Completed Field Notes: The Long Poems of Robert Kroetsch*, Toronto, McClelland & Stewart, 32-51.

MANN, T. (1989), *Death in Venice, and Seven Other Stories*, Trans. H.T. Lowe-Porter, New York, Vintage Books.

MOULIN, J. (2005), "Remanent Romanticism in Modern Poetry," *Cercles* 12: 1-13.

NEW, W. H. (2003), *Grandchild of Empire. About Irony, mainly in the Commonwealth*, Vancouver, BC, Ronsdale Press.

ROGER, A. (1997), *Court traité du paysage*, Paris, Gallimard.

SAID, E. [1978] (1991), *Orientalism*, Harmondsworth, Penguin.

SCHAMA, S. (1995), *Landscape and Memory*, London, HarperCollins.

URQUHART, J. (1982), *False Shuffles*, Victoria, BC, Porcépic.

– [1986] (1997), *The Whirlpool*, Toronto, McClelland & Stewart.

– (1993), *Away*, Toronto, McClelland & Stewart.

– (1997), *The Underpainter*, Toronto, McClelland & Stewart.

– [2001] (2003), *The Stone Carvers*, Harmondsworth, Penguin.

WORDSWORTH, W. and S.T. COLERIDGE [1798] (1991), *Lyrical Ballads*, New York, Routledge.

3

The Resurgence of Poetry
in Jane Urquhart's *The Whirlpool*

Ian RAE

University of Western Ontario

I was going to say that many of us began as poets. Margaret Atwood began as a poet [...]. Michael Ondaatje, Anne Michaels, Carol Shields began as poets. It has happened often enough: that should be paid attention to, in terms of our literature. (Urquhart, 2005: 32-3)

I owe Jane Urquhart an apology. I began *From Cohen to Carson: The Poet's Novel in Canada* with an evasion. The book opens with a quotation from a review of Urquhart's poetry collection *Some Other Garden* (2000), in which *Globe and Mail* reviewer Fraser Sutherland poses a question that I believe is crucial to understanding the develop-ment of Canadian fiction in the second half of the 20th century: "One unanswered question of Canadian literature, is why so many celebrated fiction writers begin and continue as poets" (D13). I responded to this question by demonstrating that Leonard Cohen, Michael Ondaatje, George Bowering, Daphne Marlatt, Anne Carson and Anne Michaels framed their early novels using motifs and formal devices developed in their lyric poetry and extended in their long poems. I emphasized that their non-linear narratives paired form to theme by investigating how fragmentary histories from diverse cultures interact. However, I did not devote a chapter to Urquhart's first novel, *The Whirlpool* (1986), although it certainly bears traces of Urquhart's earlier poetry; although it explores the intersection of British, American, and English Canadian cultures in 19th century Ontario; although Urquhart thanks Ondaatje as one of her manuscript readers (*Whirlpool* 239); although the book is dedicated to their mutual friend, the Canadian poet Stuart MacKinnon; and despite the fact that the poets Percy Bysshe Shelley and Robert Browning figure prominently in the narrative. My reasoning was that, unlike the poet-novelists cited above, Urquhart did not compose a first novel that is fragmentary in design and that overtly repudiates the conventions of 19th century realism. On the contrary, the often vertiginous effects produced by her novel about Niagara Falls result from the cleverly concealed way in which Urquhart smuggles the stylistic innovations of 20th century modernism into a narrative set in 1889.

At first glance, Urquhart's narrative technique in *The Whirlpool* seems firmly rooted in the dominant generic modes of the 19th century novel: realism and gothic romance. Her meticulous use of detail, emphasis on domesticity, and fairly straightforward chronology owe a debt to the realist tradition, while the images of death, mourning, nightmarish containment, and a "demon lover" borrow from late romanticism (Hancu 45) and gothic romance. However, Urquhart complicates this 19th century foundation by framing the Niagara narrative with scenes of Browning in Venice that convert aesthetic questions of poetic practice into life-or-death matters. By beginning with Browning, who writes on the cusp of modernism but is preoccupied by the legacy of romanticism, Urquhart embraces the poetic heritage of fiction, which realist authors in the 19th century sought to banish from the novel. Urquhart reminds Laura Ferri that, in terms of temporal scope, the history of poetic narrative surpasses that of prose narrative:

> It is a different form obviously, but I think that combination of poetry and narrative is not to be ignored. I mean, after all, the earliest narratives we know were presented to us in the form of poetry. I'm always amazed that people seem to think that fiction was invented in the 19th century in Britain, when we have Homer. What Homer was doing was telling a great story while using the most interesting language possible (2005: 33).

In fact, Urquhart tells Herb Wyile that during the early phases of composing *The Whirlpool* she avoided the generic heritage of the novel altogether:

> My first novel, *The Whirlpool*, was not something I consciously believed was a novel. I had been writing poetry, and I had been writing a little bit of short fiction, very short stories in sequence that had to do with my husband's family's past. I convinced myself that I wasn't writing a novel because it left me quite free to explore my husband's family's past without having to engage in the sort of self-censorship that comes into play when one is writing for publication (Urquhart, 2004: 59).

The final publication suggests that Urquhart embraced novelistic conventions at a later stage of composition, but this essay will bring into view the poetic heritage that roils just beneath the surface of Urquhart's prose. I will emphasize the importance of poetic form to her novel's design by 1) drawing connections between Urquhart's early poetry and her first novel; 2) demonstrating how the titular motif of *The Whirlpool* evokes the legacy of modernism, in particular Vorticism; and 3) illustrating how the narrative form of *The Whirlpool* can be read as a response to Margaret Avison's "The Swimmer's Moment," a poem that Urquhart uses as an epigram to the Niagara portion of the narrative.

Poetic Precedents

One basic motivation for poets to switch from poetry to the novel is the larger audience of the latter genre. In this context, it is clear that Urquhart repackages stories and themes from her poetry to shape *The Whirlpool* (1986), which in translation won *Le Prix du meilleur livre étranger* in France in 1992. For example, the character of Maud in *The Whirlpool*, the widow of an undertaker who catalogues the personal effects of drowning victims in Niagara Falls, is based on an ancestor of the author's husband, the artist Tony Urquhart, whose family introduced funeral homes to the city of Niagara Falls (Colvile, 1998: 64; Urquhart, 2004: 59-60). Jane Urquhart first explored this family history in the series of lyrics, "The Undertaker's Bride," from the collection *False Shuffles* (1982), which featured illustrations by Tony Urquhart. "The Undertaker's Bride" also introduces Urquhart readers to Kick's Hotel, the account book of drowning victims, "floaters" (20), and other items central to the novel. The titular sequence of poems in the same collection, "False Shuffles," is dedicated to the Niagara daredevil Sam Patch (74-81). Urquhart's subsequent collection, *The Little Flowers of Madame de Montespan* (1983) anticipates *The Whirlpool* on thematic and stylistic levels. *The Little Flowers of Madame de Montespan* dramatizes the relationship between Louis XIV and his mistress at Versailles. Whereas the Sun King displays a rage for order that drives him to dominate the landscape with geometry, Madame de Montespan has an eye for organic processes and entropy. This gendered contrast of modes of perception foreshadows the disparity in *The Whirlpool* between the military historian David McDougal, who uses scientific knowledge to dominate the Niagara landscape, and his wife Fleda, who celebrates the wild. Marlene Goldman's work on the sublime reveals a particular logic underlying Fleda's relation to nature, one that heightens the contrast between gendered world views. Instead of invoking the sublime "to master an experience that seems overwhelming, Urquhart's text highlights an alternative possibility, namely, using the sublime to facilitate a dialogue with the other" (Goldman, 2002: 102). Urquhart's whirlpool thus becomes a zone of interaction and negotiation, instead of a force that obliterates the self, or a logic that the self uses to overpower all opposition to it. Goldman (2005: 83) and Anne Compton (120-1) also note that Niagara Falls might make a brief appearance in *The Little Flowers of Madame de Montespan*. The poem "Terre Sauvage or the King's Nightmare" depicts a dream of Louis XIV in which the royal gardeners fail to tame the landscape of New France and the King plunges over a powerful waterfall (32-3). "Terre Sauvage" and several other poems herald her move to prose by abandoning line breaks and employing short, numbered sequences of poetic prose. For example, the poem "Museum" uses this prose poem technique to develop the concept of an "Absolute dispersal" (10) of a museum collection. Such dispersal occurs at the conclusion of Maud's story in *The Whirlpool*. Urquhart's fascination with the tension between Euclidean and organic orders also recurs in *Some Other Garden* (2000), which reprints *The Little Flowers of Madame de Montespan* and adds "Eleven Poems for Le Nôtre," the Sun King's landscape architect. The latter series first appeared as the small volume, *I Am Walking in the Garden of His Imaginary Palace: Eleven Poems for Le Nôtre* (1982). Finally, the novel's frame tale appeared in modified form as "The Death of Robert Browning" in the short story collection *Storm Glass*, published the year after the novel (Colvile, 1998: 63). Urquhart's first novel thus functions as a vortex for recirculating previously published material.

Modernist Precedents

The emphasis on motivic variation in *The Whirlpool* highlights its connection to modern literature. In his famous 1945 essay "Spatial Form in Modern Literature," republished in *The Widening Gyre: Crisis and Mastery in Modern Literature*, Joseph Frank demonstrated that modern novelists broke with the sequential conventions of realism and, instead, of depending on linear timelines and causal continuity to make connections in the narrative, introduced readers to worlds that could only be mapped through processes of recursion. This kind of modern writing foregrounds image clusters, indulges thematic obsessions, and employs patterns of iteration to produce self-similarity at different scales of the narrative design. Readers do not necessarily know where the narrative is going, but they come to recognize the way in which it moves (Frank 49). Goldman seems to be describing such a novel when she observes of *The Whirlpool*:

> [T]he central story traces the intersecting lives of five characters. There is no single hero. The text, composed of over forty discrete sections, alternates from the adventures of one character to the next. Like a merry-go-round, it offers the reader a whirling vision of colour and incident. With its shifting focus, the novel ensures that whatever plot can be said to 'exist' owes its tenuous existence not to the unifying presence of the hero, but to the reader's ability to fabricate meaning through a poetic process of association. (2005: 112)

Ralph Freedman refines this vague notion of the "poetic" in *The Lyrical Novel* (1963), where he examines how modern authors such as Virginia Woolf make use of heightened imagery and the subjective gaze in a manner conventionally associated with the lyric. For Freedman, the lyrical novel does not simply cite poetry within prose narrative, as Urquhart does extensively in *The Whirlpool*; rather, it disguises lyricism as prose narrative. Such novels favour the synchronic moment over the diachronic sequence; the associative logic of metaphor over the causal logic of successive events; the use of heightened images in place of extensive dialogue; a decelerated reading pace rather than an accelerated one; and private views of history in place of public ones.

The whirlpool in Urquhart's novel is an apt place for these subjective gazes to converge because of its natural hydraulics and because vortices were key symbols in the modernist period. Vorticism is the name of a short-lived but influential union of the wiles and artistic network of Ezra Pound and the aesthetics of the painter and writer Wyndham Lewis prior to the First World War. Pound named the Vorticist movement and Lewis edited its mouthpiece journal, *Blast*. Peter Childs demonstrates that Pound's Vorticism elaborated ideas he had explored earlier through Imagism: "Pound wrote in his *Memoir* of 1916: 'The image [...] is a radiant node or cluster; it is [...] a VORTEX, from which, and through which, and into which, ideas are constantly rushing'" (Childs 103). The Vorticists advocated a convergence of art forms and artistic energies into a unified movement that would integrate all facets of modern life. They believed that the stylistic revolutions taking place in painting, writing, and science in the second decade of the 20th century failed to overthrow the bourgeois order of the 19th century because the innovations lacked integration. Thus, in *Wyndham Lewis and the Avant-Garde*, Toby Avard Foshay emphasizes the totalizing vision of the Vorticists: "Not only painting but the whole environment needed to be redesigned in a new canon: *Architects! Where is your Vortex?* For the sensibility of isolated *individuals* to become that of integrated *persons*, a new culture on a classical scale had to be conceived, in which art defined social and economic relations, rather than vice versa" (12). The totalitarian leanings of the Vorticist aesthetic, in the hands of Lewis and Pound, are well known. However, Urquhart uses these convergences and dispersals to create interfaces between the characters' world views.

Both Lewis and Pound aimed to destroy 19th century social and aesthetic orders and recompose them according to the symmetries of the modern age. Lewis embraced the potential of turbines and other artefacts of industry to effect revolutionary change and his concept of the vortex is decidedly urban. However, the more conservative T.S. Eliot adapted the dynamics of Vorticism to the natural world and his poetry is full of references to watery vortices. Probably the best-known variation on this whirlpool motif is in the "Death by Water" section of *The Waste Land*, where Eliot describes the drowned sailor Phlebas the Phoenician:

> A current under the sea
> Picked his bones in whispers. As he rose and fell
> He passed the stages of his age and youth
> Entering the whirlpool. (Eliot 71)

Georgiana Colvile has connected this passage to the drowned poets Patrick and Shelley in Urquhart's novel (1988: 64), but there are other examples from Eliot that provide a better understanding of the formal dynamics at work in Vorticism and *The Whirlpool*.

In "Ash Wednesday," for example, Eliot converts biblical imagery into Vorticist terms that emphasize the underlying religious order in the apparent chaos:

> And the light shone in darkness and
> Against the Word the unstilled world still whirled
> About the centre of the silent Word. (Eliot 96)

The Word occupies a central position of power around which the energies of the world converge in "Ash Wednesday" and in "Choruses from 'The Rock.'" Likewise, in "Coriolan," Eliot contrasts the rush of natural forces with the secret origin of those forces: "Under the palmtree at noon, under the running water/At the still point of the turning world. O hidden" (Eliot 128). This still point of (often violent) convergence was the seat of power for the Vorticists. As George Woodcock notes, "[t]he essence of Vorticism was the concept of the still, unmoving centre" (9) and Pound believed that artists should control that focal point.

Pound's Vorticism reacted against what he perceived as the soft sentimentality of Victorian poesy. His background in Imagism caused him to emphasize a hardness, a crystalline clarity that is unlike the shifting liquid states favoured by Eliot and Urquhart. Pound's lapidary imagination is evident in his famous poem "Phanopoeia," where he configures smoke, water, skies, flame, wind, and molten metal in swirls and "bands of colour involute" (170), until ultimately they are arrested and "englobed in my sapphire" (169). Successful art, for Pound, converts liquid flux to crystalline hardness. Stephen Kern complements this point by illustrating how Lewis rejected temporal flux, semantic indeterminacy, or anything that "conspired to remove clean lines from art" (27). The clean lines of Lewis and the hardness of Pound are also synonymous with the triumph of the cerebral over the emotional, as

Foshay demonstrates in *The Politics of Intellect*, the subtitle of his book on Lewis.

Urquhart alters the masculine aesthetic of Lewis and Pound by positioning her love-struck characters on the rocky shore of the whirlpool, which they dream of entering. Urquhart's "merry-go-round" technique borrows the rotary dynamic of Vorticism, but she embraces the indeterminacy of the liquid vortex, as well as the banished passions of the Victorians and Romantics. Urquhart connects the intellect to emotions as part of the larger drive toward integrated living, and the whirlpool becomes the locus of this connection in her novel. In "Escaping the Frame: Circumscribing the Narrative in *The Whirlpool*," Laura Hancu notes the importance of "rotary motion" to Urquhart's novel (45). Hancu argues that the female characters in *The Whirlpool*, Fleda and Maud, need to find ways of breaking down the "labyrinthine societal walls" that constrain their desires and ambitions (45). Fleda is trapped in a passionless marriage to David McDougal, who is constructing a new house for her at Whirlpool Heights downstream from Niagara Falls. Wherever she goes with McDougal, Fleda escapes these domestic walls by fleeing to an imaginary world populated by Romantic and Victorian poets. The arrival in Niagara of a minor poet, Patrick, suggests to Fleda the possibility of realizing her dreams, but ultimately he disappoints Fleda: "He was not the dark man she had dreamed about during her childhood, not the one who arrived one morning and obliterated the past with his passion" (157). Patrick's poems favour nature description over subjective expression, and he does not supply the emotional corrective to life with a military historian that Fleda hoped a poet would provide.

Against the oppressive rectilinearity of a patriarchal domestic order, novelistic convention in Canada would typically introduce the curvilinear sensibilities of Aboriginals or women. However, Aboriginals are largely absent from *The Whirlpool*, and Hancu points out that "[s]pinning or sewing, both traditional means of female economic support and dark symbols of feminine power, are presented as futile activities associated with domestic imprisonment and death" (48). Indeed, Hancu argues that all rotary motion "becomes symbolic of death" in the novel (44). However, I am not completely convinced by Hancu's thesis that *The Whirlpool* is a narrative about women transcending forms of order that are imposed on them by men. These impositions are certainly present in the narrative, but Urquhart does not adhere strictly to binaries of male/female and order/deconstruction, as the body of Hancu's essay demonstrates.

For example, Maud's story, which appears in alternating chapters, complicates conventional gender binaries. Maud struggles with the constraints of managing a business and raising her young son alone. She is confined by her stiff mourner's crape and the omnipresent coffins, which suggest, respectively, a male gaze and an oppressive rectilinearity. According to Hancu's emancipation thesis, "Urquhart celebrates the metamorphic shedding of Maud's submissive posture as an indeterminate spider-like insect and her emergence as a self-defining butterfly who transcends cultural restraints" (46). However, this portrait of Maud, who lived in fear of her husband, conveniently overlooks the fact that "Maud continually and angrily wages war on 'the child'" (Colvile, 1998: 67). Urquhart implies that Maud's attacks on the boy are a response to stress and the legacy of her husband, yet even trauma does not exonerate verbal and physical abuse, which would not be forgiven in the men who work for Maud (and who do not benefit from the gentility of her class position). Furthermore, Maud copes with loneliness by cataloguing and preserving the personal effects of drowning victims. Atypically, the woman pursues a taxonomic sense of order and it is Maud's son who finally disrupts her private museum. Maud's rage for order and the symbol system of language had earlier caused her to shake and scream at her son in an effort to get him to speak. However, at the conclusion of her story, Maud reacts calmly to the boy's rearrangement of the museum articles and she accepts his interpretation of the objects' affinities as one interpretation in a series of possible arrangements. In place of binary oppositions, then, Urquhart presents a variety of ways of creating order (domestic, marital, scientific, institutional, theoretical, aesthetic, etc.) and altering it.

The Frame Tale

Since realist narrative is still the gold standard of the novel, authors need licence to indulge in the discontinuous, "metaphorical thoughts" that preoccupy Browning in the opening chapter of *The Whirlpool* (8). Urquhart gains this licence by making poets central characters in both the frame tale (which follows an elderly Browning through Venetian canals) and the Niagara narrative (which puts the fictional poet Patrick at the heart of the romantic plot). Patrick's character is loosely based on the Confederation Poet Archibald Lampman (Urquhart, 2004: 61), who resembles Patrick in that he also grew up as the son of a clergyman at Rice Lake and "found himself, at thirty-three, eking out a subsistence salary as a clerk in the capital city, grasping desperately for bits of unstructured time in order to pursue his obsession with the art of poetry" (69). Like Lampman, Patrick is a nature poet who establishes a modest reputation through American periodicals, suffers an unhappy marriage, contracts a life-threatening illness in his thirties, and experiences a radical change in world view when he falls in love with another woman shortly before his death (Connor, Early). Whereas Lampman died of his illness, however, Patrick recovers sufficiently to defy death in the Niagara region, where Lampman's ancestors settled and where Patrick has an uncle. In a novel full of intertextual references to famous English writers, the Lampman subtext goes unnamed perhaps to test the historical acumen of Canadian readers and prove McDougal's point about the neglected status of history in the fledgling country (*Whirlpool* 72-4).

By making poets central characters in *The Whirlpool*, Urquhart frees herself to record their movements and thoughts in the realist manner while at the same time departing from the restrained style and diction of the realist novel, which explicitly aimed to counteract the sensationalism of Romantic verse narratives. For example, neither Dickens nor Zola would approve of the double simile Urquhart employs in this early portrait of Browning: "Empty Gothic and Renaissance palaces floated on either side of him like soiled pink dreams. Like sunsets with dirty faces, he mused, and then, pleased with the phrase, he reached into his jacket for his notebook, ink pot, and pen" (8). Only the second half of the last sentence belongs in a realist novel, which would also favour middle-class settings over Renaissance palaces.

Browning, for his part, rejected Romanticism on moral grounds. He spurned the subjective and emotional character of the lyric voice, which the Romantics used for their long narrative poems as well as their short verses. Instead, Browning favoured more impersonal forms, such as the dramatic monologue. He extended this form into character-based narratives such as *The Ring and the Book*, which re-tells the same story of a Roman murder and trial from the perspective of ten different characters. *The Ring and the Book* is one of three volumes Fleda carries in her arms when the reader first encounters her (30). It is also the book she is reading when Patrick first spots Fleda and he connects the *Ring* on the book's cover to her wedding band (40, 71). Hancu demonstrates that the intertextual allusions give the narrative an ominous cast, because *The Ring and the Book* tells the story of an Italian nobleman who murdered his wife and Hancu sees a parallel to Fleda's sense of entrapment (54). Through this intertextual juxtaposition, Urquhart puts Fleda's public, married status into conflict with her private, emotional turmoil. Ultimately, Fleda rejects Patrick because he insists too much on the public and organic spheres to the detriment of private emotion.

The conflict between Romantic and Victorian poetics is already at issue in Urquhart's frame tale because her Browning feels inferior to Shelley, whose face he sees in Venetian statues of Pan and Dionysus (gods associated with lyric ecstasy). Browning is disturbed by Shelley's legacy as he confronts his imminent death and compares his placid old age with Shelley's storm-tossed drowning on the Ligurian coast. Against

Browning's will, complete stanzas of Shelley's poetry keep surging into his consciousness:

> "Oh God," he groaned inwardly, "now this. And I don't even *like* Shelley's poetry anymore. Now I suppose I'm going to be plagued with it, day in, day out, until the instant of my imminent death."
>
> How he wished he had never, ever, been fond of Shelley's poems. Then, in his youth, he might have had the common sense *not* to read them compulsively to the point of total recall. But how could he have known in those early days that even though he would later come to reject both Shelley's life and work as being "too impossibly self-absorbed and emotional," some far corner of his brain would still retain every syllable the young man put to paper. (14)

By the end of the novel, Browning has begun to suspect that his poems will never rival the indefinable genius of Shelley in his best works: "The formless form [Browning] never possessed and was never possessed by" (236). Whereas Browning's verse takes on the connotations of a stately death in the narrative, Shelley's poetry takes on the connotations of an enduring life force. This introduction of a vital, life-affirming poetry into an atmosphere of death is a theme that carries forward into the Niagara narrative, where one encounters Fleda, who feels trapped in a loveless marriage until she falls in love with the poet Patrick.

The Whirlpool Motif

The theme of resurgence in the Niagara narrative is guided by "The Swimmer's Moment," a poem from Avison's *Winter Sun*, which won the Governor General's Award for Poetry in 1960. As an epigram, "The Swimmer's Moment" bridges the frame tale and the romance, but the poem also haunts Urquhart's prose in much the same way as Shelley's poetry haunted that of Browning. The opening sentence of "The Swimmer's Moment," which is a standard entry in Canadian anthologies, supplies the titular image for Urquhart's novel:

> For everyone
> The swimmer's moment at the whirlpool comes,
> But many at that moment will not say
> "This is the whirlpool, then." (Avison 47)

Urquhart cites only the first two lines of Avison's poem in her epigram, which makes it more difficult to pinpoint the exact location of the whirlpool. The reader struggles to answer the ontological question of what the whirlpool *is* in the novel because the motif is in a state of perpetual transformation. Urquhart cycles the motif through a variety of scientific, historical, and political discourses; it is compared to everything from love to the cosmos; and its continual becoming is charged with erotic nuance because Patrick conflates his attraction to the whirlpool with his attraction to Fleda (102-3, 180).

Sequentially, readers first encounter the whirlpool motif on the front cover of Urquhart's novel, which in my edition (McClelland & Stewart, 1997) also features the photograph "Niagara Falls, Ont., 1859" by William England. This photograph depicts a man in dark clothing and a wide-brimmed hat sitting on a rock overhanging the estuary of the Falls. He ponders the sublime violence of the Falls and its outflow in the same way as characters in Urquhart's story contemplate the whirlpool below the Falls. Whereas Avison's whirlpool lacks a name and specific location, Urquhart situates her vortex in a very particular landscape, "the only part of the river that is entirely Canadian" (86) – a slight exaggeration since a fraction of the whirlpool falls on the American side of the water border. On the Ontario side, the nationalist historian David McDougal and his wife Fleda are building a house on a property called Whirlpool Heights (86). Major McDougal is the least important of the characters in the love triangle involving himself, Fleda, and Patrick, but his view of the whirlpool helps to establish a historical and geographical context for the events which unfold later. Unlike Patrick and Fleda, who "perceive[e] whirlpools as metaphors," the Major sees the river as an expression of scientific forces and his command of these forces initially gives him the upper hand over Patrick. (103) McDougal helpfully informs the poet that the Niagara River had two branches until glaciers closed off one branch, causing the water to return upon itself and create a whirlpool effect. For McDougal, the whirlpool represents a question of property, a land claim wrested from the Americans much as he wishes to wrest the War of 1812 from American historians who claim victory in a military stalemate that changed no borders. McDougal sees the British victory at Lundy's Lane in Niagara as proof that the American invaders were inferior, but he suppresses knowledge of the American victories elsewhere along the border.

Even given his nationalist bias, McDougal's world view is important because, as John Moss explains, most of the story "comes to us through the minds of [Urquhart's] characters. She does not create their setting in pictures; she allows us the experience of their intersecting perceptions" (Moss 80). Urquhart orchestrates these perceptions to invest the whirlpool with metaphorical connotations, whether McDougal likes such readings or not. Urquhart fashions a ring of perceptions, declarations, and interior monologues around Whirlpool Heights and puts the competing interpretations into a state of interaction. McDougal's claim on the whirlpool rests on a supposition of intellectual and physical mastery that is gradually exposed as fraudulent. For all his military bravado, McDougal only knows about war from books, as Fleda reminds the reader, and McDougal fails to rise to the occasion in the one real crisis where he is called to act. When a daredevil dies while attempting to shoot the Falls, McDougal foolishly thinks has the power to command life and death; he tries to intervene when Maud's crew from the funeral home lower a coffin to the daredevil's battered corpse on the riverbank:

> "How can they be so sure?" he had asked the doctor who, in turn, looked at him as if he had entirely taken leave of his senses.
>
> Then there is nothing I can do, David had thought helplessly, there is no part for me to play. Accustomed to shouting orders, familiar with being a centre of calm in the thick of imagined chaos, he began to feel guilty about his presence at this very real disaster. As if he were just a privileged spectator with a ringside seat. (133)

Here Urquhart invokes the qualities she habitually assigns to the whirlpool (swirling chaos, death, spectatorship) in order to highlight the Major's impotence. He is absent from the still centre, the Vorticist position of power. Yet in the contest between Patrick and McDougal for Fleda's affections, the Major wins by virtue of his inaction and the inability of Patrick to respond to Fleda's invitations.

Whereas the Major sees everything through the lens of the War of 1812 – including his wife, whom he sees as the heroine Laura Secord – Patrick is a nature poet and he associates Fleda with the Niagara landscape. He spots Fleda reading poetry at Whirlpool Heights and becomes infatuated with her and the adjacent vortex. After spying on Fleda for a while, Patrick befriends the McDougals and tries to facilitate his conquest of Fleda by studying the Major's world view. He learns about the geology and history of the landscape and his strategy of indirection lades most of his lessons from the Major with sexual innuendo. Since McDougal sleeps at a hotel while Fleda camps in a tent at Whirlpool Heights, one wonders whether McDougal abandons the lovers to their adulterous desires, and whether the Major is also talking about Fleda when he discusses the whirlpool with Patrick.

Patrick's timidity puts him at a perpetual disadvantage to the Major who, although he lacks the Romantic sentiments and Victorian graces that Fleda cherishes, at least acts on some of his passions and fills his mental world with individuals who have acted in the past. The Major's mental life manifests itself as cannonballs in Maud's garden and a Laura Secord costume begrudgingly donned by Fleda in their bedroom (50-3), whereas Patrick's poetic sensibility fails to grasp the object of its attention:

> The river was not the ocean, but it was staggering in the way he believed the ocean might be. Its size, endless movement, shocked and moved him in a

way that was basically silent. He had brought his notebook there, had the title 'Maelstrom' on his mind, but no further words would come to him. It was like a conversation he couldn't begin, never mind finish (80).

Patrick holds out the hope that he will eventually discover the "formless form" (236) to describe the whirlpool and express his desire for Fleda. In the hope of impressing Fleda and the Major, Patrick resolves to become a man of action and "swim this whirlpool" (102), much as Byron swam the Hellespont in imitation of Leander's pursuit of Hero. However, Patrick cannot decide whether to swim straight for the whirlpool's centre or to work with the circular current. He therefore consults the Major for advice on what is essentially an analogy for seducing Fleda. In the end, Patrick rejects Fleda and resolves to swim his idealized whirlpool alone.

Thus far I have detailed the male perceptions of the whirlpool. Yet if one tracks the whirlpool motif across the novel, one finds that it takes on many different connotations. Indeed, the first mention of the whirlpool in the narrative depicts it as more of a mental state than a physical location:

> Fleda's thoughts turned to the whirlpool and an acre of land that rose from it. She was, at this moment, a woman on a streetcar with a whirlpool on her mind.
>
> She was often, mentally, one or two steps ahead of her activities, her location. (31)

Urquhart usually connects the notion of the whirlpool as a cognitive event, as a turbulent confluence of distinct forces, to Fleda's musings in the novel: "In one sense the whirlpool was like memory; like obsession connected to memory, like history that stayed in one spot, moving nowhere and endlessly repeating itself" (49). Whereas the Major thinks of history in terms of linear succession, Fleda thinks of it in terms of recurrence. And indeed, the most obvious expression of this recurrence is the narrative's constant return to, and reinterpretation of, the whirlpool. This recursive action is complemented by the frame tale, which mimics the "circular journey" (48) of the whirlpool by bringing the narrative full circle to Venice such that the frame tale introduces and then echoes the Niagara story.

The whirlpool is Fleda's obsession first, but it gradually becomes Patrick's when he tries "to discover the exact moment when the whirlpool had taken hold of her life" (107). The whirlpool has a kind of gravitation power for Fleda, in addition to its hydraulic force: "In this light I am reading Browning. Pulling in around Browning, trying to avoid the pull of the open dark, the limitlessness of the stars over the whirlpool" (151). People and events spin away from Whirlpool Heights and then inevitably are drawn back to it. Patrick, too, attributes a cosmological significance to the whirlpool by comparing it with the spiral nebulae he had seen in an observatory in Ottawa. The confusion of sky and water "makes [him] dizzy, interferes with [his] sense of gravity" (177). In place of a linear teleology, then, Urquhart's narrative strings together a series of nodal points (whirlpool scenes) with a kind of gravity that increases the symbolic weight of the actions which take place near it, much as Joseph Frank observed of modernist narratives.

Whereas Patrick associates the whirlpool with Fleda, Fleda associates the whirlpool with idealized men, in particular poets. Her initial passion for Browning at Whirlpool Heights is eventually transferred to Patrick: "Every cell in her body, every synapse in her brain, demanded the presence of the poet in her life. As if all the reading, all the dreaming, had been one long preparation for his arrival" (142). For Fleda, decoding Patrick's desires and evasions becomes a matter of understanding his connection to the whirlpool:

> "I am wondering," she said, almost to herself, "if it is this that Patrick wants from the whirlpool. Perhaps he wants to carry some of it away with him in words."
>
> From deep inside the fixed idea of the poet, Fleda looked out at her husband. (174)

Gradually Fleda becomes completely immersed in the enigma of Patrick as interpreted through the whirlpool. When Patrick rejects Fleda and displaces "the fixed idea of the poet" from her reveries, she finds the rejection unbearable: "She would not be discarded, disposed of like this. She had felt his attention around her, even when he wasn't there. She had felt herself a part of his quest, his desire to break free, to attempt the whirlpool. Part of the creation of poetry" (194). While equating men with water and flux is unconventional in terms of Western gender stereotypes, Fleda's imaginings are conventional in the sense that she portrays the poet as a transcendent male who will occupy a position of power at the still centre of her fantasy. She, in turn, adopts the conventional stance of muse figure to facilitate his quest.

Patrick's perception of the whirlpool is more consistent with 19th century views, as Karen Dubinsky demonstrates in "'The Pleasure is Exquisite But Violent': The Imaginary Geography of Niagara Falls in the Nineteenth Century." Dubinsky documents the evolution of Niagara Falls as a tourist destination that serviced the emerging middle-class ritual of the honeymoon in the 19th century. The vacationing Victorians and Americans habitually projected onto the Falls the "pleasure and terror" (Dubinsky 28) they associated with sexuality: "At Niagara, gendered, sexualized descriptive imagery, the perceived 'fatal attraction' of rushing waters, tales of death and destruction, as well as invented stories of romance and tragedy [...] helped, in the 19th century, to fix an image of the Falls in the minds of North Americans as a place of forbidden pleasures" (32). These descriptive conventions are particularly significant for Urquhart's novel because, "[t]o almost all writers who gendered their descriptions, Niagara was female: the 'Queen of the Cataracts,' the 'Water Bride of Time,' the 'Daughter of History,' and the 'Mother of all Cascades'" (29). Urquhart's novel adds another entry to this feminine catalogue by creating the character of Maud, who prepares the victims of the Falls for burial: "Maud was paid fifteen dollars per body by the city, in return for disposing quickly and quietly of these unpleasant embarrassments to the mighty tourist industry." (164). Urquhart develops this snippet of her family history to make the businesswoman Maud a counterpoint to the romantic Fleda.

Maud is not in love – on the contrary, she is recovering from a bad marriage – but she, too, has an intensely subjective way of seeing the world that cannot be attributed to the heightened emotions of romantic desire. This subjective focus intensifies her perceptions, as well as slowing the pace of the plot and favouring lyrical meditation over action. Consider the simple act of entering a garden from Maud's perspective:

> Between these [beech trees], and trapped in their early summer leaves, was an intense, copper wealth of sunlight which had so transformed the contents of the garden that each shrub, each flower, appeared to be illuminated from within. Even the wire and wooden fence at the back stood altered; magnificent, its surfaces etched and clear, while in the vegetable patch directly in front of it, humble early lettuce assumed the grace of great sculpture. Beyond her own property, Maud could see the stones of Drummond Hill Cemetery glowing like white teeth on the horizon. (63)

Urquhart generalizes the condition of epiphany in this scene by soaking the landscape in the light of an otherworldly illumination. Contrary to the wishes of the realists, the quotidian aspects of the landscape are converted into high art and simile. Urquhart even uses a semicolon in a grammatically incorrect fashion to underscore the breathless magnificence of the scene.

Urquhart repeats this tactic in the subsequent paragraph:

> Unexpectedly, she was filled with awe for this small world which included only that which she could see – this landscape of garden and graveyard where no streetcar trespassed; filled with wonder that she had created some of it herself, caused, for instance, the grape arbour to exist on the left side of the garden, the roses to decorate the centre. (64)

This cascade of images separated by dashes, commas, and semicolons –
instead of periods and unobtrusive syntax – is the sign of a lyric poet
still yearning for line breaks. Indeed, one could read the Maud subplot
as a metafictional parallel to the poet (Urquhart) becoming a poet-
novelist, because the subplot charts the process of language acquisition
by Maud's son. At first the boy speaks elliptically, in "disembodied
nouns" (155) resembling modernist poetry in their inadvertent
poignancy (Compton 129). Subsequently, however, the boy moves into
a phase of mimetic prose, wherein he repeats verbatim everything Maud
says. He mirrors the actions of others by re-enacting scenes of mourning
he has witnessed at the funeral home and by reproducing dialogue
flawlessly. He eventually passes through this mimetic phase, however,
and identifies with Patrick, whom he has seen swimming. The boy's
wordplay resumes when he confuses "I" and "You" in a scene with
Patrick shortly before the dramatic climax of the Patrick's story (188).

The Avison Epigram

The effect of Urquhart's subjective focus and stylized syntax is to
draw the readers into a particular kind of attention. This attention has an
immersive aspect to it that elsewhere in the novel gets associated with
love and swimming. The use of Avison's "The Swimmer's Moment" as
an epigram helps to highlight this theme, which also transforms into a
poetic technique.

Avison is one of the most difficult Canadian modernists. Her poems
are often elliptical and abstruse, but here, too, Urquhart has been careful
in her selection. "The Swimmer's Moment" valorizes the immersive
plunge of modernism, but it is one of Avison's most straightforward
poems. It pursues a single idea from beginning to end and its narrative
arc clarifies the storyline of *The Whirlpool* as a whole.

According to "The Swimmer's Moment," the reluctance of Fleda and
Patrick to brave the whirlpool, to get their feet wet, to dive in, to commit
themselves to something other than safety will have negative consequences in the long term. The second sentence of Avison's poem
conveys this moral:

> By their refusal they are saved
> From the black pit, and also from contesting
> The deadly rapids, and emerging in
> The mysterious, and more ample, further waters. (Avison 47)

Even when Patrick decides to swim, he assures the Major that he
doesn't intend to try the rapids like the ill-fated Captain Webb (102) and
thereby fulfill Avison's prescription of reaching the further waters. By
clinging to their marital sense of duty, by habitually standing on the

riverbank but never entering the river, Patrick and Fleda commit the kind of self-effacement that Avison makes the subject of the third sentence in "The Swimmer's Moment":

> And so their bland-blank faces turn and turn
> Pale and forever on the rim of suction
> They will not recognize. (Avison 47)

For most of the novel, Patrick has no wish to yield to this suction because he fears becoming a corpse for the Old River Man to recover. However, Urquhart draws both the reader and Patrick deeper into the enigma of the titular motif. The whirlpool becomes an irresistible force as the plotlines ostensibly driving the story – the construction of the house, the growth of Maud's son, the adultery of Maud and Patrick – yield to the characters' obsession with the whirlpool enigma.

Likewise, the narrative focus of "The Swimmer's Moment" gradually shifts from ontological questions ("What is the whirlpool, then?") to epistemological ones ("What is knowledge and who dares pursue it?"). However, Avison does not follow Pound's example of trying to englobe all these questions in intellectual "sapphire" (Pound, "Phanopoeia," 169). The fourth and final sentence of Avison's poem is a meditation on the workings of empathy and despair:

> Of those who dare the knowledge
> Many are whirled into the ominous centre
> That, gaping vertical, seals up
> For them an eternal boon of privacy,
> So that we turn away from their defeat
> With a despair, not for their deaths, but for
> Ourselves, who cannot penetrate their secret
> Nor even guess at the anonymous breadth
> Where one or two have won:
> ("The silver reaches of the estuary," Avison: 47)

The chain of associations and negations in this final sentence is complex. It moves from heroism to pathos, vertical to horizontal, knowledge to hidden secret, privacy to public repute. The swirling clauses convey a feeling of being sucked into a vortex. The reader whirls amid the contrasts, accelerates toward the cliff of the colon, plummets off the line break, and then lands in the bracketed, almost hypothetical world of the "silver reaches of the estuary." Avison's poem thus prepares readers for the conclusion of Urquhart's novel, where Patrick swims the whirlpool and dies. The poem also raises questions about Fleda's fate after she disappears. Perhaps she followed Patrick and died in a copycat gesture, or perhaps she is among the "one or two" who have discovered "the anonymous breadth" of self-recreation through a transcendental gesture that Urquhart critiques but does not completely reject.

However, one could also argue that Urquhart's novel reconfigures the narrative framework of "The Swimmer's Moment": the reader enters the novel through the parentheses of the frame tale, grapples with the mysteries of death via Browning and Maud, weighs the "boon of privacy" against public repute in the romance of Fleda and Patrick, and gradually attempts to "penetrate" the secret emblematized by the whirlpool at the "ominous centre" of the novel.

For all the sexualized whirlpool imagery in "The Swimmer's Moment" and *The Whirlpool*, the latter is haunted by a fundamental impotency. Fleda and Patrick initially hesitate to act on their passions and seem to prefer the sublimations of poetry to the pleasures of the flesh. Whereas Avison used poetry as a catapult toward a heroic gesture, Urquhart cites Browning's "Amphibian" to convey the idea that poetry functions as a substitute "heaven" for those who cannot fly (199). Fleda makes a leap of faith in hope of reaching this heaven but Patrick fails to respond to her advances, as well as failing to find words that would substitute for the real. This double failure might lead readers to conclude that art is pointless, and indeed poetry comes under harsh criticism in other Urquhart novels, particularly in the post-Fist World War setting of *The Stone Carvers*: "Seems like everybody nowadays wants to express themselves. Used to be a name and the dates would do [on a monument], but no more. You kill off a generation of boys and suddenly the whole world is interested in poetry. Sometimes, God forbid, they even write the poetry themselves" (276). However, Browning's conclusion in *The Ring and the Book* offers some consolation to poetry lovers. Browning informs his readers that the goal of his circumlocutionary tale is to demonstrate "This lesson, that our human speech is naught,/Our human testimony false, our fame/And human estimation words and wind" (12: 834-6). Yet, for Browning, "Art remains the one way possible/Of speaking truth" (12: 839-40) provided that the artist approach this truth "Obliquely" (12: 856).

Returning to *The Whirlpool*, then, I would conclude that Urquhart uses to the novel to highlight some of the limitations of lyric poetry (solipsism, a fear of the mundane, a desire to live in spectacular moments that cannot be sustained), while at the same time juxtaposing and interlinking poetic world views and their material and social conditions. The aspiring novelist thus did not abandon poetry in *The Whirlpool* so much as find ways of demonstrating in prose how poetry is produced, read, circulated, and critiqued in communities. As was the case for Urquhart's peers, this repositioning of poems in historical, material, national, and canonical matrices was partly motivated by the poet's reconsideration of her identity in relation to her family, in this case the family history of her husband. However, whereas the novels discussed in *From Cohen to Carson* gesture explicitly toward avant-garde aesthetics, Urquhart has assimilated these influences into more accessible prose. For a specialist audience, she raises questions of competing classical, romantic, Victorian, and modernist aesthetic orders; for a non-specialist audience, she conveys the gist of these questions through form, sensation, and character. Urquhart's reputation as a popular writer is thus well deserved, but I hope that this collection will draw greater attention to the craft undergirding her prose.

References

AVISON, M. (1982), *Winter Sun/The Dumbfounding: Poems 1940-66*, Toronto, McClelland & Stewart.

BROWNING, R. (1990), *The Ring and the Book*, New York, Penguin.

CHILDS, P. (2008), *Modernism*, New York, Routledge.

COLVILE, G. (1998), "The Quest for a Literary and Mythical Past in Three Novels by Jane Urquhart," *Études Canadiennes/Canadian Studies: Revue Interdisciplinaire des Études Canadiennes en France* 44: 61-76.

COLVILE, G. (2001), "Anti-fleuves, corps morcelés, identités fracassées : *Le Torrent* d'Anne Hébert (1950) et *The Whirlpool* de Jane Urquhart (1986)," *Études Canadiennes/Canadian Studies: Revue Interdisciplinaire des Études Canadiennes en France* 50: 157-165.

COMPTON, A. (2005), "Romancing the Landscape: Jane Urquhart's Fiction," in L. FERRI, Ed., *Jane Urquhart: Essays on Her Works*, Toronto, Guernica, 115-143.

CONNOR, C. (1929), *Archibald Lampman: Canadian Poet of Nature*, Montreal, Louis Carrier & Co.

DUBINSKY, K. (2002), "'The Pleasure is Exquisite but Violent': The Imaginary Geography of Niagara Falls in the Nineteenth Century," in J. NICKS and J. SLONIOWSKI, Eds., *Slippery Pastimes: Reading the Popular in Canadian Culture*, Waterloo, Wilfrid Laurier University Press, 21-35.

EARLY, L.R. (1983), "Archibald Lampman (1861-1899)," in R. LECKER, J. DAVID, and E. QUIGLEY, Eds., *Canadian Writers and Their Works*, Vol. 2, Downsview, ON, ECW Press, 135-185.

ELIOT, T. S. (2004), *Complete Poems and Plays of T.S. Eliot*, London, Faber & Faber.

FOSHAY, T. A. (1992), *Wyndham Lewis and the Avant-Garde: The Politics of Intellect*, Montreal, McGill-Queen's University Press.

FRANK, J. (1963), *The Widening Gyre: Crisis and Mastery in Modern Literature*, New Brunswick, NJ, Rutgers University Press.

FREEDMAN, R. (1963), *The Lyrical Novel*, Princeton, NJ, Princeton University Press.

GOLDMAN, M. (Autumn 1996), "Translating the Sublime: Jane Urquhart's *The Whirlpool*," *Canadian Literature* 150: 23-42.

– (2002), "Encounters with Alterity: The Role of the Sublime in Moodie's and Urquhart's Historical Fiction," *Études Canadiennes/Canadian Studies: Revue Interdisciplinaire des Études Canadiennes en France* 53: 101-116.

HANCU, L. (1995), "Escaping the Frame: Circumscribing the Narrative in *The Whirlpool*," *Studies in Canadian Literature* 20.1: 44-64.

KERN, S. (1983), *The Culture of Time and Space: 1880-1918*, Cambridge, MS, Harvard University Press.

MOSS, J. (2005), "How Fiction Works: *The Whirlpool*," in Laura Ferri, Ed., *Jane Urquhart: Essays on Her Works*, Toronto, Guernica, 78-82.

POUND, E. (1926), "Phanopoeia," *Personae*, New York, Boni & Liveright.

RAE, I. (2008), *From Cohen to Carson: The Poet's Novel in Canada*, Montreal, Mc Gill Queen's University Press.

SHERTZER, M. (1986), *The Elements of Grammar*, New York, Macmillan.

SUTHERLAND, F. (2000), "Jane Urquhart's Painterly Poetry," *Globe and Mail*, 28 October 2000, D13.

URQUHART, J. (2005), "A Conversation with Jane Urquhart," interview by Laura Ferri, in L. FERRI, Ed., *Jane Urquhart: Essays on Her Works*, Toronto, Guernica, 15-41.

– (1982), *False Shuffles*, Victoria, Press Porcépic.

– (1982), *I Am Walking in the Garden of His Imaginary Palace: Eleven Poems for Le Nôtre*, Toronto, Aya Press.

– (1983), *The Little Flowers of Madame de Montespan*, Erin, ON, Porcupine's Quill.

– (1987), *Storm Glass*, Erin, ON, Porcupine's Quill.

– (1997), *The Whirlpool*, Toronto, McClelland & Stewart.

– (2000), *Some Other Garden*, Toronto, McClelland & Stewart.

– (2001), *The Stone Carvers*, Toronto, McClelland & Stewart.

– (winter 2004), "Jane Urquhart: Confessions of a Historical Geographer; an Interview with Herb Wyile," *Essays on Canadian Writing* 81: 58-83.

WOODCOCK, G. (1971), "Momaco Revisited," in G. WOODCOCK, Ed., *Wyndham Lewis in Canada*, Vancouver, University of British Columbia Press.

4

Bront(ë)ology as Emotional Landscaping in *Changing Heaven*

Georges LETISSIER

Université de Nantes

Like many neo-Victorian fictions, *Changing Heaven* probes into the process of artistic creation by occasionally adopting a deconstructive, parodic stance. Like some of them, it is not immune from the authorial fallacy at times. For instance, to account for the genesis of the book that was to make Charlotte Brontë famous, i.e. *Jane Eyre*, Urquhart – through her fictitious Emily Brontë – does not hesitate to revive the painful memory of Monsieur Heger,[1] the object of Charlotte's all-devouring passion: "Charlotte had stopped waiting. She'd started writing" (206) and, as a logical consequence, there was to be "lots of fire in it [the novel] and some wonderful charred ruins" (206).[2]

Giving psychic trauma as the source of literary creation would of course seem at best reductive and at worst specious and naive by the standards of modern criticism. In Urquhart's novel though, the fact that the diagnosis is delivered by the fictitious *persona* of a genuine Victorian novelist allows for the kind of interpretive interplay much valued in postmodern fiction writing. Yet, a certain form of ambiguity persists, as it could be argued that expressing affects through the mediation of well-known authors from the literary canon, is one way of giving a new lease of life to romance as a subgenre, or to neo-Romanticism as an aesthetic current. Anne Compton has underscored this all-pervasive presence of romance in Urquhart's fictions, by drawing from Northrop Frye's classification in *Anatomy of Criticism*:

---

[1]   See Judith Barker, *The Brontës: A Life in Letters*, Elizabeth Gaskell, *The Life of Charlotte Brontë* (1857) and Winifred Gérin, *Charlotte Brontë, The Evolution of a Genius*.

[2]   Throughout this essay, page references to the McClelland & Stewart edition of *Changing Heaven* are provided in the main text.

Urquhart's fictions, *The Whirlpool* (1986), *Changing Heaven* (1990), and *Away* (1993), are populated by prodigies, that is by obsessives, ghosts, savants, daemon lovers, and by those touched by the supernatural. Her heroes are superior in degree, in power, to regular humans and to their social environment, which in her work is usually claustrophobic, but it is precisely through their close and magical alliance to the natural environment that they gain these powers. (Compton 115)

For all its fluid multi-plotting, subtly interwoven temporal strata and poetic prose, *Jane* Urquhart's novel is chiefly about the pangs of passion, and how Ann Frear, its contemporary heroine, is progressively forced to renounce her all-consuming passion for a married man to give herself up to the transformative power of landscape *via* her obsessive, exclusive fascination for a Victorian artist: Emily *Jane* Brontë. In the same way as A.S. Byatt, also known for her engagement with Victorian writers, pleaded for the truth of the human heart,[3] Urquhart reintroduces confessional writing by suggesting that passion is imaginatively created through cultural representations and an intimate relation with language.

Changing Heaven is a self-reflexive novel highlighting the chiastic bond between art and passion; passion is shown as a privileged means to access art and, conversely, art is seen as feeding on passion, as the many allusions to fire demonstrate. To testify to the affective experience of human passion, Urquhart resorts to meteorology and, in so doing, inverts the Ruskinian "pathetic fallacy" by positing the ascendency of the cosmic over the psychic. Significantly, the novel opens on what Laurent Jenny would call *"un événement figural"* (26) or figural event with the equation between brontology (the study of thunder) and Brontëology (the exegesis of the Brontës' literary output):[4]

> Then it is a wind that has been around for a long, long time; a wind that according to the ancient Greeks, was born about the same time as chaos; or that semi-human, a Cyclops called Brontë – the Greek word for thunder. And what is thunder hereabouts, but a strong voice making itself heard in a rough wind?

This essay wishes to demonstrate that *Changing Heaven* is a poetical novel conveying the sense of an emotional present through a personal involvement with the Brontëan hypotext (not only *Wuthering Heights* but also Emily's poems and the juvenilia), and with Brontëan

---

[3] See Byatt, A.S. *Possession, A Romance.*

[4] A further twist could be given to this remark as the family name was originally "Brunty" in Ireland, and even probably O'Prunty. The Reverend Patrick Brontë, father of Charlotte, Patrick Branwell, Emily and Anne, changed his surname to "Brontë" soon after Nelson, whom he greatly admired, was made Duke of Brontë in 1799.

mythography, notably through secondary sources like Glyn Hughes's *Millstone Grit* and Peggy Hewitt's *These Lonely Mountains*. It will be argued that resurgence is the privileged intertextual mode in a text which constantly plays upon atmospheric changeability – appearance and disappearance, coming into shape and dematerializing, thus exploring in the process the whole range of variations of intensity from the substantial to the ethereal.

The perpetual present of emotional landscape

Structurally, the novel is caught in a double bind. It must call up atmospheric variations without totally eschewing temporal progression. So there is a subdued plotline in this fiction that is openly more concerned with meteorology than with chronology. *Changing Heaven* is a visual, largely *ekphrastic* narrative (Tintoretto, Goya, Velasquez, El Greco, The Titian, and also Brueghel are evoked) which explores the meteor(ic) – μετέωρος i.e. the lofty or the ascending – possibly to a larger extent than it deals with sublunary events. Significantly, the only instrument of measurement that is introduced is not a clock but the Beaufort scale, used for registering changes in wind intensity. In the novel, the latter is a metonym for shifts in states of mind: "She [Ann] is not on a boat, she *is* a boat – clear sailing, number four on the wind scale" (217). The barometric thus turns into the psychometric to record intermittent changes. The weather, mostly winds, translates subjectivity onto a cosmic level, so that the whole novel may be seen as a perpetually changing mental space crossed by most erratic and unpredictable alterations. The anthropomorphic, or rather psychodynamic, dimension of weather as mind reflector is confirmed by the fact that winds are construed as "levels of engagement [...] with life" (128). Thunderbolts, or such stochastic phenomena as bog bursts, are "the vocabulary of a landscape whose passions must speak, can no longer keep silent" (132) – thus as a resurgence of subterranean, repressed emotions, as it were. Urquhart therefore conjures up an intense, emotional experience through a secularized, elemental *psychomachia*. In other words, an intimate psychological struggle is being played out through elemental forces. And the religious has become only peripheral; heaven in the title must be understood as infinite space and not the more sacred, religiously-connoted heavens.

The novel's emotional landscape, forcefully expressed through the perennial immediacy of the weather, does not preclude any temporal movement, though. Hence a form of discontinuity between the predominating spatial and the more subdued temporal can be observed. *Changing Heaven*, like *Wuthering Heights* with its successive Catherines, does also unfold in chronological time, even if the latter may seem infinitesimal on the scale of recurrent, atmospheric phenomena: "the again and again of that revenant, the wind – its evasiveness, its tenacity, its everlastingness" (1). Little Ann Frear, whose patronym may point to a move from fear to freer, grows into an adult, and so does Arthur Woodruff (rough wood?), her thick-skinned lover. Structurally, the novel succeeds in asserting the constant present/ce of the meteorological working as an objective correlative for changing states of consciousness, while suggesting the passing of time in a minor key. As linear chronology by itself would relegate the atmospheric to a secondary position, the dynamics of the diegesis actuates the whole fictitious realm through a combination of straight, oblique and circular movements.⁵ Such a combination introduces a contrapuntal mode conducive to alternative changes of narrative patterns.

A straight line connects the three plots together. The contemporary one tells about the passionate affair between Ann, a Brontëan scholar, and Arthur, a specialist of Tintoretto. The turn-of-the-century one originates in a balloon accident in which Polly Smith *alias* Arianna Ether the aerialist perishes,⁶ and the third and final one, which is chiefly atemporal (but meteoric and meteorological), focuses on the whirling motions of two ghosts, those of the former mentioned Arianna and Emily Brontë in her afterlife. This is probably what has led a Canadian critic to see in *Changing Heaven* "an extraordinary contemporary fiction floated on the emotional weather of Brontë's *Wuthering Heights*".⁷ The linear axis is materialized by the Canadian highway taking Ann the child to her grandmother's: "An hour and a half of grey speed and you are able to enter the nineteenth century" (44). Interestingly, the highway has erased the more tortuous road that used to be like a spatial palimpsest: "a road made up of sequential experiences of earlier forms of travels" (44). In a country in which the past has been eradicated,⁸ the road only

---

5   This grid of analysis is implied by a remark inserted in the novel itself, which incidentally points to the metatextual dimension of the latter: "Ann reads the words of Thomas Aquinas concerning Angels. [...] The motion of the illumination of an angel is threefold: circular, straight, and oblique" (107). Aquinas's comment on the motions of angels is especially pertinent as a paradigm for this empyrean novel.

6   "Yes, there's a woman buried in the graveyard there [Stanbury], and her name is Lily Cove. She met her end in a ballooning accident as a result of a town fair near Haworth. What a place to crash land! She also had a manager. I had the bones of the story outlined for me by a woman I met who had been collecting little bits of folklore and stories." Jane Urquhart's answer in Katie Sykes, "Inside Other Worlds: An Interview," 55.

7   Douglas Barbour in his review of *Changing Heaven* for *The Edmonton Journal*, 17ᵗʰ March 1990, quoted in Patsy Stoneman "From Classic Text to Intertext," 90.

8   "In Canada much of the past has been thrown away. No one cares. No one records it" (183).

persists as mnemonic inscription, duly committed to memory by Ann, the Brontë scholar, together with another more famous track: the path connecting Wuthering Heights to the Grange by crossing the moors. So in a way, the Canadian road (as living memory) and the English track (as reading memory) coalesce into a latent remembrance that will be actualized once Ann travels to Yorkshire to experience it phenomeno-logically, with both her mind *and* her senses. Incidentally, this sensorial, imaginary relation to the elements can also be investigated from a Bachelardian perspective.[9] The pattern of intermittence between the actual and the virtual is indeed a constant feature. For example, Ann's destiny unfurls like the ribbon of the highway with its occasional hitches, "Grey, broken, unstoppable. Adolescence, adulthood, old age" (47), and even her commitment to literary studies is evoked in terms of spatial displacement: "uncomfortably and secretively, inside the great, dark, rattling carriages of nineteenth century fiction" (79). The spatial continuum of the highway thus revives other intertextual journeys-chiefly the steep main street of Haworth on which the novel opens, and of course, as mentioned just above, the seminal, or foundational, way between the Heights and Thrushcross Grange. Recurring at odd, unpredictable intervals, the latter is seen from above through the aerialist's bird's eye view, or at ground level by Ann walking. It is also alluded to directly through actual, original toponyms like Lower Withins, Middle Withins and Top Withins, when it is not fantasized from literary words likely to arouse the imagination, such as Gimmerton. Therefore, the paradigmatic way, whether it be the Canadian highway with its motels where Ann has her adulterous affair with Arthur, or the obsessively present path from *Wuthering Heights*, testifies to the innerness of the landscape, both as interiorized experience and mirror of the soul. The linear way is not so much evocative of an ongoing, incre-mental progression as it is subjected to sudden shifts of intensification, depending on how forcefully it imposes itself on the mind.

Changing Heaven also substitutes lateral motions for sequential succession. It explores the whole range of possibilities between the substantial and the insubstantial, or the tangible and the intangible. Such movements are strongly evocative of the way clouds alternatively come into shape and vanish into thin air.[10] Emily and Arianna, the spectral

---

[9] See in particular Maria Anne Bell's dissertation: *Courting the Elements: Jane Urquhart's Novels and the Material Imagination.*

[10] Clouds are a source of inspiration to contemporary novelists. The example of Stéphane Audeguy's *La Théorie des Nuages* springs to mind. Audeguy too taps extensively into English cultural references, from Constable to a fictitious English cloud-painter, named Carmichael. In the same way as Urquhart dabbles in the more scientific side of meteorology through allusions to Admiral Beaufort's wind scale,

characters, keep appearing and disappearing and bring each other into existence by reading each other's thoughts. This mutual telepathy comments on the process of literary creation. Speaking of Catherine, the ghost of Emily remarks: "Someone I invented. And in some way she was the invention of someone else" (83). Thus the text invents itself as it revives its hypotext in an endless process. A critic has gone as far as to introduce a reference to the Frankenstein trope to comment on this constant (re)creative activity at work in *Changing Heaven* (Colvile 71). It should of course be borne in mind that Tabitha Ackroyd, who was familiar with Yorkshire folklore, had passed her precious fabulous knowledge on to the Brontë children, so that Jane Urquhart, in her turn, through her fiction is only perpetuating this tradition of oral telling. The choreographic movements of the two ghosts interlace the three plots, bringing together the contemporary, transcontinental level involving Ann, Arthur and later John, the moor-edger, and the turn-of- the-century one with the balloon episode. The whole novel is thus caught in spatial dynamics and in this respect differs significantly from other neo-Victorian novels in which the vertical, temporal dimension is prioritized through unearthed manuscripts, or more generally the antiquarian approach. Significant instances of such historicist re-appropriation of the past, at odds with Urquhart's skyey, aerial displacements, are frequent in contemporary women's fictions currently published in Britain (Letissier 2007).

In *Changing Heaven*, this emphasis on spatial displacement is best exemplified by the circular movement characterizing the whole fiction. It plays at different levels and is proof of Urquhart's interest in Yeats.[11] Superficial signs of circularity are easy enough to spot, from the incessant twirl and swirl of the two ghosts to the expression "the turn of the century" (40) as a fulcrum for the whole narrative. The many intratextual repetitions also contribute to the same effect. A fragment from a poem by Brontë is first cited as a text in an epigraph, before being "voiced" by Emily's spectre, and then dispersed by the winds. The verse is thus returned to the element that first inspired it, and may in turn inspire other similar literary productions:

Audeguy for his part mentions at some length Luke Howard, the early 19th century Quaker who developed the cloud classification system still in use today.

[11] "Sailing to Byzantium," "Byzantium," and "The Second Coming" are of course emblematic instances of this Yeatsian pattern of circularity. On Yeats's influence on Urquhart, see interview with Jane Urquhart conducted by Anne-Sophie Letessier at the SAES conference in Orléans (May 16th, 2008). Unpublished master's thesis, Nantes University, appendix, p. 125.

"'Tis many a year, 'tis long ago, since I beheld another dwelling," chanted the woman.
"What's all that?" asked Arianna in confusion.
"Oh... just something I wrote."
Well, it seems quite strange to me."
"Yes, I was quite morbid, really. It's amazing how much I've cheered up since I've been dead."
The wind roared through the two women. (42)

Urquhart's ghosts have none of the dour austerity of many of their neo-Victorian counterparts, for the sole reason that they do not belong to the past, but rather to the realm of creation which is a continuous present.[12] Circularity is even more subtly evinced through the enunciation. *Changing Heaven* is marked by shifts and hesitancy concerning the identity of the third person pronoun "she." In an all-encompassing circular movement the novel opens and closes on a rather elusive "she": "She wants to write about the wind, about the weather" (1) and "She who loved the weather becomes the weather" (258). The persistence of the present tense is of course the first striking feature, but the inscription of the feminine pronoun in the preamble and the coda is equally interesting. As Patsy Stoneman remarks: "It [the novel] begins with an undefined 'she' (who may be Emily Brontë or may be the modern writer, Ann) [...]. So much is contained in these simple sentences that the book demands a reading like poetry, with attention to single words" (Stoneman 90). In the plot, "she" is first actualized by Ann who writes a study on weather in Brontë's works. But soon this particularized "she" becomes fused with a transcendental, *Ur* pronoun, as it were, that is both the source and the *raison d'être* of Urquhart's whole literary project: Emily's own reflexive "she," to refer to the writer that she once was and to the ghost that she is now, and will continue to be. In fact, the use of this labile, slippery "she" precludes any limited source of the enunciation. So the beginning and the end of the novel poetically suggest that the narrative voice is not so much that of an omniscient narrator as a cosmic one that may potentially be re-embodied by whoever sets out to write. The very last words "someone illuminates an upstairs room" (258) send the reader back to the title of part two "The

---

[12] "The ghosts in *Changing Heaven* are ghosts on a metaphorical level as well as on an actual level. In a way, they haunt the book. I like to think of Emily Brontë as haunting her own presence in the story. Emily and Arianna don't manifest themselves as howling, shrieking phantoms dragging their chains behind them. They are not out to drive anyone mad with fear; the ghost of Emily Brontë is very much against haunting. On the whole, they are lighthearted ghosts – but they do talk about serious issues, particularly about women and men and how they regard each other." Jane Urquhart cited in "Ghosts in the Landscape," An interview by Jeffrey Canton, 3.

Upstairs Room"(121); Dickinson's poetic fragment standing for the solitariness of creation.

"This innerness, this otherness" (48): Romantic syntheticism

Urquhart's debt to Romanticism is everywhere present in *Changing Heaven*. First, through the omnipresence of the elements this fiction is a nature novel, illustrating the Romantic principle that art does not imitate nature but *is* nature.[13] It insists on the creative process, or *Bildungskraft* and on incompleteness. Just as the Romantics favored unfinished forms such as the fragment or the dialogue, the novel cannot be concluded. The last lines not only hint at someone illuminating an upstairs room but also at variable weathers, shifting winds and changing heaven. The relentless energy of the narrative, not so much as completed form (*ergon*) but as work in progress (*energeia*) in a continuous present, is expressed through syntheticism. Syntheticism is the interpenetration, and ultimately, the fusion of all contraries. It plays on different levels in *Changing Heaven* and contributes to transforming the novel's temporality into a sustained present. The first fusion to be operated is that between high and low cultures. Episodes from the literary canon, principally *Wuthering Heights*, are interlaced with contemporary texts of a lesser caliber to feed the Brontë hagiography and to convey a sense of the eternal present of the Yorkshire area as recreated by fiction. From Peggy Hewitt's *These Lonely Mountains*, a work concerned with local history, Urquhart borrows an authentic balloon accident which she expands into Jeremy Sindbad's ultimate flight to the Arctic. So what was originally a minor, historical event and a purely contingent occurrence is treated as a time-transcending, poetic symbol. Not only does the Arctic belong to the Brontë juvenilia where it features as Parry's Land, but this flight into an ocean of whiteness cannot fail to evoke Emily Brontë's own use of sea imagery in her description of the moors stretching to infinity.[14]

The sense of temporality is partly abolished through the dialogue, or network of interconnectedness, between the arts. Urquhart underscores

---

[13] This part of the article is based on Tzvetan Todorov, *Theories of the Symbol*, more especially on the chapter titled "The Romantic Crisis," 147-222.

[14] The epigraph "How still, how happy! Those are words/That once would scarce agree together;/I loved *the plashing of the surge,*/The changing heaven, the breathy weather" (italics mine), taken from poetic fragment 78 is illustrative of the Brontëan leitmotiv of the sea that can also be found in many other poetic pieces, see 5 "High waving heather 'neath stormy blasts bending" or 76 "It is swelled with the first snowy weather;/The rocks they are icy and hoar/And darker waves round the long heather" in Emily Jane Brontë, *The Complete Poems*, 90, 34, 86.

unheard-of coincidences between Tintoretto, the Venetian painter, who made extensive use of lightning in his canvases, and the etymology of Brontë which is Greek for thunder. Besides, whereas Tintoretto was known amongst his contemporaries as "Thunderbolt" (107) which is exactly what Brontë means literally, Emily for her part resorted to storms as a metonym for outbursts of passion in her one single novel. Such connections reduce the significance of the time gap by asserting the timelessness of the elements- in the present case the troubled skies literally mirroring the stormy relationship between Ann and Arthur, the two contemporary characters:

> "All these ceilings. I'm amazed that you don't have a permanent bend in your neck."
> "You don't need to worry about that. When you go the Scuola San Rocco [...] where all these paintings are [...] they give you a mirror."
> "Yes, a mirror to look at the ceilings." (106)

The boundary lines between art, nature and life are thus erased. Tintoretto's painted female saints are likened to pictures of Emily Brontë by Arthur in his one-off effort to say something personal and meaningful to Ann: "Arthur stops, however, for a moment in front of each of two painted female saints.[...] 'There is an Emily Brontë for you, two in fact. Solitary women of words'" (222). The scene between the two lovers thus insists upon artistic fusion, through representations of tempestuous skies, to call up a Romantic instant of sheer intensity defying the constraints of time: "There are centuries contained within this moment" (222). The whole range of artistic references, from Tintoretto to the Brontës, is thus condensed into this elusive episode, when the two contemporary characters are significantly represented in the liminal space of the staircase leading to the museum exit, shortly before parting – possibly forever.

By definition, syntheticism is epitomized by moments of transition, or threshold-crossing, because in such transitory passages, any dichotomy between the outside and the inside seems to be temporarily suspended. In this respect, the novel's most emblematic scene is the rewriting, or rather *reprising* of Catherine's plea to Lockwood in *Wuthering Heights*:

> "*Let me in, let me in*... I've been lost on the moor for twenty years."
> Then the glass shatters, the arm extends past the window's teeth into the warmth of the room. The little cold hand that brings a sample of weather with it into the claustrophobic interior. The shards of glass on the dusty blanket. The delicate, damp, determined hand reaching forward. (123)

What the word for word repetition emphasizes, through this synthetic blending of the hypotext and the hypertext, is in fact more complex than what may first appear. As the passage is mentioned just after Ann, the Brontë scholar, has arrived in Yorkshire from Canada, there is the need to be at one with a new geography, to be in as close a harmony as possible with the real, tangible landscapes as with their representation through the novel's descriptions. This "let me in, let me in" conveys the incredible dream of entering physically into the text, by walking in the footsteps of the Brontës, or those of their fictitious creations. Syntheticism then resides in this temporary suppression of any ontological distinction between the text and the referential world. But such a hyperbolical moment of interchange between the hypotext and the hypertext, with *Changing Heaven* pleading to be returned to the sheer original intensity of *Wuthering Heights*, may also be seen as a traumatic experience. Urquhart's novel is indeed about textual possession and the imprisonment that goes with it: "Ann sits, now, out on the West Yorkshire moors on a rock, under a leaden sky and thinks, *I'll never be free of this.* She thinks, *let me in, let me in.* She who has only recently managed to get herself out" (123). Thus, this synthetic encounter between the two texts is also a tug of war between the inescapability of passion, be it textual or physical, literary or amatory, and the irrepressible yearning to escape it fosters: "Let *me* go, if you want me to let you in!" (*Wuthering Heights* 67).[15] Indeed, Urquhart is concerned with moments of high intensity when the instant of crossing the borderline between art and life or life and art, is frozen to crystallize tensions. Would it be stretching the point then to suggest that *Changing Heaven* remains poised on the margin of *Wuthering Heights*, successively threading in and out of the geography of Brontë's text?

"At first it was *St George and the Dragon.* Do you know it?" [...]

"There is something terribly the matter in the painting. The woman – the princess – has just had some earth-shattering news and she is trying – I'm convinced of it – to get out of the painting." (95)

Ultimately, the most telling example of fusion of contraries can be found in passion itself. For the Romantics, notably Schelling, the interpenetration of the masculine and the feminine stood for the highest form that art could attain. Such union did not so much entail the cancellation of each opposite principle as their dynamic amalgamation. Urquhart appropriates Catherine's famous exalted confession to Nelly Dean: "I *am* Heathcliff" (*WH* 122) to treat of passion as the androgynous beast:

She remembers the beast that prowled through her illness, how it was both male and female – the fused lovers – what she wanted to become, what she

---

[15] Henceforth in page references respecting *Wuthering Heights*, the title will be abbreviated to *WH*.

72

has been trying to draw Arthur into. It wasn't that she wanted *him* so much as that she wanted him to become her. [...] Like that other androgynous beast, the beautiful devil/angel in Tintoretto's wilderness, she held fragrant loaves in her outstretched hands, but they contained annihilation for him. (237, original italics)

The power of passion cannot be dissociated from the violence of the unleashed elements. The human is the expression of raw, archaic forces. Urquhart takes up from Brontë the symbiotic relationship between the natural environment and the uncontrollable hold exerted by impulses: "My love for Heathcliff resembles the eternal rock beneath" (*WH* 122). Significantly, in *Changing Heaven* the throes of passion are experienced as exposure to erratic meteorological phenomena. By travelling from Canada to Yorkshire, Ann gives herself up to the unrelenting assaults of the weather: "She has memorized the words of the first scene in *Wuthering Heights*. She cannot shake its weather, cannot stop responding to the descriptions" (123). The traumatic consequences of her painful separation from Arthur are mentally re-enacted, as a form of cosmic drama, through the paradigmatic scene of the latticed window. Ann re-imagines herself as the fir tree branch intruding into the closed (to her) territory of Arthur's geography: "*I was misperceived as a harmless piece of vegetation tapping on the glass that separated us*" (123, original italics). If there is no ease of tension in *Wuthering Heights*, similarly in *Changing Heaven* passion is kept to a maximum of intensity. The desire between Catherine and Heathcliff is doomed never to be fulfilled and to feed itself on the very impossibility of its accomplishment, like a living organism in a sense. Georges Bataille has shown that through their absolute passion, Brontë's protagonists are led to exceed the limitations imposed upon their human condition. The temptation of death should be understood as the fascination for the ultimate, absolute and ephemeral instant abolishing the possibility of duration based on calculations and compromise.[16] Yet, in *Changing Heaven*, the nihilism of passion may be deprived of any Romantic grandeur in the last resort. This is probably where the postmodernist streak comes in; the revival of deep emotional turmoil results in an interiorized, aesthetic experience conducive to artistic creation. It does not close on tragedy as in *Wuthering Heights*, with Catherine's untimely death followed by Heathcliff's own demise and his crave to be reunited in the afterlife with the exclusive object of his all-consuming passion. Urquhart devotes long pages to recording the slow, gradual recovery allowing Ann, the Brontëan scholar, to regain her mental balance,

---

[16] "*la mort est le signe de l'instant qui, dans la mesure où il est l'instant renonce à la recherche de la durée.*" Georges Bataille, *La Littérature et le mal*, 24.

73

mostly thanks to the care and dedication of John, the encloser, the moor-edger, who is also oxymoronically "a gentle man who sets fire to the landscape" (149) to prevent nature from running wild. There is then, in the last resort, an attempt to negotiate with the demands of everyday reality. Likewise, the character who comes closest to the image of the dark, Byronic hero, bent on self destruction, is Jeremy Jacobs' (aka the "Sindbad of the Skies"). But his final flight to the Arctic may be construed as a post-colonial revision of the national fantasy of "the North as the final Frontier."[17] This may well be where the political agenda of *Changing Heaven* is to be found. Jeremy Jacob's fascination for purity, which ultimately leads him all the way to the pristine whiteness of the Arctic, also implies as its corollary a denial of femininity: the radical Other. For the aerialist, the virtues of womankind amount to purity, which is "colourless, odourless, and, most importantly, weightless" (24). Instead of standing for Imperial feats of heroism, Jacob's final exploration of the Arctic North, and his subsequent death, are thus presented as the outcome of a flawed ideology, extolling an absolutist ideal of adventures, whilst denying a full right of existence to half of mankind: "the very spirit of British womanhood ascending to her rightful place with the angels in the clouds" (25).

For all its emphasis on channeling and containment, *Changing Heaven* is by no means a parodic reduction of its hypotext, *Wuthering Heights* – itself an unclassifiable tale of passion and excess. Even if the characters are brought down to human size, the contemporary novel remains nonetheless committed to the sublime. First, it makes a claim for the unpredictable – "she wants [...] to have all her predictions proved wrong" (1) – through a narrative purporting to register "the perpetual present of [its characters'] own emotional landscape" (219). Given that "people are somehow out of bounds" (205), Urquhart's fiction eschews any fixed perspectives or stable frames. Furthermore, as a metafictional novel testifying to a personal experience of reading Emily Brontë, it opens out onto the infinite spaces that may only be surmised from the confined margins of *Wuthering Heights*. Beginning from the Asmodean phantasm of having full control of the novel's territory reduced to the size of a doll's house,[18] Urquhart's fiction subsequently enlarges so as to become incomparably beyond and above

---

[17] See for example " Ghostly Voices and Arctic Blanks: from *Wuthering Heights* to Jane Urquhart's *Changing Heaven*," an article in which Catherine Lanone draws from John Thieme's *Postcolonial Con-texts*, to present the Arctic North as the litmus test for masculinity in pristine wildernesses suitably devoid of women.

[18] More precisely, we read "shrinking the world of the novel into the territory of seven small furnished rooms. Four tiny dolls live there and magnificent dramas are born among them" (20).

the narrow precincts of its hypotext, thus fulfilling Catherine Earnshaw's dearest wish. Speaking about fiction-writing, the image that comes to Urquhart is play:

> Play [...] an extension of child's play. It's like the image in *Changing Heaven* of the doll house and the kid. If you had a little invented world, you knew you could leave that world there and go down to real life and do whatever you wanted. But if you wanted to go back to the invented world, you could.[19]

Play does indeed allow for endless border-crossing and makes of creation the hub of resurgences.

References

AUDEGUY, S. (2007), *La Théorie des nuages*, Paris, Folio Gallimard. (2007), *The Theory of Clouds*, Trans. Timothy Brent, New York, Harcourt.

BARKER, J. (1997), *The Brontës: A Life in Letters*, London, Viking.

BATAILLE, G. (1975), *La Littérature et le mal*, Paris, Gallimard.

BELL, M. A. (1998), *Courting the Elements: Jane Urquhart's Novels and the Material Imagination*, Dissertation Abstracts International, 59.5.

BRANACH-KALLAS, A. (2006), "Old Environments Or New Environment? Place and Self in Jane Urquhart's *Changing Heaven*," in *Literary Environments: Canada and the Old World*, B. OLINDER, Ed., Brussels, PIE Peter Lang, 219-225.

BRONTË, E. J. (1976), *Wuthering Heights*, Harmonsworth, Penguin.

BRONTË, E. J. (1992), *The Complete Poems*, J. GEZARI, Ed., Harmonsworth, Penguin Classics.

BYATT, A.S. (1991), *Possession, A Romance*, London, Vintage.

CANTON, J. (1998), "Ghosts in the Landscape: Jane Urquhart," Interview by Jeffrey Canton, in B. DAURIO, Ed., *The Power to Bend Spoons: Interviews with Canadian Novelists*, Toronto, Mercury Press, 194-99.

COLVILE, G. (1998), "The Quest for a Literary and Mythical Past in Three Novels by Jane Urquhart," *Études Canadiennes/Canadian Studies: Revue Interdisciplinaire des Études Canadiennes en France* 44: 61-76.

COMPTON, A. (2005), "Romancing the Landscape: Jane Urquhart's Fiction," in L. FERRI, Ed., *Jane Urqhart: Essays on Her Works*, Toronto, Guernica Editions, 115-143.

FERRI, L. Ed., (2005), *Jane Urquhart: Essays on Her Works*, Toronto, Guernica Editions.

FEDERICI, E. (2006), "An Inner Landscape of Obsessions: Jane Urquhart's *The Whirlpool*, *Changing Heaven* and *The Underpainter*," in E. RUSSELL, Ed.,

---

[19] Jane Urquhart in "Jane Urquhart: On Becoming a Novelist," by Susan Zettell, 18.

Loving Against the Odds: Women's Writing in English in a European Context, Oxford, Peter Lang, 153-162.

GASKELL, E. (1995), *The Life of Charlotte Brontë*, London, Penguin.

GERIN, W. (1967), *Charlotte Brontë, The Evolution of a Genius*, Oxford, OUP.

HEWITT, P. (1985), *These Lonely Mountains*, London, Springfield Books.

HUGHES, G. (1987), *Millstone Grit*, London, Pan Books.

JENNY, L. (1990), *La Parole Singulière*, Paris, Belin.

LANONE, C. "Ghostly Voices and Arctic Blanks: from *Wuthering Heights* to Jane Urquhart's *Changing Heaven*", myuminfo.umanitoba.ca/documents/214/LanoneC.pdf (Accessed February 18th, 2009).

LETISSIER, G. (2007), "Passion and Possession as Alternatives to 'Cosmic Masculinity' in A. Heilmann, & M. Lewyn, Eds., 'Herstorical Romances'," *Metafiction and Metahistory in Contemporary Women's Writing*, Palgrave Macmillan, 116-132.

PEKKIN, J. R. (1995), "Inhabiting Wuthering Heights: Jane Urquhart's Rewriting of Emily Brontë," in *Victorian Review: The Journal of the Victorian Studies Association of Western Canada and The Victorian Studies Association of Ontario* 21. 2: 115-128.

STONEMAN, P. (1997), "From Classic Text to Intertext: *Wuthering Heights* in a Post-Kristevan World," in *Versus: Quaderni di Studi Semiotici* 77-78: 75-96.

SYKES, K. (1994), "Jane Urquhart: Inside Other Worlds, An Interview," *Quarry* 43.2: 54-62.

THIEME, J. (2001), *Postcolonial Con-texts*, London, Continuum.

TODOROV, T. (1984), *Theories of the Symbol*, Trans. by Catherine Porter, New York, Cornell University Press.

URQUART, J. (1990), *Changing Heaven*, Toronto, McClelland & Stewart.

ZETTELL, S. (May 1991), "Jane Urquhart: On Becoming a Novelist," *The Canadian Forum* 69.79: 18-21.

5

Écrire le cri : résurgences figurales dans « Italian Postcards »

Héliane DAZIRON-VENTURA

Université d'Orléans

[…] des mondes se sont ouverts et s'ouvrent sans cesse à nous, mondes qui appartiennent aussi à la nature, mais qui ne sont pas visibles pour tous, qui ne le sont peut-être vraiment que pour les enfants, les fous, les primitifs. Je pense par exemple au royaume de ceux qui ne sont pas nés ou qui sont déjà morts, au royaume de ce qui peut venir, de ce qui aspire à venir, mais qui ne viendra pas nécessairement, un monde intermédiaire, un entre-monde. (Klee 116)

Il semblerait que Jane Urquhart dans la nouvelle intitulée « Italian Postcards » tirée du recueil *Storm Glass* de 1987 revendique explicitement cette faculté de voir un « entre-monde » décrite par le peintre Paul Klee. Elle revendique l'acuité de la conscience pré-verbale, ou pré-rationnelle comme mode d'accès privilégié à la vision : « maybe she just feels that, as an adult, she can't really see these colours, those vistas, and so, in the odd moments when she does, she must necessarily be a child again » (Urquhart 114).

Si Jane Urquhart nous convie à ce retour en enfance ou retour sur l'enfance, c'est pour convoquer une douleur intolérable dont l'origine n'est pas élucidée et dont l'acuité obnubile la pensée. Kristeva décrit la douleur comme : « lieu du sujet. Là où il advient, où il se différencie du chaos. Limite incandescente, insupportable entre dedans et dehors, moi et autre. Saisie première fugace : 'douleur,' 'peur,' mots ultimes visant cette crête où le sens bascule dans les sens, l''intime' dans 'les nerfs.' L'être comme mal-être » (Kristeva 65). Par un processus de séries associatives, Jane Urquhart va lier entre elles, dans la clôture cohésive du texte, des occurrences contextuelles incandescentes, éloignées dans le temps et dans l'espace, pour en faire la cause première ou la chose ultime de la représentation. Elle va faire du cri, cet événement sonore primal, pré-verbal, la matière intersémiotique de son intrigue à travers la double médiation du texte nouvellistique et de la carte postale narrativisée, en fusionnant trois lieux distincts : les ruines de Pompéi, la crypte de l'Église de Santa Chiara et le cloître d'un monastère dans la ville d'Assise. En intégrant le cri dans l'écrit par l'intermédiaire d'un dispositif intermédial, elle procède à un retour du vocal, du phonique, de l'extra-lexical dans une écriture qui nous rappelle la présence de la voix aux sources de la littérature première en même temps que sa saturation par l'image, la figure, le fantasme. De façon synesthésique et exacerbée, Jane Urquhart nous fait voir un cri qui advient en image. Elle introduit les éléments d'un espace sonore dans un espace discursif par l'intermédiaire d'«un espace de vue» (Lyotard 373) pour ouvrir un espace de lecture interstitiel, pré-rationnel, qui ignore la séparation entre les catégories et privilégie l'effacement de la signification au profit de correspondances aigües ou diffuses entre les sens.

Le texte d'«Italian Postcards» se lit comme un ensemble apparemment clos dans lequel quatre histoires sont emboîtées. Dans cet agencement de deux séries doubles, tout commence par la remémoration de la maladie et des cataplasmes à la moutarde, «the agonizing poultice,» (115) dans lesquels la petite fille appelée Clara se trouvait enveloppée quand elle souffrait des bronches. Une série contiguë à celle-ci se développe autour des cartes postales que Clara regardait pour se distraire pendant la durée de sa maladie. Celles qui retiennent son intérêt en particulier, et qui résonnent de toute la force d'une allitération en «s», représentent les habitants de Pompéi enfermés pour l'éternité dans une gangue de lave solidifiée : «a scream in stone that once was liquid» (115).

Deux autres séries concernent également Clara, mais vingt cinq ans plus tard, lors d'un voyage qu'elle effectue avec son mari dans la ville d'Assise devenue pour elle le lieu de l'irruption d'une douleur d'être au monde qui se répand dans son corps et dans le paysage qui l'environne comme de la lave en fusion:

> Pure eruption. Shards of her broken heart are everywhere, moving through her bloodstream, lacerating her internally on their voyage from the inside out into the landscape, until every sense is raw. She can actually see the soundwaves that are in front of her. (125)

La douleur éprouvée par la jeune femme est confirmée et redoublée par la série parallèle qui se développe autour de son homonyme, Santa Chiara, l'instigatrice de l'ordre conventuel des Clarisses. Comme le corps des habitants de Pompéi conservé dans une gangue de lave et exposé dans des cercueils de verre, le corps de Santa Chiara est incorruptible et présenté aux pèlerins dans un sarcophage de verre, à travers lequel ils peuvent distinguer le cri d'horreur qui s'inscrit sur son visage :

> Frozen on Chiara's face the terrifying wonderful pain; permanent incorruptible, unable to decay. The dead mouth is open, shouting pain silently up to the electricity, past the glass, into the empty cave of the church, out into the landscape, up to the street, to the basilica where images of the live Chiara appear deceitfully serene, in the frescoes. It is the heartbreak that is durable, Clara thinks to herself experiencing the shock of total recognition. (126)

Le sentiment d'empathie « est la *reviviscence* d'un état affectif par l'intermédiaire d'une *présentation* » (Victor Basch cité par Georges Didi-Huberman 417). Ce sentiment d'empathie et d'identification, éprouvé par Clara face à Chiara, est préfiguré par la quasi homophonie de leurs prénoms mais il n'est pas circonscrit par la présentation de la sainte dans son cercueil de verre, baigné de lumière électrique. Les deux séries précédentes liées à son enfance participent également à cette commotion, à cet ébranlement de l'être, parce qu'elles présentent un certain nombre de résonances ou de correspondances avec les deux séries qui se déroulent à Assise.

Il s'est passé quelque chose dans cette nouvelle, quelque chose d'inattendu et d'intolérable, qui est de l'ordre de l'allusion à un séisme littéral, celui de Pompéi, le 23 août de l'année 79 avant Jésus Christ, mais également de l'ordre métaphorique. La jeune femme, en voyage en Italie, va faire l'expérience de ce que l'on peut appeler le retour du refoulé, la crise existentielle, le trauma, ou peut-être la douleur originaire. Le séisme qui la secoue est un événement au sens deleuzien du terme c'est à dire, celui où « il y a bien le moment présent de l'effectuation, celui où l'événement s'incarne dans un état de choses, un individu, une personne, celui qu'on désigne en disant : voilà le moment est venu » (Deleuze, 1969 : 176). Il advient à Assise, dans le jardin du cloître de l'hostellerie appelée *Oasie* alors qu'elle lit un livre intitulé *The Little Flowers of Santa Chiara* et qu'elle regarde un jeune moine s'occuper des roses et du potager. Cet événement est incorporel ou plutôt transcorporel car pour faire sens il implique des connexions aux autres séries de singularités événementielles décrites dans la nouvelle, le séisme de Pompéi, la maladie de la petite enfance, le cri éternel de Santa Chiara. L'événement de la crise existentielle de Clara, jeune adulte, est le point de rencontre et de résonance des trois autres séries : il est l'Événement constitué à partir des autres événements singuliers.

Le corps fossilisé et minéralisé des habitants de Pompéi, la dépouille incorruptible de Santa Chiara, le cataplasme de moutarde sur les poumons de Clara enfant et le cri silencieux qui s'échappe de ses lèvres vingt cinq ans plus tard forment ce que Deleuze appelle « un agencement, une série, un bloc d'intensités » (Deleuze, 1975 : 131). La distribution de ce bloc d'intensités met en relief l'envahissement de l'espace diégétique par un affect tout-puissant, un affect douloureux qui fait retour de série en série, comme une coulée de lave incandescente : comme « un flux refluant, une protension survivante » (Didi-Huberman 156). Cette résurgence de formes affectives primitives qui n'est pas de l'ordre de la linéarité temporelle mais bien plutôt de la « concomitance inattendue d'un contretemps et d'une répétition » (Didi-Huberman 168), crée un archétype durable auquel Aby Warburg a donné le nom de « formule type de pathos » ou *pathosformel*, comme en témoigne Didi-Huberman et comme Ernst Cassirer le décrit :

> [Warburg] a montré comment l'Antiquité avait crée pour certaines situations typiques et sans cesse récurrentes, diverses formes d'expression marquantes. Certaines émotions internes, certaines tensions, certaines solutions y sont non seulement encloses, mais en quelque sorte figées par un enchantement. Partout où se manifeste un affect de même nature, partout revit l'image que l'art a crée pour lui. Selon l'expression même de Warburg, il naît des formules types de pathos précises qui se gravent de manière indélébile dans la mémoire de l'humanité. Et c'est à travers toute l'histoire des beaux arts qu'il a traqué ces stéréotypes, leurs contenus et leurs avatars, leur statique et leur dynamique. (Cassirer cité par Didi-Huberman 202)

La « formule type de pathos », constituée par Urquhart en 1987 à partir du cri de Clara dans le cloître de l'hostellerie à Assise, du cri des habitants de Pompéi en 79 avant Jésus Christ, et de celui de Santa Chiara en 1253 s'inscrit dans le prolongement d'exemples picturaux célèbres de la fin du dix-neuvième siècle comme « Le cri » selon Munch (1893), ou encore du vingtième siècle comme « Le Pape Innocent X » selon Bacon (1953).[1] Pour rester dans le contexte italien, l'on pourrait également proposer comme hypo-icônes des exemples sculpturaux de la renaissance comme par exemple celui de Sainte Madeleine qui crie sa douleur devant la mort du Christ dans le groupe de statues en terre cuite intitulé « la Déploration du Christ » par Niccolò dell'Arca (*circa* 1480)[2] à Bologne, ou comme celui de la bouche ouverte des monstres de pierre du Parco dei Mostri (*circa* 1550) à Bomarzo, au nord de Rome.

Dans cette liste sélective, transnationale et transhistorique, des avatars inépuisables, l'on pourrait encore faire figurer l'exemple canadien

---

[1] Voir en particulier les études réalisées par Bacon d'après le portrait du pape Innocent X par Velasquez dans l'ouvrage critique que lui consacre Gilles Deleuze, *Francis Bacon, Logique de la sensation*, II Peintures, pp. 54, 57. Deleuze analyse l'hystérie à partir de la figure du pape qui crie dans le tome 1, p. 37.

[2] Cette statue, qui se trouve dans l'église Santa Maria della Vita, non loin de Piazza Maggiore, est reproduite sous forme photographique et analysée dans l'ouvrage de George Didi-Huberman, *L'image survivante Histoire de l'art et temps des fantômes selon Aby Warburg*, p. 179.

de « D'Sonoqua », le totem représentant la femme sauvage qui habite les profondeurs des forêts de Colombie Britannique, dont la bouche ouverte interpelle mystérieusement et doublement Emily Carr dans le recueil de nouvelles intitulée *Klee Wyck* et dans le tableau qu'elle lui consacra[3] (« Guyasdoms'D'Sonoqua », 1929-30). C'est bien la même formule de pathos qui s'y exprime à travers le même symptôme et qui produit la même forme esthétique primitive : cette bouche ouverte à travers laquelle tout le corps semble s'échapper dans un spasme hystérique. Comme le démontre Didi-Huberman « la psyché dans l'histoire laisse des traces. Elle se fraye un chemin et laisse son empreinte dans les formes visuelles » (Didi-Huberman 220-221).

En insérant deux fois dans sa nouvelle, à vingt-cinq ans de distance, une carte postale de corps statufiés en train de crier pour en faire l'événement de son récit, Urquhart se positionne clairement dans une lignée : elle se situe dans une généalogie esthétique qui repose sur la mise en visibilité d'une formule de pathos qui réduit l'écart entre l'écrit, le visuel et le sonore. Elle met en scène une collision de médiations, le sarcophage, la statue, la carte, la nouvelle, et à l'intérieur de cet emboîtement de supports, elle recourt à la synesthésie de façon répétée pour favoriser la transgression des frontières. Ainsi les cartes postales deviennent-elles le site d'effets de correspondances particulièrement marqués : leurs couleurs se répandent, elles brillent et elles crient :

> And the colours in the postcards were real after all […] they flash by on the backs of overdressed children. Near the desk of the hotel they shout out from travel posters. (116)

La synesthésie procède par déplacement, ainsi l'artisan italien qui tapisse les murs de sa chambre avec un nouveau papier peint chante-t-il des arias avec des larmes dans la voix : « Long, long sobbing notes trembling in the winter sunshine » (117). Le déplacement de l'écoulement lacrymal dans les cordes vocales déstabilise les frontières entre les sensations pour les fusionner en un seul et même épanchement symbolique et littéral: celui de la lave incandescente, qui subsume tous les autres phénomènes pour envahir l'espace psychique et diégétique mis en scène par la nouvelle d'Urquhart.

Les effets synesthésiques que l'on retrouve d'une série à l'autre n'abolissent pas seulement les frontières entre les sensations. Elles permettent l'oubli de l'écart entre la représentation du monde et celle du sujet. Tout se passe comme si le monde s'incarnait dans le sujet pendant que le sujet fusionnait avec le monde. Si les cartes postales qui

---

[3]   Voir la reproduction du tableau dans le livre que Doris Shadbolt consacre à l'œuvre picturale d'Emily Carr p. 84 et son *ekphrasis* dans *Klee Wyck*, p. 33. Ce tableau se trouve à la Galerie d'Art de l'Ontario.

représentent des paysages à l'intérieur d'une nouvelle peuvent crier, c'est que l'écart entre la carte et l'être est aboli, qu'ils ont fusionné dans une même lettre vivante. Ce qu'Urquhart s'attache à rendre, à travers la puissance d'incarnation de l'écriture, c'est la formule primitive de « l'image-pathos » (Didi-Huberman 114) : la réactivation d'une énergie volcanique qui s'exprime dans un surgissement ou une résurgence à la fois littérale et métaphorique, et où les pulsions de l'individu et les séismes géologiques se répondent. Dans sa réanimation des formules de pathos de l'antiquité, elle tente de mettre en lumière les processus de correspondances entre les formes affectives du passé et la vie psychique de personnages contemporains en les confrontant les unes aux autres sur la toile de fond unificatrice d'un « chaosmos » originel. C'est au septième jour passé dans le jardin du cloître, que le cri silencieux de Clara, récapitulatif et anticipatif, sourd des profondeurs de son être, comme un entre-deux, à mi-chemin entre la naissance au monde et l'exil hors du jardin, entre la naissance du monde et la catastrophe finale.

La correspondance entre l'ébullition des entrailles de la terre, et le réveil du pole pulsionnel primitif de l'individu souligne le lien archaïque de la terre et de la femme. L'effacement des frontières entre le vivant et le géologique permet la convergence de l'histoire individuelle, de l'histoire collective et de l'histoire de la formation ou de l'abolition du monde. Le séisme psychique éprouvé par la jeune femme peut être envisagé non seulement comme une forme de reviviscence de la catastrophe qui a affecté la ville de Pompéi, qui est elle-même une reviviscence des mouvements géologiques qui ont construit le paysage que nous connaissons actuellement, mais également comme une reviviscence des grands mythes eschatologiques, de la Genèse à l'Apocalypse. La nouvelle ne s'élabore pas seulement sur le retour des « formules-types de pathos » telles qu'Aby Warburg les a conceptualisées. Elle se définit également, en reprenant la formule de Jacques Rancière, comme « un morceau du poème du monde » (Rancière 40), un éclat, une pierre de lave, du métarécit.

Tout se passe comme si la survie de corps pétrifiés, enserrés dans leur gangue de lave refroidie, attestée par les cartes postales, décrites dans une nouvelle allait permettre l'effacement des frontières entre les catégories les plus antagonistes, les plus irréductibles ou les plus hermétiques. Les personnages de Pompéi redoublés par l'exemple de Santa Chiara à Assise ne sont ni tout à fait vivants, ni tout à fait morts : ni tout à fait organiques, ni tout à fait inorganiques, ils occupent la position inquiète d'un entre-deux, non stabilisé. Clara, enfant, se pose la question de savoir ce qu'il adviendrait des corps pétrifiés dans la lave si le volcan se réveillait à nouveau. L'éternité de leur incorruptibilité est présentée comme un suspens momentané de la décomposition, une zone intermédiaire labile qui crée une atmosphère d'inquiétante étrangeté et qui contamine l'espace de la nouvelle où tout semble reposer sur le principe de conserver du mort vivant.

Cette conservation du mort vivant se manifeste par l'oubli des frontières entre l'organique et l'inorganique que l'on rencontre d'entrée de jeu dans la première comparaison de l'incipit :

> Years later when she touches postcards she will be amazed that her hands are so large. Perhaps she feels that the hands of a child are proportionally correct to rest like book ends on either side of landscapes. (114)

En reconfigurant les mains de la petite fille en serre-livres, Urquhart opère une première transformation de l'organique en inorganique qui est rendue plus complexe par l'opération complémentaire symétriquement inverse. La carte postale inorganique enserrée par les mains/serre-livres devient un paysage comme pour s'émanciper de la médiation fournie par son support et se confondre avec son référent organique. Les frontières entre le référent et la représentation visuelle s'estompent dans le même temps que l'univers du livre s'incarne dans le corps de la petite fille : si ses mains sont des « book-ends » c'est que peut-être son corps tout entier, et pas seulement les cartes postales qu'elles enserrent, peut être envisagé comme un livre.

Ce processus de déréalisation magique repose sur l'effacement réciproque des frontières entre le dehors et le dedans que l'on peut percevoir dans la description de la chambre de la petite fille, où les cartes postales qui jonchent sa courtepointe sont décrites comme des feuilles d'arbres pendant que la chambre elle-même est dépeinte comme un paysage intérieur dont Clara conservera le souvenir toute sa vie. Les murs y sont couverts de fleurs de pommiers, la coiffeuse est recouverte d'une jupe sous laquelle ses poupées sont cachées :

> The room she lies on weekdays, when she has managed to stay home from school is all hers. She'll probably carry it around with her for the rest of her life. Soft grey wallpaper with sprays of pink apple blossom. Pink dressing table (under the skirts of which her dolls hide, resting on their little toy beds) cretonne curtains swathed over a window at the foot of the bed she occupies, two or three pink pillows propping her up. (114)

Les fleurs de pommiers sur le papier peint déstabilisent les frontières entre intérieur et extérieur ; la « jupe » de la coiffeuse encourage l'effacement des frontières entre la chambre et la petite fille et la syntaxe ambiguë qui désigne la chambre comme lui appartenant intégralement renforce également la possibilité de substitution de l'une par rapport à l'autre ; enfin la polysémie du signifiant « hide » qui en tant que verbe signifie « se cacher » et en tant que nom désigne « la peau », en particulier celle d'un animal, contribue également au passage de l'inorganique à l'organique.

Les poupées à « la peau d'animal », « cachées » sous la « jupe » de la coiffeuse, forment le pendant exactement symétrique et inversé des corps humains pétrifiés exposés à la vue de tous dans un sarcophage de verre à Pompéi. À ces poupées à la peau d'animal on peut également substituer la petite fille au corps recouvert d'un cataplasme à la moutarde ou la sainte momifiée dans son cercueil de verre. À l'opacité des cataplasmes organiques et à l'opacité de la lave inorganique s'oppose la transparence des sarcophages de verre sous lesquels les corps des habitants de Pompéi et le corps de Santa Chiara sont exposés.

Il semblerait que la permutation des bi-isotopies opacité/transparence et organique/inorganique sous-tend l'organisation structurale et métaphorique des séries sans jamais permettre le basculement unilatéral dans une catégorie ou dans une autre. Les séries se constituent et se maintiennent en participant des deux catégories à la fois, dans l'entre-deux d'une appartenance équivoque : si le sarcophage de verre est transparent, c'est pour mieux mettre en visibilité l'opacité des corps pétrifiés. Si la lave solidifiée est bien inorganique, c'est pour mieux enserrer et conserver les corps de ceux qui ont été piégés par le séisme.

L'opposition dialectique entre opacité et transparence met en tension l'occultation et la révélation. L'opposition dialectique entre organique et inorganique met en exergue le corruptible et l'incorruptible. D'un côté il y aurait la révélation, l'épanchement, la décomposition, la putréfaction, et de l'autre la stase, la solidification, la conservation, la dissimulation. Ces deux types d'oppositions qui reposent sur le passage du dedans au dehors et du dehors au dedans peuvent être envisagées en termes derridiens comme la transformation du « hors » en « fors ». De façon métatextuelle, il est également possible de les envisager comme les modalités du passage à l'art ou comme celles de l'expression du « livre imprimé en nous » (Rancière 72). La permutation des bi-isotopies transparence/opacité et organique/inorganique fait refluer le monde dans le livre et le livre dans le monde. L'inscription dans la nouvelle du cri silencieux de Clara lisant le livre de Chiara *The Little flowers of Santa Chiara* dans le jardin du cloître d'Assise met en évidence la communication des corps physiques avec la chair du monde et le corps des textes.

L'effacement des frontières entre les personnages de la nouvelle et le personnage intertextuel de Santa Chiara entraînent un devenir-livre du personnage et un devenir-livre du paysage qui est également un devenir-paysage et un devenir-personnage du livre. Ces transformations réciproques ordonnées autour de la figure du chiasme sont confirmées par d'autres séries d'allusions et de citations plus ou moins explicites à d'autres œuvres. Il y a d'abord la réécriture implicite du titre de la nouvelle « Italian Postcards » qui est sans doute une allusion au livre de Dickens de 1846, *Pictures from Italy*. Mais il y a surtout la réécriture d'un poème de John Donne qui fait explicitement irruption dans le texte par le biais d'un pastiche qui se répand non seulement sur le paysage, mais qui va et vient dans l'esprit du personnage. Ainsi depuis la fenêtre de la chambre de leur hôtel, Clara et son mari regardent-ils les lumières qui brillent à flanc de colline sur les tombes du cimetière tout illuminé et les vers de la chanson, "Go and catch a falling star/Get with child a mandrake root" transformé en "Go and light a tomb at night/Get with child a mandrake root" envahissent l'esprit de Clara, avant de s'évaporer comme de la brume.

De la même façon, dans les couloirs de l'hôtel, alors qu'elle suit le jeune moine qui leur montre le chemin de leur chambre, des mots italiens lui traversent l'esprit : « Cumbersome words such as *basilica*, *portcullis*, *Etruscan* and *Vesuvius* rumble disturbingly, and for no apparent reason, through her mind » (116). Ce grondement des mots fait refluer le volcan de l'extérieur vers l'intérieur. De façon symétriquement inversée, la déambulation de Clara, un peu plus tard, quand elle est seule, à travers les couloirs de l'hôtel fait refluer le monde dans les livres parce que poussée par la curiosité, elle ouvre toutes les portes des chambres de l'hôtel vide, et elle semble alors traverser le miroir. *Through the looking Glass* est même cité dans la nouvelle, (121) en référence à un autre livre auquel la vie de Clara se connecte directement : *The Little Flowers of Santa Chiara*. Dans cette biographie de la Sainte, son départ de la maison familiale est narré en termes de rite de passage. La jeune fille s'échappe en empruntant la porte réservée à la descente des cercueils : elle emprunte « The Door of the Dead ».

L'expérience de Clara à Assise est le double symétrique de celle de Chiara. Ce que Clara rencontre dans la crypte de Santa Chiara, devant le cri d'horreur de la sainte, c'est sa propre crypte intrapsychique, la remotivation du conflit infantile originaire, le traumatisme initial, l'obstacle à la fructification du trésor. La crypte de l'Église de Santa Chiara désigne le propre for de Clara dans lequel un corps étranger travaille son propre corps. L'étranger incorporé, encrypté, avec toutes ses forces libidinales et toutes ses contradictions, c'est la mort conservée vivante qu'elle rencontre devant le sarcophage de verre qui exhibe son homonyme.

L'homonymie entre Clara et Chiara exacerbe le clivage du moi en mettant en vis à vis non seulement la femme qui conserve en elle du mort vivant et la sainte momifiée mais également la femme vivante et l'héroïne du livre ; ce vis à vis de l'être et de la lettre constitue le chiasme fondateur du récit qui met en cause « les lieux, la mort et le chiffre », pour reprendre l'analyse de Derrida dans « Fors » (Derrida

11). La crypte littérale de l'Église de Santa Chiara encrypte la faille métaphorique de Clara mais il faut peut-être également chercher le chiffre dans les accidents du langage que présente la nouvelle et à travers lesquels la langue parle. Il y a au moins quatre accidents : le premier est de l'ordre de la fausse attribution. La narratrice attribue un poème célèbre de John Donne intitulé « Song » à Blake, elle déstabilise ainsi les frontières identitaires et ouvre la voie à l'amalgame entre Clara et Chiara. Le monastère où Clara et son mari s'installent pour leurs vacances italiennes est supposé s'appeler *Oasie*. Or, il s'agit d'un barbarisme puisque le mot *oasi*, qui désigne une oasis est invariable. Le mot doublement étranger est bien la crypte où Clara incorpore l'altérité de l'autre Claire ; de ce monastère situé à Assise, il est dit qu'il se tient sur le flanc d'une colline toscane. Or la ville d'Assise est située en Ombrie, la situer en Toscane est un mode de refus : une forme d'expulsion interne ou incorporation/dissimulation du royaume des ombres. Finalement une des chambres de ce monastère se nomme « Sala Beatico Angelico ». Nous avons là un mot valise formé de la contraction de Beato et d'Angelico. Cette chambre interdite est une église baroque, dissimulée derrière une porte ordinaire. L'étrangeté de son nom la signale comme un autre lieu cryptique, le double exactement symétrique et inversé de l'Église de Santa Chiara : le lieu des béatitudes séraphiques, d'un paradis où les morts vivent pour l'éternité, ce qui confirme la dimension sépulcrale des découvertes effectuées par Clara mais transmue l'abjection du mort vivant en représentation attractive. Ce n'est pas dans la salle « Beatico Angelico » que Clara voit le cri d'horreur de la Sainte. C'est dans la crypte de l'Église de Santa Chiara.

Ces accidents du langage représentent une mise en crise de la langue qui redouble la crise identitaire et existentielle du personnage. « Italian Postcards » est une fiction qui met en scène la reviviscence des traumatismes de l'enfance et qui répète les accidents de l'acquisition du langage de même qu'elle répète son expression première, le cri originaire. Comme l'a démontré Jean-Jacques Lecercle à propos du Nonsense, l'on peut avancer que la nouvelle d'Urquhart est une fiction de l'enfance qui, par le cri, encrypte l'enfance de la fiction.

Le dernier paragraphe de la nouvelle nous donne à voir une occurrence supplémentaire du retour involutif à l'enfance et du redoublement de la crypte intrapsychique dans le monde réel. Clara se trouve dans l'avion qui la ramène au Canada et elle a placé la carte postale qui représente le sarcophage de la Sainte dans la poche intérieure de son sac à main, qu'elle serre contre son cœur. Le cri de la Sainte est enclavé, encavé, enkysté à l'intérieur de l'avion, à l'intérieur du sac, à l'intérieur de la poche, à l'intérieur du moi. L'invagination du cri, ou le redoublement des lieux cryptiques dans lesquels il se trouve réprimé est exacerbé par le redoublement des supports sur lesquels ou à travers lesquels il est exprimé, la statue, le sarcophage de verre, la carte, la nouvelle. Pour parler comme Abraham et Torok (1976: 299), dans ce « refoulement conservateur », cette « expérience libidinale indicible », cette « identification occulte », ce qui est inter-dit, c'est d'abord la vraie souffrance d'une plaie qui reste béante, ce sont aussi les déguisements plastiques, graphiques, visuels, sonores ou muets par lesquels elle fait retour. Et ce sont finalement les contradictions mêmes de la littérature qui sont ins-cri-tes ici : comment é-crire/in-scrire le cri dans l'écart de la carte et le tracé de la nouvelle ? Comment représenter l'irreprésentable ? Comment faire parler l'opacité, comment faire taire la transparence ? Comment solidifier le corruptible et liquéfier l'incorruptible ? Comment passer du livre de pierre au livre de vie ? Comment imprimer ce qui est exprimé ? Comment nommer l'innommable ? Comment saisir la poéticité de la poésie, cet état de langage que Rancière définit comme « entre-appartenance de la pensée et du langage » ? (Rancière 40)

La réponse d'Urquhart, c'est le don du cri comme parole silencieuse et comme image celée, dans une nouvelle qui est comme « un morceau du poème du monde » et qui nous interroge, comme le dit Rancière, sur la manière « dont cette vérité s'anticipe en œuvres muettes parlantes, en œuvres qui parlent en tant qu'image, en tant que pierre, en tant que matière résistant à la signification qu'elle délivre » (Rancière 40)[4].

Références

ANONYME (1996), *I Fioretti di San Francesco : Storie di santita e di*, Rizzoli, Biblioteca universale.

ABRAHAM, N. et M. TOROK (1976), *Le verbier de l'homme aux loups*, Paris, Flammarion.

ABRAHAM, N. et M. TOROK (1987), *L'écorce et le noyau*, Paris, Flammarion.

CARR, E. (1941), *Klee Wyck*, Toronto, Irwin Publishing.

DELEUZE, G. (1969), *Logique du sens*, Paris, Minuit.

DELEUZE, G. et F. GUATTARI (1975), *Kafka Pour une littérature mineure*, Paris, Minuit.

DELEUZE, G. (1996) *Francis Bacon, Logique de la sensation*, Paris, Éditions de la différence, « coll. La Vue le Texte ».

---

[4]   Une version antérieure de cet essai, accompagnée d'une présentation de Jane Urquhart, et d'un entretien en anglais, a été publiée dans un cahier de recherches de l'université d'Orléans : Héliane Ventura, "Encountering Jane Urquhart," *Sources 19* (printemps 2006): 5-24.

DERRIDA, J., « Les mots anglès de Nicolas Abraham et Maria Torok », Préface, ABRAHAM, N. et M. TOROK (1976), *Le verbier de l'homme aux loups*, Paris, Flammarion, 7-73.

DICKENS, C. [1846] (1998), *Pictures from Italy*, Harmondsworth, Penguin.

DIDI-HUBERMAN, G. (2002), *L'image survivante Histoire de l'art et temps des fantômes selon Aby Warburg*, Paris, Minuit.

DONNE, J. (1966), *Poetical Works*, H. GRIERSON, Ed., London, Oxford University Press.

GRIMAL, P. et E. KOSSAKOVSKI (1992), *Pompéi Demeures secrètes*, Paris, Imprimerie Nationale.

KLEE, F. et P. KLEE (1963), *Paul Klee par lui-même et par son fils Félix Klee*, Trad. Maurice Besset, Paris, Les libraires associés.

KRISTEVA, J. (1980), *Pouvoirs de l'horreur*, Paris, Seuil.

LECERCLE, J.-J. (1995), *Le dictionnaire et le cri*, Nancy, Presses universitaires de Nancy.

LYOTARD, J.-F. (1985), *Discours, Figure*, Paris, Klincksieck.

RANCIERE, J. (1998), *La Parole muette*, Paris, Hachette.

SHADBOLT, D (1979), *The Art of Emily Carr*, Vancouver, Douglas & McIntyre.

URQUHART, J. (1987), *Storm Glass*, Erin, The Porcupine's Quill.

PART II

METAHISTORY AND METATEXTUALITY

6

When the Underpainting Shows Through: Jane Urquhart's Resurgent Transmutations

Marta DVOŘÁK

Université Sorbonne Nouvelle-Paris 3

In her first novel, *The Whirlpool* (1986), immediately translated in France under the more identifiable title *Niagara* and awarded the *Prix du meilleur livre étranger* (Best Foreign Book), Jane Urquhart adopted right from the start an interstitial geographical and temporal space framed by Republic and Empire. She configured as a locus of resurgence the watery zone of Niagara Falls straddling the unstable Canadian/ American border, site of military battles during the War of 1812 between a newly emancipated colony in search of expansion and the Canadas, eager to remain loyal imperial subjects. The whirlpool itself is the novel's seductive metaphor for the passage from visible, verifiable, rational reality and *logos* to another plane involving the invisible, the irrational, and the imaginary of *poiesis*. New World topography overlaps with Old World cultural matrices: in a palimpsestic fashion, the scene of the poet Browning dying in Venice and dreaming of Shelley drowning metamorphoses into three interlacing stories staging the passionate relations between language and place on Canadian soil. *The Whirlpool* anticipates Urquhart's subsequent novel *Away* (1993), a mythopoeic epic of Irish emigration suffused with Gaelic legends, reconfigured and transposed through the personal symbolism of objects: these notably generate magical metamorphosis through incongruous encounters and jarring assemblages.[1]

While the *topoi* of deracination, exile, and memory which seem to predominate in Jane Urquhart's *œuvre* have received a good share of

---

[1] The family saga beginning in Ireland in 1840 notably opens with a haunting and a possession: the oneiric scene of a young shipwrecked sailor dying in the arms of a young woman surrounded by floating cabbages and silver teapots.

critical attention,[2] the writer's focus on the visual arts in the Governor-General's Award-winning novel *The Underpainter* (1997) led me to believe that generating the writer's poetics is not so much an interest in uprooting, displacement, and cultural transplantation in themselves, as a fascination for mutation and metamorphosis.[3] I see these subtending *The Underpainter*, notably through the artistic practices of pentimento[4] and its more radical corollaries of obviation and erasure. The technique involving the intended but erratic resurgence of earlier underlying painting which the painter protagonist Austin Fraser has covered with semi-transparent glazes (pentimento) commingles with the wholly drastic techniques of obscuration in his Erasure series. He releases these paintings to the public only after waiting for two years for possible resurgences, scraping and repainting if faint shapes re-emerge through the added layers of white, treated as "chemical impurities" (41) to be eliminated rather than as the desired ghostly apparitions of pentimenti. In-between these two strategies lies the more liminal technique of obviation consisting of obscuring not by taking away but by adding, by superimposing layers of increasingly paler hues and even images so as to submerge and cancel form and detail.[5]

I sense a similar authorial fascination in *The Stone Carvers* (2001) and its opening focus on the metamorphic craft of woodcarving, "the miracle of turning wood to flesh" (*SC* 21), and I find an equally strong concern with the process of transformation in Urquhart's following novel, *A Map of Glass* (2005), whose artist protagonist, Jerome McNaughton, seeks to record mutation in movement, to "mark the moment of metamorphosis when something changed from what it had been in the past" (*Map* 11). Both *The Underpainter* and *A Map of Glass* depict transformation as inherently dysphoric. All the while celebrating

---

[2] The histories of the displaced are addressed, albeit in different ways, by critics ranging from Herb Wyile, David Staines and Caterina Ricciardi to Cynthia Sugars and Claire Omhovère.

[3] Claire Omhovère, who explores the way Urquhart goes beyond the disjunctions of postmodern historical metafiction, also detects a fascination with "Ovidian changeability" in the essay playfully entitled "Copies and (Ab)originals: The Problem of Authenticity in Jane Urquhart's *Away* (1993)" (Omhovère 183).

[4] The artist narrator relates how for weeks he paints a lived lake landscape in scrupulous detail, from the stones, water, and sky, right down to the lake-worn fragments of china washed up on shore, and then "when it's all there, [he] will take two weeks more to add the patina, the glazes, the semi-transparent layers" (Urquhart, *The Underpainter* 110).

[5] "In the underpainting, there were three lost grey children dissolving into the organic matter surrounding them... Three separate children: but as I worked on the subsequent layers of the picture, they began to cancel one another out" (*Underpainter* 133). Also see the quote in the following note.

craftsmanship, the earlier novel is suffused with the motif of absence and loss. The artist's method of creation involves a meticulously realistic portrayal subsequently invalidated by a deliberate de-construction characteristic of the epistemological crisis coterminous with modernism. Through enumeration, repetition, and echo,[6] Urquhart emphasizes the creation/decreation process which T.S. Eliot sang in "The Love Song of Alfred J. Prufrock" to a backdrop of bloody pan-European warfare and the destruction of the old world order.[7] The "voices dying with a dying fall" which Prufrock hears "beneath the music from a farther room"[8] are the dying aesthetic norms coterminous with the shattered belief-systems from which new cultural and ideological forms must emerge. Just so does this dying world order result in Austin Fraser's figures becoming "lost, missing, irreclaimable" (128). In a logical figurative extension, his canvasses become political metonyms of the collateral damage of war – the destruction of western culture[9] and the alleged impossibility (after the Great War) of meaningful representation ever arising again.[10] The spectre of annihilation is raised by Austin's friend George, just back from the war, and whose traditional craft of painting on china authorizes him to lament the obliteration of an infinite variety of enchantingly beautiful objects made by the most skilled workers and artisans, in turn metonyms of civilization, creativity, and life itself:

> Finally it seemed to me that Europe was one vast museum whose treasures were being smashed by hired thugs. We weren't making history, we were destroying it...eliminating it. Churches that had been lovingly maintained

---

[6] "I will paint Sara, the inherited house, the fist of Thunder Cape on the horizon, the frozen lake, her hands, the Quebec heater, the slowly fading fires. I will paint the small-paned window, the log walls, a curtain illuminated from behind by winter sun, the skein of grey I never saw in Sara's hair. Then carefully, painstakingly, I will remove the realism from it, paint it all out" (*Underpainter* 14).

[7] One cannot fail to think of Eliot's hybrid voice asserting that "There will be time to murder and create" and metatextually calling for homologous "visions and *revisions*," "decisions and *re/visions* which a minute will *re/verse*." T.S. Eliot, "The Love Song of Alfred J. Prufrock," in *Collected Poems, 1909-1962*, lines 28, 33, and 47-48 respectively (my emphases and slashes).

[8] Eliot, "Prufrock," lines 52-53.

[9] The underpaintings, completed only to be destroyed, function even more explicitly as objective correlatives in hindsight, when two decades later, Augusta ponders her war-time experiences as a nurse, confessing her astonishment at "how a world – a complete social system – can be constructed and then dismantled, just like that." She adds, "Everything was assembled, then dismantled. Even the pain and the death, even that was constructed, or at least planned on paper. That place was the whole world once, and it's all gone. Taken apart. If you went there now, there would be only a graveyard" (*Underpainter* 241).

[10] This once again resonates with T.S. Eliot's mouthpiece, Prufrock, who asks repeatedly "how should I presume," and "how should I begin" (Eliot lines 54, 69).

for seven hundred years were being obliterated in an afternoon. Simple men – farm boys who could trace their families back to the time of the Saxons and the Gauls or the Hun – were dying at eighteen and leaving no heirs. There will be nothing left, I kept thinking, when this is over, nothing at all. (*Underpainter* 153-154)

The bell has tolled indeed for the decorative arts: mass-produced tableware, that marker of modernity, has become more desirable than hand-painted porcelain, and – Urquhart suggests through her focalizer – an art for the people cannot re-emerge. The nostalgia that suffuses the text crystallizes in a litanic list – a chaotic enumeration of seemingly trivial objects which, extinct like the dinosaur, embody a vanished world:

Entire kingdoms of objects have disappeared from the planet, it seems, but not from my visual memory, my eidetic malediction.

Think of all the gear associated with the horse-drawn carriage, the winter sleigh; all the straps and bits and bells, the reins and shoes and blinkers. Think of the wrappers for razor blades decorated with bearded men, a tin container for coal oil, the paper rolls for player pianos, spats, moustache cups, a square box sporting a huge red blossom from which music spills. This century has been one particularly concerned with disappearance, elimination. What ever happened, for instance, to the pale-yellow tickets from the pavilion, summer 1913? Five cents a dance. (*Underpainter* 46)

The answer to the final rhetorical question is provided in *A Map of Glass*. These objects reappear, are reassembled as relics in the municipal museum where the autistic protagonist Sylvia Bradley works and worships the past. Urquhart's virtual list and subsequent 'corporeal' museum pieces call up similar stances and strategies deployed by writers such as Carol Shields, Alice Munro, and Margaret Atwood. One can notably evoke the inventory of disparate obsolete objects in a museum with which Munro begins the title story of her collection *The Love of a Good Woman*, and the archaic, pedestrian objects enumerated by Atwood in the opening story of her early collection, *Bluebeard's Egg*, meant to configure vanished civilizations. *A Map of Glass*, too, is suffused with a utopian anxiety about change, an anxiety that values stasis and views transformation as heavily entropic. Discussing transience and permanence with Laura Ferri, Urquhart has acknowledged a "desire to preserve," a desire "to freeze experience, to make it static" – a desire which I wish to stress is characteristic of the contented utopian to whom any degree of change is necessarily a regression. Urquhart posits that apprehending the fact that "the world is always disappearing from us, it's always moving away from us" is one of the impulses "which can drive an artist to a work of art" (Urquhart, "Conversation": 19). In this she both aligns herself with and distances herself from

Salman Rushdie, who has theorized the "warring myths of stasis and of metamorphosis," arguing that "metamorphosis, the knowledge that *nothing holds its form*, is the driving force of art" (Rushdie 291, original italics).

Rushdie has equally identified mutation and metamorphosis as being consubstantial with the diasporic condition (394). He points out that movement across national frontiers is not the only form of the phenomenon of migration, and that – as the very term *metaphor* etymologically illustrates – the trope essentially involves the transformation of ideas, and "the migration of ideas into images" (278). It is precisely these two levels of migration that overlap in *The Stone Carvers* which I wish to focus on, for, albeit framed by the dark, then darker, vision of the novels which precede and follow it, it deploys a fuller, jubilatory poetics of resurgence and mutation. *The Stone Carvers* flashes back and forth in time and space, along a timeline straddling a century, flitting from King Ludwig's palace and follies in Neuschwanstein and a log chapel in an unnamed, unmapped, and unscripted virgin forest in Upper Canada to Vimy Ridge and its massive war monument. A Bavarian priest, initially ordered to these backwoods by a King in quest of the exotic,[11] and searching for potential parish members, is directed toward a small settlement established next to a sawmill. The handful of log shanties in the backwoods, to which the priest gives the edenic name of Shoneval, becomes the theatre of inherited, imported, or imposed cultural practices. In an interesting twist, with the advent of the First World War, the act of dis-placement and re-placement resurges as a mass migration in reverse. The loop is looped when the sons of the Germans, Irish, and Italians who had uprooted and transplanted themselves in colonial or post-imperial soil travelled back to Europe to fight Britain's battle, often against their own kind. The grandson of the Bavarian woodcarver who had produced the sculptures for Father Gstir's chapel exemplifies the process of blurring and becoming when the Same resurges from the Other. Tilman admits to his sister Klara, the main protagonist, that while he was "over there trying to kill the Hun" (248), he could hear the enemy talking in their trenches and understood what they were saying, because he had always heard his grandfather speaking to himself in German while he was working. Human, and thus similar, preoccupations generate identification. Tilman remembers what the Germans beside him were talking about: "girls, hometowns, food," and acknow-

---

[11] Ludwig notably requests the "'good arctic priest'" to "trap three or four polar bears of highest quality and snowy whiteness to be shipped to His Majesty's property, where they would be tamed and then permitted to roam at their leisure through the Sauling" (*Stone Carvers* 25). Further page references are provided in the main text.

ledges that sometimes he forgot he was listening to German because "what they were talking about was so *familiar*" (253, emphasis added).

This part of my discussion will provide a close textual reading of how Urquhart reconfigures the persona of the migrant who, "having been borne across the world," is "translated" (Rushdie 17).[12] The translation involves more than individual loss and gain, for the migrant is "not simply transformed by his act," but also "transforms his new world" (Rushdie 394). To throw light on Urquhart's reconfigurations of migration, Homi Bhabha's essay "DissemiNation: time, narrative, and the margins of the modern nation" can serve a useful exegetical function. The novelist adopts a doubleness of representation, a narrative positionality which inscribes "the ambivalent and chiasmatic intersections of time and place" which Bhabha identifies as constituting the problematic 'modern' experience of the Western nation (141). Urquhart does address the emergence of the modern Canadian nation, and is vibrantly attuned to "the metaphoricity of the peoples of imagined communities" (Bhabha 141) sharing and transferring notions of home and belonging, articulating cultural differences and identifications. The extract below shows how she makes great use of crossed periodic sentences, the clauses of which constitute antitheses in pairs. The concordant rising and falling anaphoric parallelisms which follow stage a disposition of different forms of knowledge and a distribution of practices that overlap within a process of transcultural negotiation (Bhabha 162), from Ludwig's private performances of Wagner's *Lohengrin* in his profusely adorned Linderhof palace to Father Gstir's variegated Corpus Christi processions in Shoneval, designed to move the able-bodied men to provide another year of free labour on the stone church progressively being erected around the earlier edifice of the small log chapel:

> There followed deep inland, on both sides of the Atlantic, a period of great architectural activity. *While* Ludwig bent over the first plans for the bright, small fantasy known as Neuschwanstein [...] the parishioners in Father Gstir's log chapel cheered as the cornerstone for the great church was laid just steps beyond the door. *While* seventeen carvers worked for four and a half years on the boiseries for the king's bed chamber, Joseph Becker worked on the great altar for the church in the old barn of a nearby farm that he had managed to purchase with his wages from the gristmill. *While* dozens of hummingbirds were released to fly freely in perpetuity through the Winter Garden Room at Neuschwanstein, Father Gstir and his parishioners were assembling the same sad collection of animals for yet another Corpus Christi celebration in Shoneval. (389, emphases added)

---

12   My paper extends two previous investigations of *The Stone Carvers*.

The notions of centre and edge metamorphose constantly in the act of utterance, symptomatic of the plural (and thus evolving) belief-systems of the society being represented, and the tension between the historical contingencies articulated and the Third Space of enunciation. The indigenous spatial positioning of the utterance is visible in locutions such as "Until Pater Archangel Gstir *came* to Canada" (11, emphasis added), but is fraught with tension between metropolitan values and a postcolonial mindset. The tension becomes increasingly evident in the framework of parallelisms just examined. These correspondences, emphasized by a syntactic and rhythmic repetition, move ostensibly towards antithetical parallelism, in which Ludwig's profusely baroque tastes and solipsistic cultural amusements are dysphorically contrasted with the neo-Gothic sobriety and communal values of the simple settlers. The triple "while" parallelism quoted above is followed by a duplicate "and while" closing the series and ending the novel:

> And while the magnificent chandeliers were hung in the palace of Linderhof from ceilings whose Gods and Goddesses, Rhine Maidens, and Swan Kings were barely dry, Father Gstir lit forty candles in the log chapel to replace the light that had been blocked out by the increasingly high stone walls that now completely enclosed the little structure. And, finally, several years later, while Ludwig floated in a boat on a pool designed as part of a stage set for one of his *separatvorstellungen*, or private performances of Wagner's *Lohengrin*, a different kind of theatre was being enacted in Shoneval, Canada, where a few dozen young farmers, who had been working all day to dismantle it, took the wooden chapel, log by log, out of the wonderful tall oak doors of their large and splendid new stone church. (90, original italics)

The initial euphoric qualifier above commending the ostentatiously ornate royal decorations is invalidated by the juxtaposition with the homely material and the humble/feeble natural light of the New World settlement. The final sentence, binary in structure, contains a confrontation of multiple binaries of an axiological nature. A quasi-paganism (foregrounded by the use of capitalization, traditionally reserved for the Deity in monotheistic religion) is pitted against the Christian ethos of salvation through faith, but also through good works (fused as early as the opening chapter in the alliterative locution "work and worship" [6]). Passion is contrasted with action, decadence with renaissance, as kingly idleness is set firmly within the sphere of simulacrum, artifice, and specious spectacle, while the utterance overtly takes on the dimension of a eulogy celebrating the values of manual labour and the resourcefulness of a pioneer society. The dialogical discourse furthermore constitutes the locus of the Other through the literary device of *peregrinism*, the interpolation of a foreign term, which in this case, as it often does, serves parodic or satirical purposes, to the advantage of the familiar –

and implicitly wholesome – English. The discernable enunciative distance and the agency of identification are in no way pure or holistic, to borrow Bhabha's terms, but are constituted "in a process of substitution, displacement or projection" (Bhabha 162). Urquhart's novel is profoundly heteroglossic, for resurging into the diffused narratorial voice is the speech of current opinion, itself an amalgam re-emerging from generation to generation. A belief system hidden in a hybrid utterance is at times at odds with an ideological stance articulated covertly, and then overtly, in a subsequent descriptive pause (a privileged locus of the relocation and reinscription of transgressive or contesting agencies [Bhabha 193]). In the following extract, we can see how conflicting positionings on the teleology of progress erupt:

> The backwoods was no place for even the middle-aged, as everyone was necessarily engaged in the act of turning one thing into another, an occupation that required an athletic form of labour, a labour that never ceased. The carver transformed barley into flour and wood into statues; the seamstress made bedsheets into altar cloths; the men in the sawmill helped turn forests into wastelands, while the farmers attempted to turn wastelands into fields. The priest was hoping to turn a barren hilltop into the site of a pilgrimage church whose bell would ring out to an established village and whose song would carry over beautifully cultivated fields. All of them were trying to force western culture into a place where it undoubtedly had no business to be. It was hard work. (24-25)

The figuration contains both positive and negative overtones. We can find two communication systems intersecting in this double-styled utterance. One is an authoritative or normative speech code and mindset which has become the postcolonial *doxa* among the intelligentsia in settler societies (the ideological positioning of a collective voice discernible in the dysphoric verb "force" and the modalizer "undoubtedly" condemning cultural translation). The spurious dimension of the Sisyphean transformative activities is underlined by the repetitive, crossed periodic sentences involving chiasmus (forests into wastelands/ wastelands into fields) and by the qualifying verbal locutions (attempted to turn/hoping to turn). Interweaving and negotiating these discursive dynamics debunking an epic stance is an inherited post-imperial semantic and axiological belief system celebrating the migrants. The laudation of transmutations with Promethean contours, present in the temporal layering and enunciative stance, operates within the field of the affect. The narrator guides the reader towards a positive value judgment: the work is "hard," "athletic," and unceasing (24). Interestingly, the sentence modifier positing certainty ("undoubtedly") – pleonastic alongside the already emphatic value judgment "had no business to be," is cast into doubt, and authoritative belief systems are relativized.

Such polyphonic resurgences of voices and viewpoints enable Urquhart throughout the novel to deconstruct or revisit certain social, historical, and political developments. In a passage which reverts to inner focalisation, Father Gstir, an *exemplum* or figure of the colonizer, catches his first view of the Canadian valley he will contribute to transforming. His migrant's eye view doubles what he sees with what he and the other settlers will turn the scene into (a replication of Bavaria). Colonial jubilation and postcolonial distancing commingle, as the free indirect discourse carrying the utterance of the focaliser is overcoded and countered by the diffused authorial voice: "Rock outcroppings and shallow caves *suitable for* the statues of saints, bubbling springs that were *surely* holy places, towering deciduous trees *miraculously* overlooked by the axe" (15, emphases added). The authorial utterance discernable in the locutions of belief effectively establishes distance and questions the suitability of imported cultural practices. Yet, when lost, these cultural practices are mourned. The immigrant woodcarver Joseph Becker finds himself "carving at the outer reaches of the world among people who would be able to comprehend neither his ability nor his limitations" (45), calling to mind the artistic and literary Susanna Moodie, dismayed at an alien environment devoid of congenial minds. In this collision of worlds, European craftsmanship and knowledge which find no place on New World soil are celebrated, and acculturation filtered through multiple *ubi sunt* prisms. During the Depression, accepting odd jobs for a meal, Joseph's grandson Tilman remarks that the noble limewood held almost sacred by the great sculptors of Nuremberg and Ulm is routinely chopped and burnt as kindling. The subsequent celebration of ancient craft is simultaneously a lament on Canadian cultural 'illiteracy':

> Tilman, carrying a full load of this material into the farmer's shed, recalled that his grandfather could *read* wood, was able to determine from the grain how a piece might crack or warp as the moisture departed from it, where the flesh of it might glow when it was rounded, glazed, and rubbed, and how it would catch the light when coaxed into a particular shape. (201)

Urquhart's is the doubleness of hybridity rather than a binary hierarchical or oppositional structuring. Her discourse of cultural difference involves rearticulating the sum of knowledge from the de-centred position of the displaced or marginal. The church bell which Father Gstir has for years pleaded to obtain finally arrives, and, through a shift from omniscience to inner focalisation, the reader is given to understand the staggering displacement of ancestral knowledges and arcane skills which must needs accompany the dis-placed bell if it is not to remain mis-placed in an inappropriate landscape:

He attempted to negotiate the indistinct path back to the Europe of his youth, to remember just what was entailed in raising a bell to its place in a church tower and how the bell should be positioned once it arrived there. Various terms such as "headstock," "strike note," "timbre," and "the flight of the clapper" entered his mind. Sonority, he knew, was something to be considered, but he couldn't quite remember why or how. He recalled one bell ringer he had known in Bavaria saying something about "percussive grandeur" and then making reference to gudgeons. What on earth was a gudgeon? There would have to be wheels. There would have to be discussions concerning acoustics. Was there anyone at all in this wild country with whom one could carry on such discussions? (147)

The staggering responsibility of erecting and maintaining in "this wild country" what he sees as the apotheosis of human creation and inventiveness strikes Father Gstir down with a stroke. The novel teems with other such resonant objects which are sites of resurgence, in which ancestral knowledges and arcane skills reappear. There is the red waistcoat Klara tailors for her lover before he dies in the war, functioning as a concretization of the metaphysical notions of transformation, return, and resurrection. There is the oil lamp – like love whose brightness can be controlled, intensified, or allowed to diminish. There are the lines, circles, and curves of the names of the dead carved in stone at the Vimy Ridge war monument, both abstraction and concretization of presence and absence, calling to mind Linda Hutcheon's observation that "postmodernism is the *process* of making the *product*; it is *absence* within *presence*; it is *dispersal* that needs *centering* in order to be dispersal; it is the *idiolect* that wants to be, but knows it cannot be, the *master code*; it is *immanence* denying yet yearning for *transcendence*." (Hutcheon 49, original emphases) There is notably the transmutation of sounds called out "at summer dusk from a back porch door" and all that remains of "torn faces, crushed bone, scattered limbs" (275). There is particularly the torch bearer which is "everyone's lost friend, everyone's lost child" (337) transformed into stone by carvers exclusively brought over from Italy, where the art of stone-carving has best been handed on, according to Walter Allward, the Canadian sculptor who masterminded the project.

Significantly, Giorgio, a young Italian Canadian friend of Tilman's, trained in woodcarving, but unable to earn his living from an art that a New World economy has marginalized, migrates back to Europe to join the Italian carvers on the Vimy monument work site. This migration in reverse is a mirror reflection of Tilman's identification process with the Germans he had to combat, for Giorgio recognizes in the community of imported Italians "certain tribal similarities" (282) with the Italian Canadian community of his childhood. Although he belongs to the second generation of Italian Canadians, he speaks fluent Italian, and the workers welcome him "like a lost brother" (282), sheltering and feeding him until he can be hired. When Giorgio has climbed the rope ladders and scaffolding to work in the elevated hut that serves as a studio, which, enchanted, he considers to be "part swing and part tree house," he spontaneously sings "When the wind blows, the cradle will rock" (289). The line, which the North American receptor exposed to an inherited English culture will – at most – consciously identify as the second verse of the well-known (but here unnamed) nursery rhyme "Rock-a-bye Baby," or – at the very least – unconsciously identify as known material, is defamiliarized and made strange through the incomprehension and horrified reactions of his audience. Playing with the paradigms of distance and normativity, Urquhart pushes the instabilities of situational defamiliarization and recontextualization to the limits, demonstrating that the discourse of cultural difference is dialogical, that the object of identification is ambivalent, and that the agency of identification is "never pure or holistic but always constituted in a process of substitution, displacement, or projection" (Bhabha 162):

> When asked which opera the tune came from, he eventually sang and then translated into Italian the whole nursery song for the two other carvers of the studio, who were horrified by this English verse they believed must be about infanticide. Giorgio was pestered for the rest of the story: Who put the cradle up in the tree? Was the mother dead? Perhaps the child was the result of some passionate and forbidden union, or a princeling whose existence would upset the order of royal succession? A complete narrative developed in full view of the silent plaster models, while the men busied themselves preparing the work space that would enable them to transform these into stone. (289-90)

While the characters translate the plaster into stone statues, and the protagonist translates the song from English to Italian, the author translates a commonplace ditty into an exotic one, through a technique similar to the *perverb*, or perverted/adapted proverb. Common knowledge is denaturalized and questioned, shedding its totalizing status of universal given to take on that of a limited, cultural construction. This is revealed to be both spatially and axiologically ex-centric, the site of unnatural or monstrous tenets. The logic of articulation based on the rules of nonsense is deconstructed and reinterpreted through a prism of cultural judgment grounded in a humanist quest for meaning and order. By shifting the ground of knowledge, by rearticulating the lullaby of the baby tumbling from the treetops cradle and all from another signifying position which equates it with infanticide, Urquhart generates a sudden shock of signification. She contests the homogenization of experience, suggesting that the interpretation of cultural difference resides not only in *what* is said and done, but also *where* it is said or done. In spite of the manifest complicities, Giorgio's return to the community of his origins enacts what Bhabha terms "the repetition that will not return as the same... where adding *to* does not add up but serves to disturb the calculation of power and knowledge" (162), producing other spaces of signification and other strategies of identification. Giorgio and his fellow stonecarvers are implicated in different symbolic and socio-political systems (Mother Goose/opera; democracy/aristocracy), and their forms of identity call for cultural translation.[13] In turn, the transfer of meaning can never be total between systems of meaning which are differential, when not outright alien. The author seems to fall in line with Bhabha's suggestion that the "uncanny structure of cultural difference" (163) enables us "to coincide with forms of activity which are both at once ours and other".[14]

All the while refuting homogenization and totalization, Urquhart tends to privilege the conjunction of interconnections and hybridization over the disjunction of alterity. In this final part of my discussion, I wish to engage with a second level of resurgence. I shall investigate an additional tier which overdetermines Urquhart's reconfiguration – that of the transformation of ideas as writerly process. I shall address the resurgence of the idea in the image, and show how the writer enacts the migration "from the World to the Book," allowing her readers to travel through the page, "to end up inside and also behind the writing" (Rushdie 276). I shall also demonstrate how she reverses Rushdie's paradigm and generates the resurgence of the Book in the World.

Giorgio and Klara, also skilled in carving, explore on the Vimy site the elaborate maze of tunnels which the army had dug underground. The maze participates in Urquhart's trademark strategy of synecdoche and recourse to the objective correlative. It is a network which reconfigures the correspondences between interdependent continents, elements, and cultures, calling up once more Bhabha's uncanny structure of simultaneous difference and similarity:

> Eventually Klara began to view the whole landscape, all the land given to Canada by France, the sky above, and the depths of the chalky earth below as part of an interconnecting system, one aspect of which could not survive without the other. The tunnels were like extended tangled roots reaching up to the monument above, feeding its construction by their very existence. (356)

---

[13] Interestingly, the defamiliarization of the popular song retrieves a dark side which it has shed in contemporary North American society, for this ditty of another time and place was indeed once suffused with ominous hints of potential infanticide.

[14] Claude Lévi-Strauss, *Work of Marcel Mauss*, p. 35, qtd in Bhabha p. 163.

Here worlds are telescoped in sundry manners. The inscription on a wall of a boy soldier who had "scratched his name and *still alive and kicking* in the same roughshod manner as he might have decorated the surface of a pioneer desk in a one-room country school" (356). The names of places the soldiers had chiselled into the underground rooms and passageways: Place de la Concorde, Centreton Ball Park, or Convocation Hall. These resurgences of the extra-textual world go beyond the referential dynamics of realism. They are synecdoches of our societal/global interconnecting system, and they are echoed by organic metaphors for migration and cultural cross-pollination, such as the young trees from Canadian forests which have recently been transplanted to the Vimy site. Giorgio hopes they will grow to be healthy "in a land where they were never meant to be," just as his family had grown and finally become rooted "in a land far from the soil of their birthplace" (372). The plant metaphor is mirrored by the objective correlative of the spindly wisteria taken by his family from the homeland to Canada, which hangs frail and listless, "barely leafing in the spring until one year it burst triumphantly into blossom in early June, its flowers hanging like an overstated offering of pale grapes at an emperor's feast" (373), the sign of a transformative moment in the process of familial and cultural translation. Concomitantly, when describing how the foundation of the war monument was installed, Urquhart represents hybridization through dysphoric organic metonymy. Through its framework of chaotic enumeration the chaos of the world erupts:

> Body parts and clothing, bibles, family snapshots, letters, buttons, bones, and belt buckles were unearthed daily, and under the plot of earth from which the central staircase would one day rise, the fully uniformed skeletal remains of a German general were disinterred. In the seven years since the battle, several poplars had made a valiant attempt to take root on the battlefield, and some were now taller than a man. In almost every case when they were removed to make way for the road, bits of stained cloth and human hair and bones were found entangled in the roots. Once, a mine half a mile away exploded, unearthing a young oak tree and the carcass of a horse, intact, activated, it would seem, by the fractional movement of the underground growth of roots. (271)

A desired amplification intensified by polysyndeton (cloth *and* hair *and* bones) is produced by the list, which translates the abstract into concrete terms, disparate, disjunctive items conjoined only by alliterative sound (buttons/bones/belt buckles). The descriptive pause obeys its function. It serves as a privileged locus of the relocations and reinscriptions of axiologies and agencies, either consolidating or contesting. It notably provides a representation of an organic universe contaminated by human technology, commingling to a point of agency and interchangeability: the healthy tree roots clogged unnaturally by the human remnants of war in turn detonate explosions through the natural process of life and growth.

The images of the Vimy war monument are embodiments of Urquhart's double exploration of migration and transmutation – the migration across the world, but also the migration from world to book, or even from story to page. The self-reflexive hymns to craft come to rest on a metalinguistic, or rather metaformal, contemplation of writing as formal sign or icon. Giorgio significantly begins "a love affair with the alphabet," passionately interested in how words "occup[y] the surface of stone, the placement, the depth," and fascinated by the magical changes affected by light and mathematical centring, primordial for the desired effect of permanence which the letters take on (277). The reader is invited to think of the eleven thousand names carved on a huge stone wall surmounted by a magnificent sculpted monument not as arbitrary signifiers, but in terms of shape and texture. Through inner focalisation, the author suggests that "even on impermanent, short-lived paper, even in foreign languages you would never understand, words had a presence unlike any other presence. They carried authority in a way no other collection of lines, circles, curves, squares could" (280). The authority and permanence of shape is none the less overcoded by a metaphysical dimension evoking eternity and infinity: "'Alpha and omega,' he would whisper to himself when he was working. 'Moses and the tablets'" (280).

As a corollary to her deconstruction of words to icons, shapes on a surface, Urquhart engages the receptor in a reflection on language as empty acoustic image. She does so through the othering effect of *peregrinism*, the foreignizing literary device which deviates here from its common dysphoric function generating distance, so as to present the unfamiliar in a seductive light. After years spent on the road as a hobo begging for scraps, Klara's brother Tilman returns a second time to France, where he does not speak the language, and where he is subjugated by the musicality of the names of dishes on French menus. He enumerates them sensually for Klara: *Gratin de homard au porto, Truffe St-Hubert, Caneton de la belle époque, Flan de langoustines George V, Écrevisses à la crème, Bouillabaisse Marseillaise*. She is receptive to "the soft cadences of the French phrases," signifiers without a signified, whose assonances and consonances she finds "a most soothing lullaby" (317). Still, one cannot fail to remark another resurgence, for the Edenic sensuousness of sounds is intensified by its association with the comforting notion of food, which in turn is consolidated by the widely-held tenet concerning the refinement of French cooking. It is furthermore enhanced by being associated with other pleasurable sensations involving not only smell but also sight and touch: "He would also describe for her the tablecloths, the napkins, the large silver-plate spoons, and the elegant china edged in gold leaf, things that in a thousand years, Klara would not have thought could have held his attention" (317).

Ultimately, the writer's metalinguistic investigation does not fail to include a reflection on the power of words. She resorts notably to holophrastic textual segments in which a single word expresses a range of ideas and emotions. When the chef at the Hôtel Picardie restaurant invites the non-francophone Tilman to visit the kitchen, in lieu of conversation they bandy proper nouns back and forth, namely the names of battles which evoke for both an affect as well as a cognitive anchoring in experiential event with which they can identify. "'Shrapnel,' he said, knocking twice on Tilman's wooden leg. 'Verdun,' he added. The Canadian understood then that this kind man carried in his body fragments of the catastrophe of the battle of Verdun [...] then brought his fist down on his artificial leg. 'Vimy Ridge,' he said. 'Vimy'" (325). Urquhart varies the technique of the syntagm-sentence, in a manner similar but opposite to the practice favoured by the modernists. While Samuel Beckett, Virginia Woolf, and James Joyce strived to erase all signs of a referential situation along with punctuation to return to the "original" expression of unspoken thought, Urquhart on the contrary erases all but the referential sign. When Giorgio wishes to discover the identity of Klara's lost dead lover, knowing only the village he came from, he consults the Master File which lists the missing alphabetically, next to an adjacent column indicating their home town, which he must peruse first. The reader is confronted with a series of proper nouns devoid of both propositional content and organizing principle:

> Grimsby, Maple Creek, Fernie, Clinton, Lévis, Vernonville, Rimouski, Colborne, Truro, Humboldt, Walkerton, Parry Sound, Lilac, Medicine Hat, Moose Jaw. Who were the settlers who had titled these places? Could they have imagined the names they had invented would lie, as the result of an immense slaughter, in an official document on a foreign desk? Vernon, Collingwood, Val d'Or, Nanaimo, Lunenberg, Kingsville, Swift Current, Trois-Rivières, Hull, Winnipeg, Alderville. (368)

Even for receptors unfamiliar with Canadian geography and unaware that the areas touched by the death of sons reach from the Atlantic to the Pacific, the list of acoustic images meant to call up a referent rather than a signified is nevertheless fraught with significance. Perlocutionary rather than informational, it evokes the sound poems of Bernard Heidsieck, in which chant and repetition of recognizable words, such as the names of towns, serve to privilege pure vocal or "abstract" sound at the expense of significance, yet, through accumulation and echo, simultaneously suggest and expand meaning.

Discussing her writerly strategies in my graduate seminar at the Sorbonne Nouvelle on 5 April 2005, Urquhart declared that a certain landscape, architecture, or object were usually her starting points for a novel, as could be family anecdotes or tales told. The Vimy battlefield and monument provided the catalysis for *The Stone Carvers* just as the glass ballroom floor buried under a burned-down hotel, only to surface years later, triggered her subsequent book, *A Map of Glass* (in press at the time). When questioned, the writer asserted that she never works out a preliminary outline of events, just as "a child never determines a plot," maintaining that "memory and childhood are the key to the way we create." She affirmed that it is after the first draft that she "shakes the material [she's] been playing with and gets down to work". The glimpses of Urquhart shaking her material, making image and idea interact, inviting us to "travel through the page, to end up inside and also behind the writing" (Rushdie 276) is an indissociable part of the pleasure of the text. When the small Tilman has been harnessed and chained to stop him from running away from home one more time, his little sister Klara frees him and watches him walk away, "his chain trailing behind him like print on the page of the road, like the end, or the beginning of a story" (71). In the same manner as this conceit, we watch Urquhart travel down the metatextual road of her pages.[15] My analysis suggests that underlying the strong metatextual dimension which centripetally draws the focus back from the world to the word, there is a reversal of Rushdie's paradigm. Urquhart once more loops the loop, generating the resurgence of the Book in the World in an overlapping metaphorical, metaphysical dimension. This neoplatonic strain striving to pierce *eikos* (appearance or reality) generates meaning as "*imamnence* denying yet yearning for *transcendence*" (Hutcheon 49).

References

ATWOOD, M. (1989), *Bluebeard's Egg and Other Stories*, London, Virago.

BAKHTIN, M. (1996), *The Dialogic Imagination: Four Essays*, Ed. M. HOLQUIST, Trans. Caryl Emerson and Michael Holquist, Austin, TX, U. of Texas P.

BHABHA, H. (2001), *The Location of Culture*, London/New York, Routledge.

DVOŘÁK, M. (2008), "Rock-a-bye Baby, or Tribal Similarities Revisited in Jane Urquhart's *The Stone Carvers*," in C. Sturgess and M. Kuester, Eds.,

---

15 Jane Urquhart participated in the panel at which part of this paper was originally presented (Orléans, May 2008), and to my delight confirmed my observations. See the ensuing discussion with the writer included at the end of this volume.

Reading(s) from a Distance: European Perspectives on Canadian Women's Writing, Augsburg, Vussner-Verlag: 33-40.

DVOŘÁK, M. (autumn 2008), "Resurgences of the Extra-textual and Metatextual in Jane Urquhart's *The Stone Carvers*," *Commonwealth Essays and Studies* 31.1: 31-36.

ELIOT, T.S. (1975), *Collected Poems 1909-1962*, London, Faber & Faber.

HEIDSIECK, B. (1999), *Respirations et brèves rencontres*, Paris, Al Dante/Niok.

HUTCHEON, L. (1990), *A Poetics of Postmodernism: History, Theory, Fiction*, London, Routledge.

MUNRO, A. (1998), *The Love of a Good Woman*, Toronto, McClelland & Stewart.

OMHOVÈRE, C. (2007), "Copies and (Ab)originals: The Problem of Authenticity in Jane Urquhart's *Away* (1993)," *Anglophonia* 21: 179-188.

RICCIARDI, C. (2005), "Away and the Meaning of Colonization," in L. FERRI, Ed., *Jane Urquhart: Essays on Her Works*, Toronto/Buffalo/Chicago, Guernica, 65-77.

RUSHDIE, S. (1992), *Imaginary Homelands: Essays and Criticism 1981-91*, London, Granta.

STAINES, D. (2005), "*The Stone Carvers*," in L. FERRI, Ed., *Jane Urquhart: Essays on Her Works*, Toronto/Buffalo/Chicago, Gernica, 42-44.

SUGARS, C. (spring 2003), "Haunted by (a Lack of) Postcolonial Ghosts: Settler Nationalism in Jane Urquhart's *Away*," *Essays on Canadian Writing* 79: 1-32.

URQUHART, J. (2002), *The Stone Carvers*, Toronto, McClelland & Stewart/First Emblem Edition.

– (1997), *The Underpainter*, London, Bloomsbury.

– (2005), *A Map of Glass*, Toronto, McClelland & Stewart.

– (2005), "A Conversation with Jane Urquhart," conducted by Laura Ferri, in L. FERRI, Ed., *Jane Urquhart: Essays on Her Works*, Toronto/Buffalo/ Chicago, Gernica, 15-41.

– (2005), Talk delivered at the Sorbonne Nouvelle, Paris, 5 April 2005.

WYILE, H. (winter 2004), "Jane Urquhart: Confessions of a Historical Geographer," *Essays on Canadian Writing* 81: 58-83.

7

Collection, Canadian Nationalism, and Colonial Resurgences in Jane Urquhart's *Away*

Barbara BRUCE

Carleton University

"Nations, like narratives, lose their origins in the myths of time and only fully realize their horizons in the mind's eye." (Bhabha 1)

In Canada in the 1980s and 1990s, nationalism was a current and contentiously debated issue, prompting Canadians to contemplate what it means to be "Canadian" and how Canada as a nation might develop in the future. The 1980 Québec Referendum, the Constitution Act of 1982, the Meech Lake and Charlottetown Accords, the Multiculturalism Act of 1988, the Canada-United States Free Trade Agreement of 1989, the North American Free Trade Agreement of 1994, and the second Québec Referendum in 1995 fuelled the issue, along with "challenges to official multiculturalism and its secondary status within Canada's bicultural model of nationhood, challenges launched by Quebec separatists, First Nations groups, and people of colour" (Brydon 165). The debates and challenges led to a "crisis of identity" in Canada, one Eva Mackey characterizes as "particularly fierce and brutal" (Mackey 8). However, the "renegotiating of Canada and Canadianness," Diana Brydon observed in 1995, "takes place within a postcolonial context not always fully understood or recognized by either participants or analysts" (Brydon 165). Jane Urquhart, though, was one participant who recognized the postcolonial context, as she demonstrates in her historical novel *Away* (1993).

Through tropes of collection, which are central to the novel, as well as other references to material culture, Urquhart warns that Canada's imperial and colonial histories threaten to undermine contemporary Canadian nationalism to the point that the nation is at risk of being subsumed – collected – by industry and other nations. Urquhart suggests that, to prevent the erosion of Canada, nationalism generated through official histories and by hegemonic institutions that mask a legacy of violence, destruction, and displacement must be tempered with the inclusion of narratives of the Other, such as women and minority or ethnic groups. This tempering can be effected by both preserving and sharing personal and familial stories in collections and narratives: that is, by creating and circulating alternative histories. This idealization of collection is comparable to the novel itself, since it represents Urquhart's preservation of alternative Canadian histories, albeit fictionalized.[1] At a time when Canadians were occupied with questions of identity and debating the pros and cons of a free trade agreement with the United States, Urquhart employs tropes of collection in *Away* to represent synecdochically the means through which the dominant culture attempts to impose unity, but which actually effect the fragmentation and destabilization of the nation. The author thus cautions against the loss of Canadian stories and histories and the sense of commonality and belonging they generate, which can result in the loss of communal cohesion and thus leave Canada as a nation vulnerable, particularly to appropriation by the United States.

In the novel, Urquhart extends Jonathan Kertzer's characterization of literature and nationalism as "eager but fractious allies" (Kertzer 12). Kertzer observes that "Literature makes the nation both possible and impossible, imaginable and intolerable" (Kertzer 12). The "life" of a nation comes from literature and "all the arts of cultural persuasion, because they articulate a national life by telling its story and by supplying its motivating principle – justice" (Kertzer 12). However, literature also "exposes the national life as unjust, and even monstrous, because it has the paradoxical ability to criticize the ideology in which it is immersed and by which it is compromised" (Kertzer 12). Urquhart recognizes that the museum and private collection constitute a third ally of literature and nationalism, since, in a way, they also tell stories that are integral to the formation of the nation and the rise of nationalism, but which have the potential to expose the injustices of nationalism.[2] For example, museums founded in recent decades by First Nations tell the

---

[1]   *Away* is a fictionalization of Urquhart's family history of an "extended Irish family that immigrated to Canada around the time of the potato famine" (Urquhart, 1998: 198). Urquhart intertwines this "unofficial" history with the "official" history of the assassination of D'Arcy McGee. The Sedgewicks brothers are also based on actual people: "Aubrey DeVere and his brother." The former had "sailed with his tenants when they immigrated to Canada and then came back and presented to Parliament the terrible facts about conditions on the vessels later known as 'coffin ships'" (Urquhart, 2004: 71).

[2]   In her 1986 novel, *The Whirlpool*, Urquhart asserts a continuity between writing and the museum, referring to the objects in the local museum as "three-dimensional documents" (*Whirlpool* 231).

Other side of the story of colonization: through acts of repatriation, these museums collect already-collected objects or, in other words, meta-collect them and display or redisplay them to counter dominant discourses and reveal the brutalities of colonial, national, and museological processes.[3] Often, though, it is more difficult for museum-goers to see and understand what they are and are not being told in the museum, since the objects and their display can mask their own stories. As the reader does in literature, then, the viewer must "read between the lines" of such collections, a practice Urquhart advocates in *Away* by exposing the impulses of collection and their implications in constructions of the nation and nationalism.

My analysis of collection as trope in *Away* begins with the collector characters, Osbert and Granville Sedgewick, Anglo-Irish landlords in the north of Ireland in the mid-19th century. Growing up in her Irish-Canadian family, Urquhart heard stories "about the history of Ireland and how dreadful the British were" (Urquhart 1995), but she resists creating in her novel simplistic Irish/British, good/bad binaries. Instead, Urquhart constructs the Sedgewick brothers as men who are "as well loved by the peasantry as any pair of landlords could ever hope to be" (*Away* 41). These "well-meaning, eccentric, non-absentee landlords" (Wyile 32) come from a long and similarly-minded line of "Anglo-Irish landed gentry" who "had exhibited nothing but surprise, delight, and a certain charmed mystification whenever they examined the details of their surroundings" (*Away* 39). Generations of Sedgewicks, however, were not content to examine their surroundings as they found them; instead, the Sedgewicks became "Dedicated collectors of almost everything," who "dragged an extravagant amount of information and unprecedented numbers of specimens and objects into their damp, ill-lit halls, going about the task with such zeal it soon appeared they wanted all of County Antrim under glass" (*Away* 39). Not distinguishing between natural and cultural histories, Sedgewicks "scoured the coastal cliffs for birds' eggs, flora and fauna, the moors for ancient carved stones, and the cabins of their tenants for quaint bits of folklore and songs" (*Away* 39). Osbert and Granville live up to this legacy by collecting in their own fashion: Osbert collects by sketching and painting the views around their

---

[3] The U'mista Cultural Centre and the Kwagiulth Museum are two examples, which James Clifford discusses in his essay "Four Northwest Coast Museums." Clifford observes that the "repatriation of objects from national museums to new tribal institutions […] seemed to be a striking example of how a dominant practice of collection and display has been turned to unanticipated ends. Master narratives of cultural disappearance and salvage could be replaced by stories of revival, remembrance, and struggle" (Clifford 214).

estate and creatures he finds in the landscape, while Granville collects the Irish people, history, and mythology in poetic laments.[4]

While they are not "blatantly exploitative villains" (Wyile 32), the Sedgewicks, past and present, are still possessive and controlling colonizers, which is revealed by their insatiable need to collect everything in their demesne. The Sedgewick family, having been in Ireland since England colonized it in the early 1600s (*Away* 39), stands in the novel as a synecdoche of British colonization, and the tropes of collection emphasize that, no matter how benevolent it can seem, colonialism is an all-consuming and destructive system, as I will demonstrate. That the Sedgewicks limit their collecting activities to their own county does not mean that the detriments of colonialism are limited and contained; instead, we can read this landlord family as representing the idea that, from within the limits of colonized territories, colonizers extracted resources, wealth, and power century after century. Collection in the novel also represents the Sedgewicks' and thus the British desire for an ideally contained and controlled Irish population. Here, collection and historical fiction are comparable: both are means by which the collector/author can order and control historical artefacts and information, respectively, as s/he desires. When an author includes or meta-collects collector and collection as tropes in an historical fiction, however, the ultimate power is, of course, the author's. By meta-collecting the colonizers' collection in her novel, Urquhart does what the Sedgewicks did not do: she makes it public[5] and lays bare its politics and the stories and histories that such collections typically mask. Urquhart employs tropes of collection to suggest that the imposition of the colonizer's desire to order, control, and exploit Ireland and its inhabitants is detrimental to both colonized and colonizer in ways that cannot be undone or repressed and that resurge in a developing Canadian nationalism.

Reading collection as representative of the desire for power and control is premised on the idea that, in the collection process, the object is fundamentally altered: "any thing can be possessed, invested in, or, in terms of collecting, arranged, sorted and classified" (Baudrillard 11), and, once collected, its "finite use value when filled is played against the measureless emptiness that marks [its] new aesthetic function" (Stewart

---

[4]   The Sedgewicks' *Encyclopaedia Britannica* is represented in *Away* as another kind of collection, a collection of knowledge, which also stands in the novel for the inequity of power under colonialism. However, it also differs significantly from the collection of material goods and so should be the topic of another study.

[5]   Granville did publish a collection of his laments, but that it was published by a "London firm" (*Away* 40) reinforces the idea that his collection is not for or even about the Irish, but rather about the colonizer's sense of mastery over the colonized.

159). The object is emptied and brought under the collector's control: it does not resist possession; it does not assert its own subjectivity and thus is, in Jean Baudrillard's pithy formulation, "the perfect pet" (Baudrillard 11). Unlike human beings, Baudrillard explains, objects do not come into conflict with one another, and so they "are the sole things in existence with which it is truly possible to co-exist"; objects "extend my person rather than confine it" and "incline obediently towards myself, to be smoothly inventorized within my consciousness" (Baudrillard 11). Unlike people, or even animals, who assert their agencies and thus have the potential to challenge, limit, or otherwise destabilize the subject's sense of self, objects are a means by which the subject can define and represent himself without fear of that self-definition being challenged or belied. An object, then, "is ideal in that it reflects images not of what is real, but only of what is desirable," which also makes it an "ideal mirror" (Baudrillard 11) and implies that collection is an inherently narcissistic activity. In a collection, numerous mirrors or "perfect pets" are organized and arranged as a whole,[6] and they all "submit to the same *abstractive operation* and participate in a mutual relationship in so far as they each refer back to the collecting subject. They thereby constitute themselves as a *system*, on the basis of which the subject seeks to piece together his world, his personal microcosm" (Baudrillard 7, original emphasis).[7] Collection "enables individuals to create themselves" (Pearce, 1995: 197), but it also reveals the collector's desire for control over and power within his world. What these theories of collection lead to is the idea that the "pets" are not as perfect as they seem: they inform on their master, reveal his need for control, power, and the ideal; therefore, while collected objects represent power and control for the collector, they are also in a way evidence of his vulnerability. This is certainly the case in *Away*.

While Osbert and Granville see their presence in Ireland in benevolent terms, the novel reveals collection to be an alibi. When the tenants fail for the first time ever to appear at the estate house on rent day, Osbert and Granville begin to face the reality of the potato famine

---

6   Collections, "however large or small," in turn constitute the museum (Pearce, 1992: 2), or, as Stewart puts it, the museum is "the central metaphor of the collection" (161).

7   Baudrillard's masculinization of the imaginary collector is, of course, problematic, not only in light of the work done by feminist theorists in recent decades to denaturalize the masculine norm, but also because Pearce maintains in her work that historically "women seem to have actually collected things as much as men, but frequently in ways which emerge much less often into specific and recorded social practice" (Pearce, 1995: 222). That said, in the desire to avoid the awkwardness of "s/he," "her/him," or "her/his," and since Urquhart's collectors are male, I also use the masculine norm when discussing the imaginary collector.

and worry how the Irish will act: "Surely they wouldn't rise up, would they, against us?" Granville asks. "Not when we appreciate their history and all those songs and stories and the like. [...] I for one, understand the sorrows of Ireland. I, in fact, have given a voice to the sorrows of Ireland" (*Away* 103). The brothers' appreciation for Irish history and culture and their sense of unity with their tenants, manifested through collection, become their alibi when colonial oppression leads to disaster. This ironic alibiing recalls Mary Louise Pratt's idea of the "anti-conquest," a term she uses to "refer to the strategies of representation whereby European bourgeois subjects seek to secure their innocence in the same moment as they assert European hegemony" (Pratt 7) in lands subjected to European imperialism and colonialism. The Sedgewicks may believe they are innocent because of their appreciation for the culture they collect, and they collect because of their appreciation, but the novel consciously shows that collection is violent and disruptive, not at all innocent.

When they collect the oral culture of their tenants, the landlords "patronize" it, both aesthetically and by condescending to it, diminishing its power and undermining its purpose by removing it from its vital social context. For the Sedgewicks, the songs and folklore are something to be studied, rather than circulated actively from person to person, generation to generation. In her work on *Away*, Anna Branach-Kallas suggests that the Irish people "filter their perceptions of reality through Celtic legends," but that, when Osbert and Granville "scrutinise Gaelic myths, these traditions become meaningless, ridiculous and lose their mysterious depth" (Branach-Kallas 133). More than this, though, the living culture of the colonized is for the colonizer only something to be recorded, which, like collecting an object, historicizes it: fixes it in and out of time. The Sedgewicks render Irish culture past through the processes of collection.

Away thus emphasizes the idea that, historically, anthropological collectors have tended to collect what they believe, or choose to believe, is traditional and ignore or fail to see the modern as it is performed in the ongoing present. In the novel, the Sedgewicks, anxious about the missed rent day, leave their estate to check on their tenants, some of whom are attending a wedding dinner that proves to be a solemn occasion, since "For many this would be the last time they would taste wholesome food" (*Away* 106). When Osbert and Granville hear the wedding guests playing and singing traditional songs – songs the brothers have collected – they realize that, in collecting pieces of the Irish culture, they have denied its modernity:

'I believe,' said Osbert, when the song had finished, 'that they are unable to pay. I believe that's why they didn't come.'

'Yes,' agreed Granville, wiping perspiration from this forehead, 'yes... that must be it. Should we turn back?'

Osbert wanted to turn back; back to the cases of kept things, to the Cave Walk, the long rooms of Puffin Court. But he was suddenly ashamed of his desire to avoid the misery. 'I think we should go,' he said quietly. (108-109)

Thinking of Irish culture as past has allowed the Sedgewicks to ignore the present and not question their roles as colonial landlords or face their responsibilities for unfolding events. In an interview, Urquhart recalls Alice Munro saying to her, "we write about the past because we can see it whole. We may not see it accurately, but we know what transpired, how events unfolded, whereas in the present you're in the middle of it, you're experiencing it; there's no sense of completion [...]" or distance (Urquhart, 2004: 60). The Sedgewicks more than just see the past, however: surrounded by their collection, they live in the past, because it can be comprehended, reduced to key moments, figures, and objects, and, therefore, ordered and controlled. They believe it is part of their roles as colonial landlords to protect and preserve their tenants and their culture; the roles of landlord and curator are thus aligned. When the Sedgewicks are forced to deal with the Irish present/presence, they feel powerless and at a loss. In *Away*, collection blinds, or facilitates the willful blindness, of the collectors to the complexities and detriments of the imperial and colonial worlds and their roles in them, and Urquhart reveals that, to justify itself, colonialism as a system depends on the willingness not to see the viability, potentiality, or even humanity of colonized peoples.

Another strategy for justifying colonization is to dehumanize or objectify the colonized by subsuming indigenous cultures into the natural world. As I noted above, the Sedgewick collectors have not distinguished between natural and cultural histories, a failure that implies that, for the colonizer, indigenes are merely part of the landscape that they believe is theirs for the taking. Before he and Osbert are forced to face the reality of their tenant's present/presence, Osbert reveals the degree to which in his mind his Irish tenants are merely part of the landscape when he meets and addresses Mary, who is on the beach gathering seaweed. He approaches her only because he wants to make a record of this "woman who had been away" and uses her activity as "a key to communication" (*Away* 86). Unable to comprehend her actions in any way other than in terms of his own collecting, he asks her why she is taking so many "specimens of this particular kind of seaweed" (*Away* 87). Mary, realizing that "that this man had been blind to them, her people" and does not understand the kind of life-giving gathering she has undertaken, explains that the seaweed is used as fertilizer for potatoes (*Away* 87). Osbert "felt it prudent, under the circumstances, not to show his reaction. Instead, he assumed a sympathetic expression. 'They haven't been growing properly, have they?' 'No, sir,' she answered quietly" (*Away* 87). Osbert reveals his ignorance not only about the lives and life-styles of the colonized, but also about the severity of the potato famine. Even once he has gained this information, he does not yet realize the desperation of their situation and wants only to find a way to shift his conversation with Mary "into the area where he would be able to glean some useful information for his - folklore collection" (*Away* 87). As members of the Anglo upper class, who make their living on the rent their tenants must pay them, the Sedgewicks are able to give all their time and energy to collection, which for collectors "acquires a sacred character of apartness from the profane world" (Pearce, 1992: 50), allowing them to look only inward, block out that world and blind themselves to their tenants as human beings and the reality they are living beyond the walls of the estate. Even rent day is less about the rent than it is for giving Granville a chance to expand his collection, "to scout for more folklore and to enquire into the quaint and amusing events that made up his tenants' simple lives" (101), although, in some sense, collecting folklore and anecdotes is another type of rent he charges his tenants for the privilege of living on his land.

As a synecdoche for colonialism in the novel, collection is more than alibi and justification: it is also suffering and death. The poems Granville writes, as I noted above, are all laments "concerning the sorrows of Ireland" (*Away* 39), whether those sorrows concern the Earl of Essex's massacre of Irish women and children in 1576 or "a Sea Mollusc Trapped in Osbert's Aquarium" (*Away* 85), and the stories and folklore they collect from the Irish have "always" been about "incredible hardships" (*Away* 65). This more than foreshadows the potato famine: it suggests that how the colonizers perceive and construct the colonized is realized in time. Even collecting through sketching and painting becomes deadly as Osbert, "stirred by the mania for natural history that was sweeping like an *epidemic* through England, began to collect the strange, delicate life-forms that existed in the coastal tidepools" (*Away* 85, emphasis added). Rather than preserve only one of each specimen, Osbert keeps the collected sea creatures in a bucket so that he can inspect, sketch, and paint them, then, once the creatures die, he "head[s] for the shore to search for fresher specimens" (*Away* 85). Osbert rips his specimens out of their context, studies, and kills them in the name of science, doing his part to impose on his colonized part of the world what Pratt, writing about the Victorian era's passion for scientifically inventorizing and collecting nature, calls "a finite, totalizing order of European making" (Pratt 38).

Urquhart's choice of the word *epidemic* in the quotation above to characterize the rise in popularity of collecting and cataloguing in the name of science is particularly apt: Deborah Root describes the Western need to consume and exploit in terms of "a highly contagious disease with hideous effects whose sufferers are nevertheless highly rewarded in this culture" (Root 11). As well, *epidemic* reflects the devastation the collecting trend wrought on Europe's colonies and links Osbert's collecting activities to the potato famine: at the same time as he is killing bucketfuls of sea animals and throwing "the whole putrid soup into the rose garden" (*Away* 85), millions of Irish are dying of starvation and disease, a situation brought about largely by the limitations British colonization imposed on the Irish. Urquhart further emphasizes the negative impact that relentless colonization and European scientific pursuits had on all living beings in subjected lands in noting that, while he "worked carefully, scooping the creatures out of the pool with a glass jar," Osbert "lost some, those of such fragility that they came apart when subjected to anything other than the ebb and flow of the sea water that replenished their habitat. He cursed, then, quietly under his breath, and reached for a larger, stronger example of the same species" (*Away* 85-86). In contradiction of Darwin, even the fittest are hard-pressed to survive in the face of such an invading force. Osbert, however, "paid little heed to the gorgeous small world he was disturbing. His specimens would gain significance and reality only when he got them home, put them under the microscope, and accurately reproduced them on paper. But by then, of course, they would be dead" (*Away* 85). Through Osbert, the novel lays bare the colonialist assumption that the colonized are not meaningful in their own right, but rather are meaningful only in terms of how they fit into existing systems of thought and might be exploited.

The idea of collection as death is further exemplified in the Sedgewicks' collection of taxidermized specimens: "*One* of every creature, great or small, that crept or ran or flew or swam in and around County Antrim was now on display [...]" (*Away* 40, emphasis added). Urquhart's description of the collection recalls the biblical description of Noah's Ark, which is often looked to as a touchstone of collecting: in the 17th century, for example, Jesuit scholar, scientist, and collector Athanasius Kircher "considered Noah's Ark to have been the most complete natural history museum" (Alexander 42). While Urquhart does not go so far as to replicate the overt violence and horror of Timothy Findley's version of the myth in his 1984 novel, *Not Wanted on the Voyage*, neither does she view it with Kircher's positive connotations or in the biblical version's terms of benevolent preservation, procreation, and re-creation, as Noah strives to keep the paired creatures God puts under his temporary care alive (Genesis 6: 19-22 King James Version). In Urquhart's version, the single specimens are all taxidermized, never to be released to "breed abundantly in the earth, and be fruitful, and multiply upon the earth" (Genesis 8: 17). There is no emergence from the Sedgewicks' "ark": no procreation, no life.

Considering the story of Noah, John Elsner and Roger Cardinal observe that the collection of "that which had been created and was doomed became inseparable from the creation of a new and better world. In the myth of Noah as ur-collector resonate all the themes of collecting itself: desire and nostalgia, saving and loss, the urge to erect a permanent and complete system against the destructiveness of time" (Elsner 1). These themes of collecting are also present in *Away*, but Urquhart's evocation of the Noah's Ark myth denies the idea that a collection can stand against "the destructiveness of time." Despite the efforts of the Sedgewicks to preserve life in death, and despite the fact that to Granville "his stuffed puffins and demesne seemed eternal" (*Away* 44), many of the specimens are faded and decayed: the teeth of taxidermized hounds are "yellowed" with time (*Away* 40), while collected butterflies are no more than "colourful, if faded, detritus" (*Away* 100). The rooms and furnishings of Puffin Court, too, are "dusty" (*Away* 40), "musty" (*Away* 85), and "much worn by previous generations of Sedgewicks" (*Away* 101). Like their forebears, Osbert and Granville live in the past, surrounded by their collection and the taint of death; unlike their forebears, the brothers themselves belie the collection with its connotation of preservation, since they are, like their tenants, dying, although not from the famine: childless bachelors, they are the end of their line. The novel thereby suggests that the oppressiveness of the colonial system is destructive not only for the colonized, but also, ironically, for the colonizers. In her reading of Urquhart's *The Whirlpool*, Marlene Goldman proposes that, when a system produces an insider versus outsider dynamic, it "is bound to be harmful to both parties" (Goldman 169). This idea is also at work in *Away*'s consideration of colonization and is represented specifically by the collection: the collector/colonizer and collected/colonized both are oppressed by and dying within the system of British colonialism.

The Irish tenants, however, are not tidepool creatures with no hope of escaping the bucket; instead, their creativity and the vocal assertion of their presence represent a degree of resistance against collection by the colonizers. Before the famine, for example, some of the elder tenants "kept their minds busy inventing new folklore to relate at their firesides during Osbert's and Granville's note-taking visits so as not to disappoint the young masters" (*Away* 41). This creativity undermines the idea implied in the Sedgewicks' collection that Irish folklore is past, as well as the "authenticity" of their entire folklore collection, at least from an ethnographic point of view. The novel thus figures fiction as an instrument of resistance. The collection of (past) songs is also disrupted, as I noted above, when Osbert and Granville overhear the fiddler playing and village women singing traditional songs at the wedding, after the groom's father, in the face of the famine, has declared, "We're not dead yet" (*Away* 106). The songs and the declaration defy the death of the indigenous Irish culture as represented by the Sedgewick collection. The villagers make present, de-collect, their culture.

The politics of collection and class are further revealed in the implements Mary uses to gather seaweed: "Though she didn't know this, the knife she carried had lived indoors for two centuries after serving as a weapon in Cromwellian times. The creel was one woven in sorrow by Brian's grandmother when she was mad with grief over the death of her first-born son" (*Away* 82). The impoverished tenants have a significantly different relationship to their objects than the elite: they do not have the "luxury" of exchanging the use value of an implement for aesthetic value, of living in the past through collection, but therein lies their strength. Baudrillard differentiates between implements and collected objects through the idea of possession, which "cannot apply to an implement, since the object I utilize always directs me back to the world" (Baudrillard 7). Mary's implements, in contrast to the Sedgewicks' collected objects, represent presence and an active engagement with the world, while also recalling stories of defeat, loss, and grief, but also of resistance and survival: Cromwell may have put down the resistance, a child may have died, and particular stories may have been lost, but the Irish people, culture, and history continue. Fittingly, it is the sound of "the knife rasping on rock" that alerts Osbert to Mary's presence when she is gathering seaweed into the creel (*Away* 86), giving Mary the opportunity to reveal to Osbert that, despite colonization and his collection, the Irish are present and able to resist him in a small but significant way.

While Brian, Mary's husband, gives into despair that it is too late and Irish culture is lost, Mary knows that she carries within herself "fragments of the old beliefs" that "had not been completely stolen from her... had become dormant, instead, in a kind of winter sleep. Any kind of return would be accepted by her, unquestioningly" (*Away* 75). Only when Mary and Brian emigrate, though, do the repressed beliefs return. These "fragments of the old beliefs" are set in opposition to the fragments of Irish culture held in the Sedgewick collection, which can only be passive and past as long as it is under their control. The Sedgewick collection, characterized in terms of death, rather than the rescue from death, suggests that colonial collection exacerbates the "historical decay or loss" in the culture of the colonized and threatens its eradication, a word the Oxford English Dictionary defines as "The action of pulling out by the roots […]." The brothers, though, are oblivious to the effect their collection and their very presence have on the Irish until it is nearly too late. In fact, once he realizes the Irish are dying, Osbert ensures that some at least survive by, ironically, uprooting them.

Although Cynthia Sugars argues that in the novel Mary's "psychic state of being 'away' functions as a metaphor for the migrant's state of mourning" (Sugars 11), I would suggest that the tenants are in mourning before migration. When the tenants are waiting to emigrate, the Sedgewick brothers provide them with a pamphlet that lists items the author, Colonel Tarbutt, believes "should be taken along on a journey to the northern portion of the new world" (*Away* 117). The alphabetical list, which includes a bizarre range of items, from "ancestral armour" to "engraved prints of Windsor Castle, Buckingham Palace, and the Queen" to "tennis racquets, umbrellas, and Wellingtons" (*Away* 117), emphasizes the class and cultural differences between British emigrants like the Colonel and the Irish peasants. The list, along with the Sedgewicks' collection and the shipwreck that brings to the tenants one last boon of cabbages, silver teapots, and barrels of whiskey before the famine, stand in stark contrast to the tenants' "vanished possessions," including a chair, a brooch from an ex-lover, pitchers, spoons, the head of a china doll, livestock, musical instruments, pocket-watches, and even a wheelbarrow (*Away* 118), which the Colonel's list prompts them to remember "with a terrible sense of loss" (*Away* 119). Under the oppression of colonization, they have lost, had to sell, or had taken from them the possessions that symbolize who they are in terms of history, prosperity, ownership, and heritage. In the Freudian understanding, mourning is "a turning away from reality," Sugars explains, "through which 'the existence of the lost object is psychically prolonged,'" while the "'shadow of the object,' as it falls on the self […] functions as a kind of internal haunting – in the case of diaspora or exile, as the trace of the superego effects of lost ancestors" (Sugars 11). For the Irish, however, this haunting begins before migration occurs. The loss of their possessions, including livestock, not only threatens the ability of the tenants to survive, it also disrupts, even severs, their links to their ancestors while they are still in Ireland. In a sense, then, they are exiled or haunted in their own homeland, but they are also ghosts, shadows of their former selves, consumed by the devastations of colonialism and famine. The tenants in Ireland are "both here and not here" (Sugars 25), and it is in this state – already haunted, already ghosts – that they set sail for Canada. Mary's "Awayness" (Urquhart, 2003: 81) more than prefigures her "exilic transplantation" (Sugars 12): it symbolizes synecdochically the alienation of the Irish from their homeland and heritage in their homeland under British colonization.

Away suggests, however, that colonization also alienates the colonizers. As I have argued, collecting, science, and writing (creative and scientific) are linked in the novel as the colonizers' alibis for doing nothing to rectify a dire situation, until it is nearly too late. Granville and Osbert see just enough to inspire collection, poetry writing, and scientific observation, but not to comprehend what is really happening beyond the walls of their estate or apply their knowledge to find a solution. It is only near the end that they realize that their colonial and collecting life has produced little and destroyed a great deal, and that they too are like ghosts, "here but not here." As colonizers, Osbert and Granville are not integrated into the community, but remain foreign to the country of their birth, which Osbert realizes when he meets Mary: "Everything about him had been manufactured somewhere else, in another country; everything, including his bones and the cellular construction of his flesh. She, however, had been built out of the materials of this country" (*Away* 90-91). In time, the Sedgewicks become haunted by what they have collected. The "mournful song" Granville heard sung at the wedding, which recalls his collection of Irish folk songs, keeps "running and running through his mind during the moments when he wasn't mentally cursing his father and his father's father for leaving such sensitive souls in the possession of this unholy mess" (*Away* 112). And Osbert, once the chosen tenants depart for Canada, is haunted by the "thought of the tidepool and the beautiful creatures he had wrenched from it and the light in the woman's face, and fear and loss came to sit beside him at his table until he covered his ears to free himself from the wailing that seemed to be pouring out of all the familiar objects in his room" (*Away* 130). His beloved collection and scientific work become unbearable memory cues that haunt him for his part in oppressing the Irish. In time, Granville escapes in death, while Osbert tries to escape by selling "the demesne, all the stuffed wildlife, the cases, the library, the walks – everything – to the first person who wanted it" (*Away* 219). However, *Away* suggests that the act of de-collection cannot undo the damage done over centuries of imperial and colonial oppression. The shift to the "New World" in the latter part of the novel does not represent a new beginning, but rather the resurgence of past wrongs and continued hauntings.

At first, it seems as though Brian and Mary's life in Canada will differ significantly from their life in Ireland. This optimism is suggested in a further contrast Urquhart sets up between implements and collected objects. Unlike the Sedgewicks, Brian and Mary use their implements to create a home and a livelihood and empower themselves: "Brian had been able to purchase crocks and sealer jars, cutlery, tools, dishes, farm implements, and finally, for his wife, a wheel and loom. Starting, as they had, with nothing, the two adults were like gods creating a universe. [...] Household goods were fondled or stroked like pets, and under such care developed an animate life, a soul" (*Away* 153-54). The references to "gods creating a universe" and to objects as pets evoke the collector and collection, but Urquhart distinguishes empowerment through collection versus empowerment through utility by contrasting the death of the Sedgewicks' objects and specimens with the life of Brian and Mary's implements. Similarly, unlike the knife and creel Mary used in Ireland, the new objects do not carry old sorrows. Mary even "raised a brood of chickens," naming them "after remembered things – Rathlin, Antrim, Moyle, Crannog – and in doing so, destroyed, for a time, the awful power of memory itself. There was no desire in her to make and sing poems [...]" (*Away* 153). The escape from memory, though, is temporary. Unable to remain present, Mary leaves her home, drawn into the past, while Brian relives past sorrows with his children (*Away* 197-98), seeing the oppression of the Irish continue in the "flourishing Orange Halls" of Upper Canada (*Away* 198). Both Mary and Brian die young, "exhausted and withered" (*Away* 203) by the system of colonization. Revealing "how problematic the weight of cultural heritage can be in a new land" (Wyile 35), the fates of Mary and Brian, and later Liam and Eileen, also suggest a critique of the naïveté of those like Aidan and D'Arcy McGee, who believe that Canada could become a country "in which there would be no factions, no revenge for old sorrows, old grievances. [...] A sweeping territory, free of wounds, belonging to all, owned by no one" (*Away* 337-38). Canada is no *tabula rasa*; instead, Urquhart suggests that the destructiveness of its progenitors, British imperialism and colonialism, resurges in Canada's rising nationalism.

As a colony, Canada cannot offer refuge from colonialism, which is also figured in Osbert, who arrives at the O'Malley homestead on stilts, seemingly "walking on water, towards the acres of light" (*Away* 214). Sugars suggests that "the text tricks its readers [...] into thinking that" Osbert is a ghost (*Away* 13), but he is a ghost: consumed by the system of colonization in Ireland, he is in Canada the spectre of colonization, as well as a false saviour. Osbert purchases the O'Malley homestead, then oversees "a man he'd hired from Madoc to install a decorative wrought-iron fence around the gravestones" of Brian and Mary as he is "pasting a variety of brilliant-coloured leaves into an album he'd made himself out of birch bark bound together with fence wire" (*Away* 282), images that further evoke the ideas of collection as death and rigid containment. The graves and album are metonymic symbols of Osbert's return as a collector/colonizer: he once again takes over his Irish tenants' land, buying it with the money he received from the sale of the symbols of colonization – his demesne and collection – which reinforces the idea that Canada is not a "New World" at all.

Through Osbert's re-collection of the O'Malleys and their land, Urquhart suggests that modern capitalism and industrialization have emerged from imperialism and colonization. Osbert begins to pan for gold on the O'Malley land, even though in Ireland he had believed that gold was "a binding force without which the planet would simply fly to pieces" (*Away* 64) and that some of Ireland's sorrows "were undoubtedly based on the fact that gold was not prevalent in the makeup of the country's rocks" (*Away* 64). He was oblivious to the fact that his own collected objects were Ireland's "gold." In desperation, Osbert had sold his collection to a whiskey factory, and, in Canada his beliefs about gold are overridden by greed: "Let us sing the praises of flowing streams: the one that bubbles through the demesne at Puffin Court and makes whiskey; the one that hurries towards the Black River and gives us nuggets of gold" (*Away* 225). These transitions from home to factory and homestead to goldmine emphasize the idea that capitalism and industrialism are extensions of colonial exploitation, while Osbert, as a re-colonizer and industrializer, epitomizes the novel's rather clichéd idea that the future is jeopardized when past mistakes are repeated, an idea that is also figured by collection. With Mary in mind, Osbert laments that, since "Gosse wrote a book about nature near the sea," England's "people of culture crowded the beaches seeking the tidepools, lifting the life out of them with nets" (*Away* 225); he cannot see, however, that, in panning or mining for gold, he too is "lifting the life out of" what he calls the "forest tidepool of quivering life" (*Away* 225). The lust for gold will bring its own destructive crowd and destabilize the "stable spot in the universe" he desires (*Away* 225).

Liam and Eileen, the children of Mary and Brian and, therefore, of colonialism, facilitate Osbert's industrialization by selling him their homestead, for which their "family would be visited by the curse of the mines" (*Away* 225), a metaphor for the idea that contemporary industrialism is one way Canada is haunted by its colonial past. The colonization of Ireland also "haunts" Liam's "capitalist ethic" (Wyile 36), which he picks up from Osbert, along with his mannerisms and speech (*Away* 223). Like the Sedgewicks, Liam becomes a landlord, not comprehending that he is as guilty as the British for buying land they had taken from the aborigines. However, Urquhart sidesteps the participation of the Irish immigrants in the colonial oppression of Native peoples with Liam's wedding to Molly, the half-Native, half-Irish daughter of his tenant, Doherty. This pairing is part of what Anne Compton calls "Urquhart's mythologizing mission" (*Away* 212), her perpetuation of the myth of Canada's benevolent treatment of Native peoples, a myth that has been "an important element in developing a national identity based on the notion of difference from the USA – a difference that was tied to the idea of Canadian tolerance. The contradiction is that this notion of Canada's tolerance coexisted with brutal policies of extermination and cultural genocide" (Mackey 14). The novel glosses over the death of Molly's Ojibway mother, a figure that can be read as representing the loss of Native cultures, focusing instead on the part Molly plays in the success of Liam's colonial project (*Away* 302). Perhaps wanting to celebrate the fortitude of her foremothers, Urquhart instead all but erases the Native peoples from the Ontarian landscape, reducing Molly and Exodus Crow to benevolent guardians of the white immigrants and a means for the colonizing Irish immigrant to achieve his goals.

At the end of the novel, symbolic objects also figure the haunting of the current generation by past colonial mistakes. Although not a collector, Eileen keeps a "braided skein of red and black hair," which represents her mother's love for the dead sailor and her own for Aidan; "a black feather" to symbolize Exodus Crow; and "a shard of turquoise china" that Brian had used to show Mary the colour of the Mediterranean Sea (*Away* 351). These objects represent both Eileen's connection to her fragmented heritage and the idea that she is trapped in and by the past, as she was when she became caught up in her father's Irish nationalism and inadvertently set up the assassination of D'Arcy McGee. The novel "warns against the comforting seductions of extremist national or ethnic politics" (Smart 68), but it also suggests that such extremism is inevitable: Canada cannot escape the violence of its imperialist and colonialist roots, a violence that also informs modern capitalism and industrialism. In the end, the "curse of the mines" is not visited directly on Liam and Eileen, but rather on their children and grandchildren, whose houses are destroyed and who are pushed from their land by the unrelenting movements of sand, caused by "careless farming practices" and industry (*Away* 11, 349). In particular, Esther, the inheritor of Eileen's objects, bears the burden of the past. The curse links the system of colonization, its exploitative nature, and its transitions into industrialism and nationalism to the disconnection of the people from the land and their heritage. Urquhart has said of that she is "terribly attracted" to the place in Ontario where "there is an ancestral history" for her family, that she "feels as if it's mine" (Urquhart, 2003: 81), and she carries into the novel the romantic notion that the family farm and rural living offers a better sense of belonging, self, and one's place in history than urban living. In the last pages of the novel, and like Osbert and Granville, Esther dies childless, the end of her line, as the cement company eats up the last O'Malley homestead.

Despite its romanticizing tendencies, *Away* offers a strong critique of the nature of contemporary Canadian nationalism as the offspring of colonialism, in which industry and urbanization are allowed to erode and insatiably consume the family farm, viable farmland, small communities, and human labour. This shift to industrialization and urbanization, the novel suggests, fragments communities and families, creating a sense of alienation; it causes a severing of roots, a disconnection from the unofficial histories and narratives that are instrumental to the construction of Canada as a nation and of a Canadian consciousness. In the novel, the lake-boats *Sir John A. Macdonald* (*Away* 352), *Daughter of Confederation* (*Away* 353), and *The New Dominion* (*Away* 356), loaded with limestone quarried from the devastated O'Malley homestead, are ironic symbols of the selling-off of Canada. Like Ireland, the novel suggests, Canada is being colonized or re-colonized, "collected" piece-by-piece: "Now the land itself fragments, moves away from piers [...] towards other waters, other shores" (*Away* 356). Here, "the land" could refer to the farmland, to the actual earth, but also synecdochically to the nation itself, and, while "other waters, other shores" indicates global destinations, I would suggest that Urquhart is implicating the United States in particular and thereby reflecting the anxieties of many Canadians in the 1980s and early 1990s about the impact a free-trade agreement with the United States would have on Canada. Those who opposed a free-trade deal feared that Canada would become "a de-industrialized warehouse economy and little more than a resource colony of the United States" (Bashevkin 104), a process we see at the end of *Away*. Urquhart, who has called herself "a staunch Canadian Nationalist" (Urquhart, 1986b: 34), suggests in *Away* that the threat posed by the United States to Canada is analogous to that of England to Ireland in the colonial period. She reiterates this belief in an interview when she says that the stories handed down from her Irish-immigrant forebears about "real and imagined injustices, and the difficulty of keeping your sense of self when there's a great imperialist power looming over you" are stories Canadians "can relate to looking south of the border" (Urquhart, 1998: 194).

Away, then, employs collection tropes to bring to the fore a see-mingly irresolvable tension between the desire to preserve one's heri-tage and the inherent danger in getting trapped in the past that one has preserved. If the nation is, as Hugh Seton-Watson defines it, "a commu-nity of people, whose members are bound together by a sense of soli-darity, a common culture, a national consciousness" (Seton-Watson 1),

Away warns that, when the capitalist drive for wealth and power, a drive that has developed out of imperialist and colonialist ideologies, becomes a nation's "common culture" at the expense of the connection to its histories and myths, the sense of solidarity weakens, and the nation is at risk. In response, but not unproblematically, *Away* implies anti-American sentiments and attempts to preserve fragments of Canadian histories and from them to construct pieces of mythology for a more inclusive nation. Collection figures the harmful containment of British colonialism that resurges in Canada as a nation, but de-collection cannot solve the problems that this collection has caused. In the face of the "renegotiating of Canada and Canadianness" that was ongoing in the last decades of the 20th century, Urquhart in *Away* expresses concern that no resolution can ever be reached that would satisfy even a small majority of Canadians, given the tensions inherent in a nation that has grown out of imperialism and colonialism, and that how we define ourselves as Canadians may become a moot point as Canada is increasingly subjected to America's corporate and cultural imperialism – the Canadian nation "collected" piece-by-piece.

References

ALEXANDER, E. P. (1979), *Museums in Motion: An Introduction to the History and Functions of Museums*, Nashville, Association for State and Local History.

BASHEVKIN, S. B. (1991), *True Patriot Love: The Politics of Canadian Nationalism*, Toronto, Oxford University Press.

BAUDRILLARD, J. (1994), "The System of Collecting," Trans. Roger Cardinal, in J. ELSNER and R. CARDINAL, Eds., *The Cultures of Collecting*, Cambridge, Harvard University Press, 7-24.

BHABHA, H. K. (1990), "Introduction: Narrating the Nation," in *Nation and Narration*, H. K. BHABHA, Ed., London, Routledge, 1-7.

BRANACH-KALLAS, A. (2003), *In the Whirlpool of the Past: Memory, Intertextuality and History in the Fiction of Jane Urquhart*, Torun, Pol., Wydawnictwo Uniwersytetu Mikolaja Kopernika.

BRYDON, D. (1995), "Reading Postcoloniality, Reading Canada," *Essays on Canadian Writing 56*, 1-19. Rpt. in C. SUGARS, Ed., (2004), *Unhomely States: Theorizing English-Canadian Postcolonialism*, Peterborough, Broadview, 165-79.

CLIFFORD, J. (1991), "Four Northwest Coast Museums," in I. KARP and S. D. LEVINE, Eds., *Exhibiting Cultures: The Poetics and Politics of Museum Display*, Washington, Smithsonian Institution Press, 212-254.

COMPTON, A. (1998), "Romancing the Landscape: Jane Urquhart's Fiction," in W. M. BOGAARDS, Ed., *Literature of Region and Nation: Proceedings of the*

6th International Literature of Region and Nation Conference [...], 2, Saint John, SSHRC and University of New Brunswick in Saint John, 211-229.

CRANE, S. A. (2000), "Introduction: Of Museums and Memory," *Museums and Memory*, S. A. CRANE, Ed., Cultural Sitings, Stanford, Stanford University Press, 1-12.

ELSNER, J. and CARDINAL, R. (1994), Introduction to J. ELSNER, and R. CARDINAL, Eds., *The Cultures of Collecting*, Cambridge, Harvard University Press, 1-6.

ELSNER, J. and CARDINAL, R. Eds. (1994), *The Cultures of Collecting*, Cambridge, Harvard University Press, 1-6.

FINDLEY, T. [1984] (1985), *Not Wanted on the Voyage*, Toronto, Penguin.

GOLDMAN, M. (1997), *Paths of Desire: Images of Exploration and Mapping in Canadian Women's Writing*, Theory/Culture, Toronto, University of Toronto Press.

KERTZER, J. (1998), *Worrying the Nation: Imagining a National Literature in English Canada*, Theory/Culture, Toronto, University of Toronto Press.

MACKEY, E. (1999), *The House of Difference: Cultural Politics and National Identity in Canada*, Sussex Studies in Culture and Communication, London, Routledge.

PEARCE, S. M. (1992), *Museums, Objects, and Collections: A Cultural Study*, Washington, Smithsonian Institution Press.

PEARCE, S. M. (1995), *On Collecting: An Investigation into Collecting in the European Tradition*, Collecting Cultures, London, Routledge.

PRATT, M. L. (1992), *Imperial Eyes: Travel Writing and Transculturation*, London, Routledge.

ROOT, D. (1996), *Cannibal Culture: Art, Appropriation, and the Commodification of Difference*, Boulder, Westview Press.

SETON-WATSON, H. (1977), *Nations and States: An Enquiry into the Origins of Nations and the Politics of Nationalism*, London, Methuen.

SMART, P. (1994), "Weighing the Claims of Memory: the Poetry and Politics of the Irish-Canadian Experience in Jane Urquhart's *Away*," *International Journal of Canadian Studies* 10: 63-70. CD-ROM. International Council for Canadian Studies.

STEWART, S. (1984), *On Longing: Narratives of the Miniature, the Gigantic, the Souvenir, the Collection*, Baltimore, Johns Hopkins University Press.

SUGARS, C. (2003), "Haunted by (a Lack of) Postcolonial Ghosts: Settler Nationalism in Jane Urquhart's *Away*," *Essays on Canadian Writing* 79: 1-32.

URQUHART, J. (1986a), *The Whirlpool*, Toronto, McClelland & Stewart.

– (1986b), "An Interview with Jane Urquhart," conducted by Geoff Hancock, *Canadian Fiction Magazine* 55: 23-40.

– (1993), *Away*, Toronto, McClelland & Stewart.

– (1995), "Home from Away: Jane Urquhart Walks the Landscapes of Her Past and Her Imagination and Turns Them into Compelling Fiction," Interview conducted by Elaine K. Naves in *Books in Canada* 24.4: 7. Proquest 7, 6 July 2004.

– (1998), "Ghosts in the Landscape: Jane Urquhart," Interview conducted by Jeffrey Canton, in B. DAURIO, Ed., *The Power to Bend Spoons: Interviews with Canadian Novelists*, Toronto, Mercury Press, 194-199.

– (2003), "Finding Your Place in the Story: A Conversation with Jane Urquhart," Interview conducted by Margaret O'Shea Bonner, *New Quarterly* 88: 71-90.

– (2004), "Jane Urquhart: Confessions of a Historical Geographer," Interview conducted by Herb Wyile, *Essays on Canadian Writing* 81: 58-83.

WYILE, H. (1999), "'The Opposite of History Is Forgetfulness': Myth, History, and the New Dominion in Jane Urquhart's *Away*," *Studies in Canadian Literature* 24.1: 20-45.

8

Talking Crow: Jane Urquhart's *Away*

Marlene GOLDMAN

University of Toronto

As Héliane Daziron-Ventura and Marta Dvořák argue in the introduction to this volume, co-extensive with the principle of resurgence are spatial tensions "between depth and surface, disappearance and reappearance, latency and manifestation." With respect to the temporal realm, resurgence promotes "a consideration of the rewriting and reconstruction of the past, of its surfacing or its erasure, of concealment and reappearance." In tracing the concept of resurgence in Jane Urquhart's writing, my essay focuses primarily on how Urquhart's novel *Away* (1993) explicitly addresses the Irish immigration to Upper Canada and simultaneously conveys the historical burden of Irish identity. As a result, Urquhart's contemporary, magic realist Canadian novel instigates a return to some of the most heated and racialized debates in the 19th century concerning Celtic identity and the foundations of Irish national identity. I argue that *Away* provides readers with a very useful opportunity to explore the uncanny return and reactivation of the 19th century tensions between the Irish and British discourses of romantic nationalism that were carried across the ocean to the New World.

Away draws on ancient Irish Celtic tales of "otherworld" spirits to trace the experiences over four generations of a rural Irish Catholic family that flees the Great Hunger of 1846 and emigrates to Upper Canada. The story opens with the retelling of a miraculous event: in 1842 on the island of Rathlin, the narrator's great-grandmother, Mary, visits a beach after a storm that leaves the ocean glistening with silver teapots, bobbing green cabbages, and barrels of whisky. Clinging to one of the barrels is an exhausted young man. Mary drags the stranger to shore and, before expiring, he murmurs the word "Moira" and dies. As the narrator tells us, Mary recognizes immediately "that he came from an otherworld island, assumed that he had emerged from the water to look for her, and knew that her name had changed, in an instant, from

Mary to Moira" (*Away* 8). From that moment on, the entire village understands that Mary has been "taken" by the Formoire, the ones from the sea. This magical encounter endows Mary with significance, transforming her from a dispossessed and impoverished Irish peasant girl into a powerful woman who has knowledge and possession of an otherworld spirit. As Mary explains, "Everything about him was hers now, all hers forever" (*Away* 5). Mary is hastily married off to Brian, the local schoolmaster, and they emigrate to the New World. But after the birth of her second child, Mary again falls under the spell of her daemon lover. This time, she sheds her domestic life entirely and abandons her children so that she can live with his spirit by the shores of Lake Moira.

In relating the family's story, which begins with Mary and Brian O'Malley and their two children, Eileen and Liam, *Away* also explores the larger complexities surrounding the formation of what Mark McGowan terms "the Irish collective memory" of the Famine and the diaspora, and Irish nationalism both in Ireland and the New World.[1] Although varying in many details and by no means constituting a unified genre, the diverse narratives that convey the Irish collective memory share common elements: first, "the 'potato famine heritage' is integral to the Irish"; second, "the Irish are Catholic"; third, "they have emerged from poverty, ignorance, and social degradation"; fourth, "the Famine was created artificially by British conquerors and landlords who were determined to rid Ireland of her Catholic vermin"; and, finally, "Irish Catholics are the Famine's children who passed through 'Hope's Gate' in Canada" (McGowan 2).[2]

As noted, *Away* relies on magic realism to generate a version of Ireland's colonial past and the Irish collective memory that challenges the prevailing, dominant discourses of British and Canadian

---

[1]   In using the phrase "the Irish collective memory," I am drawing on Mark McGowan's insight that as "a people come to identify themselves – their beliefs, their historical past, their culture, their sense of common purpose, in other words, their sense of peoplehood – there will emerge commonly accepted strands of what might be called a collective memory" (16). According to McGowan, in the case of the Great Irish Famine, "one often learns less about the 'historical moment' than one does about the dreams, desires, fears, self-identification, and ethnicity of those who embrace the moment as their own, weaving it into their own sense of peoplehood" (16).

[2]   Nowadays, the essential ingredients of the Famine memory are formally engraved in the popular culture: "the Famine was *the* Irish migration event; these Irish were Catholics who had suffered their 'time on the cross"; these Irish were the oppressed, the poor, the victims" (McGowan 11). Both the Irish collective memory and *Away* fail, however, to account for the experience of those thousands of Protestant and Catholic Irish who emigrated before and after the Famine. As McGowan asserts, in the "new historiographical assessment of Irish immigration, the Great Irish Famine has become an endpoint of a much longer migratory movement from Ireland to British North America, rather than the focus of Irish migration" (2).

nationalism. *Away*'s use of magic realism reveals that nations are not merely "imagined communities" but, more specifically, collective identities borne of fantasies that arise, in part, in response to suffering and loss. Viewed in this light, magic realism can be used by displaced and dispossessed members of a community to fashion a consoling vision of survival. Indeed, critics of Canadian literature have repeatedly analyzed how history is transformed into myth in the service of unifying the nation and offering consolation (see Vautier and Kertzer). My aim in this paper, however, is to examine *Away* to discover why the process of myth-making fails.

One of the most intriguing features of *Away* is the way in which the narrative illustrates the tensions surrounding the resurgence and "the rebirth of Ireland (and Irish culture, language, ethos and values) elsewhere 'off island,' the ultimate postmodern paradox" (Scheper-Hughes 29). In *Away* magic realism is instrumental in disseminating the Irish collective memory and the related ideologies of Primitivism and Celticism that permeate the novel. During the mid-19th century, when the novel is set, these ideologies helped to fashion an Irish collective identity in the face of terrible deprivation and loss. Primitivism has been famously defined as the "discontent of the civilized with civilization" that gives rise to the idealization of the primitive (Garrigan Mattar 4). Primitivism can thus be understood as a product of disillusionment and the resulting nostalgic desire to return to what has supposedly been lost, not on an individual but on a cultural level. As critics note, however, Primitivism is not so much a thing as a process "of self-referential idealization that can constitute an ideology, a poetic mode, a form of satire, a social contract, a religious instinct, an intrusive element in a 'scientific' discourse, or an instrument of tyranny" (Garrigan Mattar 3). During the 19th century, Primitivism provided a "cultural counterweight to the modernization and rationalization of society encompassed by the Enlightenment through its display of commitment to the preservation and transmission of the past, particularly the past of Scotland, Wales, Ireland, and the out-lying regions of English" (Pittock 36). Primitivism was also intimately bound to Celticism since the latter was "the main stream of the Primitivism that became fashionable throughout Europe" (Pittock 36-37).[3]

For the purposes of my essay, it is important to appreciate that Celticism exists in a dialectical relationship with what has been termed

---

[3] In her essay "The Irish Female Presence in Jane Urquhart's Fiction," Libby Birch reads *Away* in terms of the Celtic literary revival. Rather than offer a historical or political perspective of this discourse, Birth celebrates the text's portrayal of its protagonist as the symbol of "a vanquished Celtic goddess" whose culture is "buried in the mists of time" (115).

"Anglo-Saxonism." Simply put, the spirits and magical beliefs associated with the ancient Celtic Irish aristocratic culture as it was "imperfectly preserved, adapted, and transformed by a repeatedly colonized and disenfranchised Catholic peasantry" (Scheper-Hughes 25) co-exist with the supposedly rational, colonial "Anglo-Saxon" approach to daily life. The most important aspect of the latter's creed was the belief that the Anglo-Saxon people or race, "as clearly distinguished from all other races in the world, had a peculiar genius for governing themselves – and others – by means of a constitutional and legal system that combined the highest degree of efficiency with liberty and justice" (Curtis 6-7). In Ireland, the Anglo-Saxonist mythology set up "a counter-current or cultural resistance movement," known as Celticism or the Irish Revival. "Drawing on many different talents and disciplines, Celticism tried to accomplish for the 'Irish race' what Anglo-Saxonism had managed to do for the 'English race,' namely to raise the people concerned to an exalted position of cultural and racial superiority [...] Ethnocentric Irish men and women sought to combat heavy doses of Anglo-Saxonist venom with a Celticist serum of their own making" (Curtis 15). Celticist scholars viewed the modern Irish as direct descendants of a "pure and holy race [...] whose ancient institutions, veneration for learning, and religious zeal made Saxon culture during the two or three centuries before the Norman Conquest look nothing less than barbarian" (Curtis 15; see also Pittock 5-6).

Viewed in terms of Celticism the diasporic upheaval irrevocably severs a people from their roots, their life-giving and sacred land.[4] Yet, in *Away*, the diaspora confers land and newfound wealth on the once-impoverished O'Malley family, a transformation that, ironically, puts them in an analogous position to their former, contemptible Anglo-Irish landlords *vis à vis* North American Native peoples. Portraying the Irish in terms of the collective memory as a unified, dispossessed, primitive tribe eternally victimized by the British Empire thereby obscures the Irish settler-invader's complicity in the imperial and colonial project. In effect, the unequal power relations between Native North Americans and Irish settler-invaders are obfuscated by *Away*'s reliance on the characteristic archetypal tropes of Celticism and magic realism which promote a "mythic participation" in what Jorge Louis Borges termed "a 'universal history' that is always present, available, communal" (Parkinson Zamora 508). To establish a connection between the Irish

---

[4]   Citing Fintan O'Toole, Nancy Scheper-Hughes explains, "The people and the land are no longer coterminous and 'the lie of the land is that there *is a place* [at all] called "Ireland" inhabited by the Irish people [...] [when] over the past 150 years much of [Irish history] has happened elsewhere [...] the central fact of that culture is that it knows no borders [...] it is porous and diffuse' (29).

and the genius locus of the New World, *Away* invokes magic realism to identify the Irish characters with the Canadian landscape and, on occasion, to transform Irish characters into replicas of indigenous peoples. In this way, magic realism serves the necessary yet politically-suspect work of indigenizing the Irish settler-invaders. This rhetorical move, however, undercuts "the impulse to generate a specific political and cultural assessment of the impact of imperialism and colonialism on the distinct groups" (Parkinson Zamora 504). Moreover, in its attempts to legitimize the right of the Irish to possess the land, the text uncannily replicates the European romantic reification of Native North Americans. As writer and critic Thomas King observes, in the second half of the 19th century, Europeans became obsessed with a mythical Indian, "the wild, free, powerful, noble, handsome, philosophical, eloquent, solitary Indian [...] who could be a cultural treasure, a piece of North American antiquity. A mythic figure who could reflect the strength and freedom of an emerging continent. A National Indian [...] If North Americans couldn't find him, they could make him up" (King 79). *Away* conjures this mythic figure in its portrait of Mary's Indian friend, Exodus Crow. In what follows, I explore the problems associated with *Away*'s reliance on romantic and stereotyped images of the Indian and the figure of the crow, which serve to indigenize the Irish and simultaneously reduce Native North Americans to spectral images.

In a multi-media presentation entitled "Canadian Blackbirds: Crow and Raven in Canadian Literature and Art" held in 2001, Russell Brown, Donna Bennett, Lora Carney and myself – all of us scholars of Canadian literature and visual culture – observed that the figures of the crow and the raven functioned as a "way to construct a tradition for a new literature in a new land, providing a meeting place of the inherited and the new."[5] In the Greek proverb of the Oldest Animals, repeated in Hesiod, Plutarch, Erasmus, and other texts, the crow lives nine times as long as humans do, and ravens much longer than that, and both are thus figures of time itself (though both must die as the universe continues). In Anglo-Saxon poetry, crows and ravens are sinisterly identified as the

---

[5]   The first session, which drew on the research and writing of Russell Brown, Donna Bennett, Lora Carney and myself, was held at the ACSUS conference at the Hyatt Regency, San Antonio Texas. 14-18 Nov. 2001. (It was also presented 26 May 2002 at the ACCUTE conference, University of Toronto.) As Russell Brown and Donna Bennett observe: "For settlers in British North America, the new land gave new importance to literal crows and ravens, which turned out to have a special significance for Canada. The raven was one of the few birds that wintered over in the Canadian north. Thus the raven offered itself as a kind of natural symbol of Northern endurance and survival."

birds of battle because they are drawn to carnage.[6] In the narratives of Native peoples, the raven and the crow are portrayed as creators and tricksters whose presences trouble and vitalize the landscape. Precisely because the figure of the crow is not purely indigenous to North America, but bore a prior and potent meaning before being transported to the New World, in *Away*, the figure of the crow serves as a reminder of the seemingly inescapable hold of the romantic European interpretive framework. As Herb Wyile explains, in Celtic mythology, fairies or the Sidhe "often take the form of birds," which merges "with the trickster tradition so important in Ojibway and other native cultures, giving the novel a conspicuous dash of the syncretism that is such an important feature of Latin American magic realism (Wyile 29-30). Whereas Wyile and other scholars celebrate this fusion, I find myself troubled by its political repercussions.

In her essay on the native in literature, Margery Fee observes that non-Native writers, especially those from marginal groups, frequently adopt Native imagery and Native peoples themselves to assert nationalist claims.

> A variant of mainstream nationalism uses the First Peoples' position as marginal, yet aboriginal, to make a similar claim-by-identification for other marginal groups. Those who do not wish to identify with "mainstream" Anglo-Canadian culture, or who are prevented from doing so, can find a prior and superior Canadian culture with which to identify. (Fee 17)

To legitimize the Irish people's right to possess the land – essentially to effect their indigenization – *Away* similarly relies on the figure of the crow and the metonymic connections among this figure, Celtic mythology, and the spiritual traditions of Canada's indigenous peoples.[7]

In its depictions of the three central characters, Mary, Liam, and Eileen, *Away* illustrates how their respective encounters with the crow nurture and supposedly authenticate their claim to the land. Initially, the crow appears in human form. Seven years after her disappearance, Mary's friend, the Ojibway Exodus Crow, emerges from the forest bearing Mary's frozen body. Before explaining the reason for their

---

6   That identification surfaces in visual and literary works as Alex Colville's paintings, Timothy Findley's novel *The Wars*, and Patrick Lane's poem "Temenos." It is also present in Susanna Moodie's *Roughing It in the Bush*, when one of Moodie's neighbours says of a detested land speculator: "And pray, what brought you here today, scenting about you like a carrion-crow?"

7   Old Irish mythology does not refer to the crow, per se, but the raven is considered an oracular bird. "to have the foresight of the raven" is a proverbial saying which refers both to the raven's knowledge and his prophetic gifts. And "to have raven's knowledge" is an Irish phrase meaning to see all, know all."

mother's mysterious departure, Exodus Crow outlines the significance of his name:

The crow was my father's spirit-guide and, in time, became mine. He is a wise bird who survives hardships and who loves that which shines. He is a bird with a strong voice who insists on being heard. Because he sits high on the top branch of the tallest tree in the forest and flies even higher than that, he can see many things at once and so is a good guide. Because he flies fast and calls loudly he is a good messenger. (*Away* 74-75)

He goes on to explain that he is called Exodus Crow because his mother, who read the *Bible*, loved the name Exodus, even though according to her, that biblical book was not worthy of its name because it was filled with battles for land and the making of laws" (*Away* 175). The allusions to the Book of Exodus are especially significant because, as Mark McGowan, observes, sometimes "the Irish were likened to the Jews," and "[h]omilies cited the Book of Exodus wherein the Chosen of God were released from bondage and called upon to do mighty deeds" (McGowan 10). In *Away*, Exodus Crow's introduction recalls these associations to God's Chosen People and more generally aligns him with both Native and biblical wisdom and spirituality. By referring to his mother's rejection of the Judeo-Christian book, Exodus Crow specifically identifies himself as pacifist and a Primitivist symbol of natural virtue.[8] Despite his mother's rejection of the biblical book's contents, both Exodus and the members of his generation – not to mention subsequent generations – remain concerned with "battles for land and the making of laws." By portraying Exodus's mother as dismissive of law making and territorial battles, the narrative again seemingly promotes nostalgia and amnesia over pragmatic action. Ironically, both Exodus's mother's response and Mary's escapist fantasies constitute a similar response to terrible sufferings borne of displacement, dispossession, and loss. Viewed in this light, *Away* demonstrates the extent to which disparate peoples in the New World were caught up in the conscious and unconscious project to imagine a nation, a New Jerusalem, a Promised Land, in an effort to mitigate suffering and to magically restore a lost home.

Exodus Crow goes on to tell the family about his unexpected encounter with Mary by the shores of Lake Moira; he thinks at first she is an animal or a ghost (*Away* 178). When he realizes that she is a white woman alone and starving in the forest, he provides her with food. As in so many texts by non-Natives, Exodus Crow plays the role of the

---

[8]   It is ironic that *Away* emphasizes the rejection of martial efforts to gain land and assert a tribal identity since, as I am arguing, a major aim of one strand of the narrative is to legitimize the claim of the Irish to British North America.

"magical helper" common in myth and fairytale (Fee 22). His portrayal recalls Thomas King's account of the pattern that began to emerge in the second half of the 19th century that would culminate in the creation of "a singular semi-historic Indian who was a friend to the White man, who was strong, brave, honest, and noble. A figure who kept his clothes on and who spoke reasonable English" (King 83). The shift from fiend to noble friend that King traces is in fact merely the flipside of the same coin. Even in the more positive Primitivist versions of the stereotype, the indigene remains "a semiotic pawn on a chess board under the control of the white signmaker" (Goldie 10). Exodus Crow recounts how after accepting his aid Mary told him stories about Ireland, her homeland, and its mythical inhabitants. As he says, he believed her because "it was as if his own mother were telling the stories of the spirits" (*Away* 180). Here Mary demonstrates her characteristic ability to transform grown men into children in touch with their primal imagination. In turn, Exodus Crow relates Ojibway stories about the spirits that live in the forests and Mary assures him that she believes these stories. Eventually, Mary explains why she abandoned her family and came to live in the forest: "I am loved by the spirit of this lake" she says, and "I will stay near him now until I die." Again, Exodus Crow tells Mary's family, "I said that I believed her because I did" (*Away* 182). This scene and others like it that emphasize credibility and verification of magical thinking have a political valence. Simply put, they condition the reader to accept magic over realism, presumably in light of the recognition that, at an earlier point, so-called realism was, in fact, artificially or magically produced.

Yet Exodus Crow and Mary share more than a belief in the spirit world. After several years pass, Exodus Crow listens as Mary speaks about "the time of the stolen lands of her island, and of the disease, and of the lost languages and the empty villages" (*Away* 184). Exodus Crow then confesses to Mary that "some white men had seized my people's land and killed many animals for sport and abused our women." Hearing this, Mary embraces him, saying that "the same trouble stayed in the hearts of both our people" (*Away* 185). Read in the light of the urge to legitimize the Irish's possession of the New World, this episode forges strategic links between Irish and Native mythical worlds, implying that a spiritual kinship exists between Canada's indigenous peoples and the Irish. Here as elsewhere suffering, as presented through myth, unites a people. This kinship is so strong that after meeting Mary only once, Exodus Crow has a vision that tells him what he should do: "I should help this woman to stay near her spirit and to live there in the forest" (*Away* 183). More important, the text enhances this supposed kinship by forging yet another connection between the Irish and the Native peoples based on their mutual experience as colonized peoples. The text's reliance on magic realism promotes the tendency to forge universal, archetypal connections. But myth obscures history, and this is a familiar compromise: the universals, commonalities, archetypes, and truths that unify people efface the specificities of diverse subjective experience of historical events. As a result, myth also obscures the agency and responsibility of various groups for perpetuating or acquiescing in others' suffering.

Away thus maintains a tension between a mythic and spiritual perspective – all peoples are on similar paths involving suffering – and a post-colonial, political, and historical perspective which I adopt in this chapter – that insists on drawing causal links and identifying specific agents and victims. The mythic perspective is evident in a scene that takes place shortly before Mary emigrates, when her beloved spirit shows her

> the world's great leavetakings, invasions and migrations, landscapes torn from beneath the feet of tribes, the Danae pushed out by the Celts, the Celts eventually smothered by the English, warriors in the night depopulating villages, boatloads of groaning African slaves. Lost forests. The children of the mountain on the plain, the children of the plain adrift on the sea. And all the mourning for abandoned geographies (128).

Framed in this way, the Irish diaspora is simply another example in a series that also includes the dispossession of Native North Americans.

If, as I am suggesting, Mary's relationship with the figure of the crow establishes grounds for the Irish's claim on the new world, then her children's subsequent encounters with the crow serve to deepen and strengthen this initial claim. When he returns with Mary's body, Exodus Crow insists that it is his mission to give Liam back his mother. After climbing into a willow tree and pondering how to achieve this, Exodus Crow suddenly departs. Eileen tells Liam: "first he turned into a bird, then he flew away, high up, very high over the trees" (*Away* 194). As the narrator explains, each spring "from then on, Liam would set out in search of Exodus... Years later he would say that this was the time when he learned the woods" (*Away* 196). In the service of indigenization, the text repeatedly plays on the archetypal notion of the mother. While it is clearly impossible for Exodus to bring Mary back to life and thus restore her to Liam, he does give Liam Mother Nature, a gesture that recalls Mary's consistent identification with nature throughout the novel. As the narrator explains: Liam "would not find Exodus and eventually, he forgot that this had been his original intention. He would find, instead, rock and bark and swamp and cedar and strange, narrow liquid highways the colour of mahogany" (*Away* 197). Ultimately, surrounded by nature (and rivers the colour of his mother's hair and the ship imagined by the would-be-immigrants) Liam has an epiphany: "he knew he wanted to make things grow, wanted, above all, to nurture, to be a farmer" (*Away* 197). The novel further reinforces Liam's connection to the land and to the aboriginals by portraying his marriage to Molly. She and her father are squatters on the land that Liam purchases. Part Irish and part Ojibway, Molly is a woman who "[c]arried the cells of both the old world and the new in the construction of her bones and blood" (*Away* 302). Ironically, when Molly and Eileen first meet in the forest, both girls simultaneously exclaim: "I live here" (*Away* 271). In depicting Molly's satisfying marriage to Liam, the text predictably resolves the Native/non-Native contest of ownership by presenting the blessed marriage between Irish and Native and by conveniently fusing the two tribal identities in what Sugars refers to as "a dubious process of indigenization" (Sugars 18).

Taken together, Liam's experience – his confusion about his mother, his meeting with Exodus Crow, and his recognition of his vocation – mirrors a familiar pattern in many Canadian works that rely on Native imagery.

> Typically a white speaker or main character is confused and impelled by a strong desire to know more about the past: personal, familial, native or national. The confusion is resolved through a relationship with an object, image, plant, animal or person associated with Native people. Occasionally, the relationship is with a real Native person. The resolution is often a quasi-mystical vision of, or identification with, Natives, although occasionally it simply takes the form of a psychological or creative breakthrough [...] The movement from observer to participant, outsider to insider, immigrant to 'native' [...] is often commented on specifically. (Fee 16)

In *Away*, Liam's experience of the Famine and his subsequent discovery of his vocation also recall the prophetic overtones of Mary's panoramic supernatural visions of Irish history over the ages. These prophetic episodes, in turn, can be read in light of the reworking of the Famine by Irish nationalists into a "providentialist vision" (McGowan 3). Exodus Crow reinforces this sacred vision when he insists that Liam must hear his mother's story. "Like Crow I will be heard. Your sister wants to hear the story, your father wants to hear the story. But you, who will move forward and make the change, *must* hear the story" (*Away* 175). His oracular pronouncement intimates that Liam must hear the story to fulfill the family's heroic destiny first prophesied by Mary in Ireland when she saw little Liam begin to dig in the earth, "caking the undersides of his delicate new nails with mud" (*Away* 80). In Herder's theory of romantic nationalism, 'soil' denotes not just place, but the spirit of place (Kertzer 48). Viewed in this light, Mary realizes that, like her, Liam has a primal connection with the spirit of the land.

Eileen's relationship with the crow likewise establishes the claim of the Irish to the land, albeit in a slightly different fashion. After Exodus Crow's departure, Eileen spends a great deal of time sitting in the willow tree, conversing with an actual crow. Speaking of the crow, Eileen explains that he was "her bird; her secret. She had tried once or twice to share him with her brother but his lack of belief had eliminated the possibilities for the crow in any other life but hers" (*Away* 220).[9] Like Mary's spirit, Eileen's crow furnishes her with accurate and helpful information. On one occasion, readers are told that Eileen watched as the crow dove into the creek and "returned with what appeared to be a piece of the sun in his mouth" (*Away* 22). After teasing Eileen, his beak held open by "solidified light," the crow eventually drops "his most recent gift into her palm" (*Away* 222). The gift turns out to be gold and, shortly after receiving it, Mary's children are paid a fortune for their property. This enables Liam to realize his dream of buying even more arable land and becoming a prosperous farmer.

This episode featuring crow's gift to Eileen, a nugget of gold likened to "the sun in [crow's] [...] mouth," specifically recalls the Native story of raven stealing the light. In keeping with this story, the gift in Urquhart's novel has both positive and negative consequences. As crow tells Eileen, "the only problem was that from now on her family would be visited by the curse of the mines" (*Away* 225). While this episode, like the others mentioned above, aims to authenticate the settler-invader society's claim to the land, it is particularly troubling. As Fee generally observes: "Several English-Canadian works describe the transfer of something symbolic of the land from Native to white [...] sometimes a Native voluntarily hands a totem [...] over to a newcomer, thereby validating the white's land claim and blessing the relationship between old land and new land-owner" (Fee 21; see also Monkman 5; Kertzer 131-133). In *Away*, this "totem-transfer" implies that crow, essentially the Ojibway spirit of the land, willingly offers his land to the Irish, whom he loves, for appropriation and exploitation.

Ultimately, Eileen forgets about her relationship with Exodus Crow and her conversations with her feathered friend in the willow tree. Again, this forgetfulness is in keeping with non-Native portrayals of First Peoples, in which the Indian is relegated to "the side of childhood, innocence, and nature" (Fee 26), representing what is, according to Fee, "past, lost, almost forgotten" (Fee 25). In other words, the Native is

---

9 As Thieme argues, in Canadian texts, animals sometimes stand for "a world which may exist before Western rationalist thought imposes dualistic modes of description. They represent life before discourse, before history, and before gender stereotyping" (qtd. in Slemon 419).

relegated to the realm of the uncanny and repressed, primitive beliefs. It is only later, as an adult, when she hears the Irishman and Father of Confederation Thomas D'Arcy McGee speak in the House of Commons that Eileen is reminded of the wisdom of her beloved crow. "Eileen was shaken by sudden recollection; the privacy within the curtains of a willow; a dialogue with a blue-black bird [...] She remembered now, for the first time, that as a child she had listened to a wise man" (*Away* 338). Daniel Francis observes that settler-invader societies had two characteristic responses to arriving second in the new world: conquering the Native peoples or transforming themselves into Indians (Francis 122-23). *Away* repeatedly figures attempts at the latter. First Mary literally goes Native and proclaims that Native and Irish peoples share similar spirit worlds and similar fates. Second, thanks to Mary's friend Exodus Crow, Liam finds his home in Mother Nature, and eventually marries a *Métis*, thereby ensuring that his children are part Native by blood. Finally, the Irish politician D'Arcy McGee is transformed into a Native, by virtue of his likeness to Exodus Crow. In the novel's concluding pages, an Irish orator becomes the mouthpiece of the wisdom of Canada's Native peoples. Taken together, the text's reliance on Celticism and romantic nationalism is responsible for reactivating a host of stereotypes of the Irish and for reinstalling caricatures of Native peoples ranging from the exotic, magical friend, to the Roussauian symbol of natural virtue, to the "wise elder." Moreover, after playing the role of guide, helper and shaman to Mary and her children, the Native vanishes from the text. In effect, both Mary and Exodus Crow vanish, in keeping with the prevailing romantic view of the Indians and the Irish as members of a doomed and degenerate race (see King 83-84).

Unfortunately, while every effort is made to demonstrate the kinship between the Irish and the aboriginals, no effort is made to identify their differences. Yet, as Donald Akenson explains, "the success of imperialism was contingent upon the displacement of indigenous populations, upon the legalized theft or confiscation of land previously held by the native inhabitants, and upon the breaking of aboriginal cultures. The Irish participated energetically, efficiently, and enthusiastically in all of these processes and they were very well rewarded for doing so" (Akenson 151). Despite their image of being rebellious and anti-imperial in general and anti-British Empire in particular, the Irish have actually been among the greatest supporters of the second British Empire and the Commonwealth. Drawing on Ronald Robinson's theory of "collaboration," Akenson outlines how the Irish served as "the ideal prefabricated collaborator: 'the white colonist'" (Akenson 142). According to Akenson, Ireland's greatest boon to the United Kingdom Empire

was through the massive numbers of everyday settlers that it provided [...]
From 1815 until the Great Famine, the first overseas choice of Irish migrants
[...] was British North America (modern day Canada). This was a set of
British colonies most of which had been founded by people opposed to the
principles of the American Revolution and extremely loyal (among English-
speakers) to the Crown (Akenson 148).

As he explains:

> [W]hether they settled in the British or American empire, the members of
> the Irish diaspora were an integral part of the nineteenth century and
> twentieth-century tidal waves of European imperialism. In the empires-of-
> settlement (which includes the English-speaking world), the success of
> imperialism was contingent upon the displacement of indigenous popula-
> tions, upon the legalized theft or confiscation of land previously held by the
> native inhabitants, and upon the breaking of aboriginal cultures. (Akenson
> 151)

As my reading of *Away*'s treatment of Native figures and the crow
suggests, it is crucial to revise simplistic views of magic realist texts as
unequivocally opposing the imperial centre. Instead, it is more fruitful to
consider how spectral figures signal barely repressed investments in
romantic nationalist paradigms. It is useful, as Jennifer Andrews argues,
to attend more carefully to how Canadian magic realist fiction "may
perpetuate and profit from romantic constructions of 'otherness'"
(Andrews 16).

With respect to the notion of resurgence, although it might appear as
if *Away* successfully and rapidly indigenizes the Irish and exorcises the
ghost of tribal nationalism, the spectres of romantic nationalism are not
so easily banished. For his part, Kertzer warns that "no discourse is
autonomous or pure, and those that pretend to be brand new have merely
mystified their lineage" (Kertzer 193). Citing Ralph Cohen, Kertzer
insists that histories are always "complicit with the paradigms they claim
to supersede: 'it is thus impossible to generate anew history without
being contaminated by the language and genre of the old'" (Kertzer
193). To Eileen's surprise, the new nation described by McGee "was
one in which there would be no factions, no revenge for old sorrows, old
grievances. Everything about it was to be new, clear; a landscape
distanced by an ocean from the zones of terror. A sweeping territory,
free of wounds, belonging to all, owned by no one" (*Away* 338).
Moreover, McGee was addressing them "not as the representative of any
race, any province, but as the forerunner of a generation that would
inherit wholeness, a generation released from fragmentation" (*Away*
338). I would argue, however, McGee's vision and Eileen's are two
sides of the same coin. Whereas Eileen's romantic nationalism remains
fatally oriented toward the past, McGee's remains fixated on the future,

so that both preclude an engagement with the present. Moreover, McGee's vision of the New Jerusalem is predicated on historical amnesia, as if one can by an act of will and imagination erase racial formations and install wholeness – an example of "domineering universalism" which presents itself as a benign antidote to tribalism.[10]

While seemingly purged of tribal nationalism, the appeal of McGee's vision and, by extension, the narrative as a whole, lies in their uncanny similarity to the assimilationist discourse of British imperialism. Historically, Celticism often coincided with an overarching assimilationist policy. The Celticist scholar Matthew Arnold argued that "the fusion of all the inhabitants of these islands into one homogenous, English-speaking whole [...] The swallowing up of provincial nationalities, is a consummation [...] a necessity of what is called modern civilization" (qtd. Pittock 64). Many other writers likewise indulged in Celticism "only in the context of 'the larger responsibilities of united [British] nationality and race'" (qtd. in Pittock 72). *Away*'s tendency to incorporate archetypes and a historical comparisons is thus in keeping with this assimilationist agenda. For a vast number of writers, whose "western gaze echoed the association of the Celtic lands [...] with marginality, mortality and decline," the image of the Celt abused by the Saxon became "a type for the general experience of mankind" (Pittock 73). The movement to construct and deconstruct Celtic identity at one time thus served the aims of British nationalism:

> Part of the manner in which homogenous identities succeed derives from not only the suppression of diversity, but also the suspension of belief in that diversity or its value among those who are its heirs. This is part of the process of consolidating the "imagined community," in Benedict Anderson's phrase [...] In postcolonial terms, the systematic downplaying or rubbishing of Celticism and Celtic culture was part of the British imagination in which many of the Celts themselves took part [...] The display of national culture could only be approved if it consented to disown its nationality. (Pittock 102)

In *Away*, both Mary's Celtic Primitivism and McGee's equally visionary image of the modern nation are thus dialogically related and

---

[10] As Kertzer explains, a common narrative of romantic nationalism portrays that nation as a sleeping giant that awakens, recalls its ancient glory, and resolves to fulfill its heroic promise. In this potent mixture of fact and fantasy, national history is both framed and validated by epochs that transcend history. It is inspired by a mythical pre-history ... and fulfilled by utopian post-history (e.g. the classless society, the peaceable kingdom)" (11). Sugars shares my criticism of McGee's vision, noting that it is "compromised by its commitment to a select 'settler' branch of the Canadian polity that takes as its privilege the ability to omit questions of race from any discussions of national unity" (18).

constitute an uncanny repetition of the 19th century tensions between Irish and the British discourses of romantic nationalism that were carried across the ocean to the New World. In its treatment of the spirit of the nation, as we have seen, *Away* resurrects the legacy of Celticism and its counterpart, assimilationist British nationalism, in the guise of a new form of assimilationist Canadian nationalism. Although the most zealous proponents of both forms of nationalism die, namely, Mary and McGee, their spirits continue to haunt the Canadian nation-state.

References

AKENSON, D. (1993), *The Irish Diaspora: A Primer*, Toronto, P.D. Meany.

ANDREWS, J. (1999), "Rethinking the Relevance of Magic Realism for English Canadian Literature: Reading Anne-Marie MacDonald's *Fall on Your Knees*," *Studies in Canadian Literature*, 24.1: 1-19.

BIRCH, L. (1997), "The Irish Female Presence in Jane Urquhart's Fiction," *Canadian Woman Studies* 17.3: 115-119.

CURTIS, L. P. (1968), *Anglo-Saxons and Celts: A Study of Anti-Irish Prejudice in Victorian England*, Connecticut, University of Bridgeport Press.

FEE, M. (1987), "Romantic Nationalism and the Image of Native People in Contemporary English-Canadian Literature," in T. KING, C. CALVER, and H. HOY, Eds., *The Native in Literature*, Toronto, ECW, 15-33.

GARRIGAN, MATTAR, S. (2004), *Primitivism, Science, and the Irish Revival*, Oxford, Oxford University Press.

GOLDIE, T. (1989), *Fear and Temptation: The Image of the Indigene in Canadian, Australian Fiction, and New Zealand Literatures*, Kingston, Montreal, and London, McGill-Queen's University Press.

KERTZER, J. (1998), *Worrying the Nation: Imagining a National Literature*, Toronto, University of Toronto Press.

KING, T. (2003), *The Truth about Stories: A Native Narrative* [Massey Lectures], Toronto, Anansi.

MC GOWAN, M. (2006), *Creating Canadian Historical Memory: The Case of the Famine Migration of 1847*, Ottawa, The Canadian Historical Association.

PITTOCK, M. (1999), *Celtic Identity and the British Image*, Manchester and New York, Manchester University Press.

SCHEPPER-HUGHES, N. (2001), *Saints, Scholars, and Schizophrenics: Mental Illness in Rural Ireland*, Berkeley, University of California Press.

SLEMON, S. (1995), "Magical Realism as Postcolonial Discourse," in L.P. ZAMORA, and W.B. FARIS, Eds, *Magical Realism: Theory, History, Community*, Durham, Duke University Press, 407-426.

SUGARS, C. (2003), "Haunted by (a Lack of) Postcolonial Ghosts: Settler Nationalism in Jane Urquhart's *Away*," *Essays on Canadian Writing* 33: 1-35.

VAUTHIER, M. (1998), *New World Myth: Postmodernism and Postcolonialism in Canadian Fiction*, Montreal, McGill-Queen's University Press.

WYILE, H. (1999), "'The Opposite of History is Forgetfulness': Myth, History and the New Dominion in Jane Urquhart's *Away*," *Studies in Canadian Literature* 24.1: 20-45.

ZAMORA, L.P. (1995), "Magical Romance/Magical Realism: Ghosts in U.S. and Latin American Fiction," in L.P. ZAMORA and W.B. FARIS, Eds., *Magical Realism: Theory, History, Community*, Durham, Duke University Press.

ZAMORA, L.P. and FARIS, W.B. (1995), "Introduction: Daiquiri Birds and Flaubertian Parrot(ie)s," in L.P. ZAMORA and W.B. FARIS, Eds., *Magical Realism: Theory, History, Community*, Durham, Duke University Press.

ZAMORA, L.P. and FARIS, W.B., Eds. (1995), *Magical Realism: Theory, History, Community*, Durham, Duke University Press.

9

Jane Urquhart, Arbiter of the Aesthetic

Karis SHEARER

Post-doctoral Fellow, McGill University

When Penguin Canada published *The Penguin Book of Canadian Short Stories* (2007), selected and introduced by Jane Urquhart, the press could hardly have anticipated the controversy it would cause in certain corners of the Ontario-Quebec literary community. After all, they had chosen as editor an internationally-renowned poet, novelist, and short-fiction writer – an author whose literary work has been recognized by both Canadian and international juries for prizes that range from the Governor General's Award to the International IMPAC Dublin Literary Award to *Le prix du meilleur livre étranger* in France. In selecting Urquhart as editor of this trade anthology, Penguin had secured a writer of both national and international prestige, a writer who held both popular[1] and academic appeal[2] – whose name, therefore, must have seemed sure to attract a wide range of readers to the anthology. And it no doubt did. Nevertheless, the publication of *The Penguin Book of Canadian Short Stories* also caused a minor uproar and prompted an extensive debate about literary value. In response to the anthology, a number of Canadian writers wrote lengthy diatribes, objecting to everything from the appropriateness of Penguin's choice of editor, to Urquhart's understanding of the short story genre, to her choice of authors and selection of stories. Two journals, *The New Quarterly* and *Canadian Notes and Queries*, both quickly responded to the Penguin anthology by each publishing a *"Salon des Refusés"* issue. Much of the

---

[1] Urquhart's third novel, *Away* (1993), for instance, spent longer than any other Canadian book – 132 weeks – on *The Globe & Mail*'s National Best Seller list.

[2] An MLA (Modern Languages Association) database search, for example, returns 49 results for articles on Urquhart and her work. Similarly, a Proquest Dissertations and Theses database search returns 26 results: between 1998 and 2007, in North America, there have been 9 PhD dissertations and 15 MA theses that deal with Urquhart's work. – an average of approximately 2 per year.

critical discourse produced in response to the anthology, however, is characterized by problematic assumptions about the stability of aesthetic value and by a misunderstanding of the role anthologies play in the production of cultural capital; indeed, some of these troubling assumptions are perpetuated by the anthology itself. When placed in an historical context that includes major moments in Canadian canon-making, the Penguin anthology emerges better understood as a cultural production that, instead of transmitting value, *creates* it.

> All value is radically contingent, being neither a fixed attribute, an inherent quality, or an objective property of things but, rather, an effect of multiple, continuously changing, and continuously interacting variables or, to put it another way, the product of the dynamics of a system, specifically an *economic* system.
>
> – Barbara Herrnstein Smith (30, original italics)

Since the early 1990s, the question of how Canadian canons are formed – and what is at stake in such an axiological question – has been productively debated by such critics as Donna Bennett, Frank Davey, Carole Gerson, Robert Lecker, and Tracy Ware. Despite their differences, these critics have generally taken a materialist stance on canon formation, agreeing that canons are formed through the relationship of production (initial publication) and reproduction (in the form of quotation, reviews, critical articles, anthology selections, and the like). What role, then, do anthologies such as *The Penguin Book of Canadian Short Stories* play in this canon-making process? If the cultural capital of a given short story is created in part through the reproduction of this story, then anthologies can be said to influence 20th century Canadian canons through their organizing, evaluative, and recovery functions. As Alan Golding explains, certain "texts are considered worth keeping in print in a readily available form, while others survive only in the darker corners of university libraries. One way this selection works, one fundamental means by which the selective canon is formed and transformed, is through the [...] anthology" (3). But even the resurgence of those texts living "in the darker corners of university libraries" is possible through their inclusion in a new anthology, which is the case for several of Urquhart's selections. When asked in an interview about how her background reading for the anthology led her to "writers who have fallen out of collective memory," Urquhart reveals that she wanted to

> revisit Hugh Garner, for example, a man who wrote about the underclass before the term was invented. [...] Even more interesting was the discovery of a writer like Sam Selvon who [...] became the break through [*sic*] Caribbean writer in England, opening the way for all that would grow in

that rich field. It is fascinating to think that while he has been almost forgotten by us, he is still celebrated, years after his death, in Britain and the Caribbean. (Urquhart, 2008: 36-37)

Other examples of the resurgence of forgotten texts in the anthology include Adrienne Poy's [Clarkson's] "Ring Around October," originally published in *Macleans* magazine (1961) and Virgil Burnett's text "Constance" (1983). I use the term "resurgence" because these texts – if not also their authors – are irregularly, if ever anthologized and thus are not part of what Urquhart's interviewer correctly terms "collective memory." Indeed, it is precisely Urquhart's inclusion of these stories in the Penguin anthology – their reproduction – that opens the possibility for them to return to the Canadian imagination.

The evaluative and recovery function of anthologies – so nicely demonstrated by Urquhart's selection and narration of the recovery process – are, however, directly at odds with the way in which Urquhart herself characterizes aesthetic value in the anthology's introduction when she evokes the familiar claim that the best stories are determined by the test of time:

> I was able to make my own selections with an almost clear conscience because I knew that, as a poet friend of mine once so brilliantly and accurately said, 'Time is the great anthologist.' This is not an abdication of responsibility, this is the simple truth. Posterity has always been an unpredictable reader. No one knows which stories or novels will remain alive, or where one or two hundred years from now the pulse will continue to beat. (Urquhart, "Introduction" x)

This is hardly "the simple truth," as is indicated by the explanation of her selection process that Urquhart offers to her interviewer. If time were "the great anthologist" or the authoritative arbiter of the aesthetic, then by this logic there would be no need to "discover" or recover stories by writers such as Selvon and Burnett. If these stories are valuable, the logic suggests, "time" will have assured they remain in print and one would need only to look at any contemporary anthology to see what has maintained its value over the years. Of course, this isn't the case, since time itself is never a neutral factor that can be dissociated from historical context, nor can the term "art" be removed from its historical and cultural specificity. Although a text deemed valuable by a culture at a given moment in history may continue to have value many years later (*Paradise Lost* comes to mind), it will necessarily do so for *different* reasons, since the values of a culture shift throughout history. Furthermore, to suggest that time does the work of anthologizing is to abdicate or at least deflect responsibility for editorial choices as though they were self-evident. According to Jane Tompkins, such editors' beliefs about the nature of literary value – i.e. that it is 'inherent in the works themselves,' timeless and universal – prevent them from recognizing their own role in determining which are the truly great works. In describing their own activity, therefore, they speak as if they themselves had played virtually no part in deciding which authors deserved to be included, but were simply codifying choices about which there could be 'no question' (Tompkins 188-189).

What renders Urquhart's introduction unusual is that despite her appeal to the transcendence of literary value, she also shows herself to be aware of the material constraints of anthology production, as well as conscious of her own role as an arbiter of the aesthetic; thus, two axiological positions co-exist in the introduction, signalling a fundamental contradiction.

From a materialist position, the selection process itself is a complicated one involving other contingencies such as space – a factor fundamentally linked to the economics of publishing. For example, Laura Moss describes some of the dilemmas with which she and co-editor Cynthia Sugars were faced when assembling their anthology of Canadian literature, published around the same time as Urquhart's anthology:

> Lynn Coady's story "Play the Monster Blind" has roughly 11,200 words. To my mind, it is one of the best short stories recently published. However, in the anthology of Canadian literature I am currently co-editing with Cynthia Sugars, we seriously have to ask if we have 28 pages for this short story. Is it worth 2.3% of our total allotted pages? Does the story compose 1/43 of the Canadian canon we want to represent? Coady's "Big Dog Rage" is only 12 pages. Does that make it a better story for the anthology? If Coady is in, who is out? Bliss Carman or Sky Lee? Or both? Or neither? What is the provenance of the most highly canonized works? How organic is Canadian literature, really? Looking at the pragmatics of creating a Canadian literature anthology leads me to consider the practical limitations of canon formation. (Moss 7)

These practical limitations that Moss describes are ones linked to the economics of producing an anthology: for instance, an editor may wish to include a story in an anthology but ultimately find that the permissions costs are beyond what the press has allotted. Similarly, a story may find its way into an anthology not because it is the one the editor finds aesthetically most valuable, but because it is sufficiently short or its rights are sufficiently inexpensive. As Moss attests, the "possibilities of canonical expansion are at least in part governed by the sheer volume of work published, publishers' restrictions on page lengths, permissions drawbacks, and a lack of time for any one critic" (Moss 8). In her introduction, Urquhart acknowledges this practical limitation, albeit in a manner that turns a material problem into a whimsical analogy: "There is never enough space, I have learned, for all that we want in life, so stories left out of an anthology serve as a wonderful metaphor for unfulfilled desire" (Urquhart, "Introduction" x). At nearly 700 pages, *The Penguin Book of Canadian Short Stories* is already almost 50% longer than what is probably its nearest market-rival, the 460-page *Oxford Book of Canadian Short Stories* (1997), edited by Margaret Atwood and Robert Weaver. In a later interview, Urquhart refers to the length of the anthology as a constraint in more practical terms, admitting that Penguin did suggest "how long the book should be," a limitation that proved to be somewhat flexible, since she "increased the size by two hundred pages" (Urquhart, 2008: 35) – probably able to do so since as a major commercial press, Penguin is in a position to compromise on page-limit. Still, as interviewer Kim Jernigan (editor of *The New Quarterly*) suggests, "[g]iven the cost, [Urquhart] did well to persuade the editors at Penguin to allow [her] those additional pages" (Urquhart, 2008: 36). In addition to space, Urquhart reveals a further constraint on her selection: "because Lisa Moore was working on her own *Penguin Book of Contemporary Canadian Women's Short Stories* at approximately the same time, we conferred with each other in order to ensure we did not duplicate (stories, not authors)" (Urquhart, 2008: 35). By situating the anthology in the context of its production, Urquhart offers a better sense of the contingencies that affected what works came to be valued via their inclusion in this trade anthology.

None of these contingencies is acknowledged by the anthology's most caustic critic, John Metcalf, who ironically holds a position on aesthetic value similar to that of Urquhart: that aesthetic value is innate, timeless, objective, and self-evident. His article, "Thinking about Penguins," launches an attack on Urquhart that is based on three problematic assumptions: first, that aesthetic value is inherent and literary value is stable; second that the popular and the literary are mutually exclusive terms; and, third, that memoir and short fiction are mutual exclusive genres. Metcalf protests what he sees as Urquhart's failure to recognize the "best" writers of short stories in Canada; the anthology, he objects, "flatly does not represent the best in Canadian short fiction" (Metcalf 5), as though the best of Canadian short fiction existed *a priori*, or outside of critical judgement of anthologists such as Urquhart.[3] According to Metcalf, "*any* aesthetic surely should have

---

[3]   Dan Wells, editor of *Canadian Notes and Queries*, makes the same presumption in "Tweaking the Beak: An Introduction to TNQ/CNQ *Salon des Refusés*" when he asks the rhetorical question: "Is it not the job of an anthologist and editor, in some

included – at a minimum – Mike Barnes, Clarke Blaise, Mary Borsky, Libby Creelman, Cynthia Flood, Keath Fraser, Douglas Glover, Terry Griggs, Steven Heighton, Hugh Hood, Mark Jarman, Norman Levine, K.D. Miller, Bharati Mukherjee, Patricia Robertson, Robyn Sarah, Diane Schoemperlen, Ray Smith, Russell Smith, and Linda Svendsen" (5, original italics). *Any* aesthetic? In Metcalf's fantasy of transcendence and endurance, these writers – nearly all of whom are white – are so "universal" that their work should be said to represent a feminist aesthetic, queer aesthetic, postcolonial aesthetic – the list is presumably endless. Here Metcalf assumes literary value exists outside of, or independent from social and historical forces and arbiters of the aesthetic such as Jane Urquhart.

His position is surprising considering that Metcalf is himself an editor who must work regularly with the material constraints of the publishing industry. Metcalf, Urquhart, and Jernigan are in their editorial roles fall into a category Pierre Bourdieu calls "agents":

> Given that works of art exist as symbolic objects only if they are known and recognized, that is, socially instituted as works of art and received by spectators capable of knowing and recognizing them as such, the sociology of art and literature has to take as its object not only the material production but also the symbolic value of the work, i.e. the production of value of the work [...] It therefore has to consider as contributing to production not only the direct producers of the work in its materiality (artist, writer, etc.) but also the producers of the meaning and value of the work – critics, publishers, [...] and the whole set of agents whose combined efforts produce consumers capable of knowing and recognizing the work of art as such, in particular teachers. (Bourdieu 37)

Within this "whole set of agents," editors in Canada play an influential role in determining what is held to be of literary value or of cultural significance. As Roy Miki explains,

> editors have exerted a powerful influence in the making and shaping of establishment CanLit, more so in this country with its geographical spread, its small population of readers. [...] In the post-war years especially, the products of their "tastes," not only the literary journals but also the plethora of anthologies, have been instrumental in the canonization of writers and critics, and in governing what comes to be judged of *national* relevance [*sic*] (Miki 35, original italics).

As the editor of a nationally and internationally distributed anthology, Urquhart is in a position of *some* power as far as the canonization of writers goes and Metcalf is correct to point out that "[b]ecause of the

---

measure, to preserve what needs preserving?" – as though "what needs preserving" were self-evident.

history and widespread influence of the Penguin imprint all books bearing the Penguin colophon have undeniable cachet" (Metcalf 5). However, even more powerful are editors of academic anthologies such as the ones Laura Moss and Cynthia Sugars recently edited for Pearson Education (an imprint of Penguin). If, as John Guillory, Leslie Fiedler, Barbara Herrnstein Smith, and Carole Gerson have suggested, the 20th century literary canons have been "constructed by, or on behalf of, institutionalized education" (Gerson 91), then anthologies targeted toward university classrooms will have more potential for shifting canonical value than a volume such as the Penguin anthology which lacks any kind of scholarly apparatus (footnotes, extended author biographies or bibliographies, etc).

Rather than seeing the figure of the editor as one of Bourdieu's agents, Metcalf would more likely consider the role as editor to be one of a cultural custodian. When referring, for instance, to Penguin's appointment of Urquhart as editor of the anthology, Metcalf uses the word "entrust," as in "they entrusted the task" (Metcalf 5), three times. This language constructs the role of editor as a guardian, keeper, or custodian of the "best" that has been written, also echoing the Arnoldian role of the critic whose task is to discover in a disinterested manner the "best that is known and thought in the world" (61). I would suggest the editor is better seen as a worker – someone hired by a press to perform the tasks of selection, evaluation, and recovery – and Urquhart certainly confirms this by presenting herself as a labourer in both her introduction and subsequent interview on editing. In her introduction, she emphasizes her work as an editor and a reader, describing how she read the introductions to dozens of short story anthologies over a span of two years (Urquhart, "Introduction" x); commenting on the editing process post-publication, Urquhart once again discusses the "extensive reading" that preceded her selection, referring as well to the informal consultations she had with "both celebrated and newer practitioners of the form," with a "veteran writer of Canadian short fiction," and with "a well-known literary expert" (Urquhart, 2008: 35). The emphasis on the labour of reading and consulting works against the notion of the "best" literature being self-evident, although by the post-publication interview, Urquhart seems also to be invoking this labour as a means of justifying and defending her editorial choices and her authority as editor. That this is the case is further signalled by her repeated reference to the external recognition of both those people she consulted and those writers and stories she selected in order to give them added authority; Urquhart uses words such as "celebrated," (Urquhart, 2008: 35) "veteran," "well-known," "expert," "extensive" (Urquhart, 2008: 36) to describe people, while referring to the literary prizes awarded to Adrian Poy's and Gayla

Reid's stories, respectively. Urquhart's strategic defense of her selection as well as her role as editor is not surprising given Metcalf's aggressive attack on her as Penguin's choice of editor.

What is particularly striking about Metcalf's article – aside from its viciousness – is the way in which it assumes the popular and the literary to be mutually exclusive. It is Urquhart's status as a popular writer to which Metcalf most objects. Ignoring the recognition given to Urquhart's work by the many institutions traditionally understood to be arbiters of the "literary" (universities, prize juries, literary critics), Metcalf paints Urquhart as a Canadian "Maeve Binchy," whose "popular hands" are not worthy of being "entrusted" with the task of selecting representative stories (Metcalf 5). The anthology, he claims, is "edited by a popular entertainer largely innocent of the field." The scorn he expresses toward Urquhart's status as a popular writer comes off as rather ironic given his esteem for the Penguin imprint's "undeniable cachet." Two things are worth noting here: the first is that Urquhart's novels (published mainly by McClelland & Stewart) circulate in the trade paperback mass-market and are produced in what Bourdieu calls the large-scale field of production. The Penguin anthology, similarly, belongs in this same mass-market, large-scale field of production, making the pairing of anthology and editor a logical one from a marketing perspective. According to Bourdieu's theory, as art objects, the position of both Urquhart's literary work and the Penguin anthology occupy within the field of cultural production is one of reduced symbolic capital because of their widespread distribution. The second thing worth noting, then, is the shift in academic theory and criticism that has more recently sought to challenge the notion that best-sellers, or popular texts that circulate widely amongst readers ("chick lit," graphic novels, women's life writing), are necessarily unliterary. Filled with barely-concealed misogynist undertones the derisive language Metcalf uses to dismiss Urquhart's editorial abilities includes such expressions as "she trills," "uplifting drivel," "not an aesthetic idea in her head!" "not a clue," "her fancy," "hankers after" (Metcalf 5), all of which serve to undermine her authority as editor.

While Metcalf suggests that Urquhart is "largely innocent of the field," I want to argue that on the contrary, Urquhart's editorial decisions show her to be well versed in the field of Canadian anthologies and that one anthologist's editorial practices in particular serve as an unacknow-ledged precedent for the editorial decisions evident in *The Penguin Book of Short Stories*. Michael Ondaatje's *The Long Poem Anthology* (1979) and *From Ink Lake: Canadian Stories* (1990) can be linked to the Penguin anthology by the editorial practices evident in them; indeed, a number of Ondaatje's editorial choices resurge in Urquhart's anthology. Urquhart has been criticized for excerpting novels in her anthology (Saikali), yet it was Ondaatje who first took the editorial liberty of excerpting sections from novels – Elizabeth Smart's *At Grand Central Station I Sat Down and Wept*, Joy Kogawa's *Obasan*, and Ethel Wilson's *Swamp Angel*, among others – for *From Ink Lake*. Moreover, rather than organizing his anthology chronologically, Ondaatje arranges the stories to create what he calls a *collage* (Ondaatje, 1990: xvi), expressing a desire to "relax the rules of entry" both in terms of a "wider social context," but also a "larger literary range." Urquhart, too, avoids chronological arrangement, opting instead to group the stories as though "situating [...] works of art in an art museum where pictures are assembled for a purpose within a series of rooms or galleries" (Urquhart, "Introduction" xii). Like Ondaatje, Urquhart's objective is to expand the parameters of the volume, to "open up and make more interesting the definition of the short story" (Urquhart, "Introduction" xi) and in doing so she settles on the memoir as a means of accomplishing this. Acknowledging that the memoir *seems* "on the surface" to "be an engagement with complete disclosure," Urquhart includes an excerpt from what she calls Alice Munro's "semi-fictional family memoir" (Urquhart, "Introduction" xii). Ondaatje also emphasizes works that blur the boundaries between traditional memoir and fiction (he cites *Obasan*), between autobiography and fiction. The blurring of generic boundaries is, of course, a technique Ondaatje practices in his own work, *Running in the Family* (1982), an excerpt of which Urquhart includes in the Penguin anthology. In the introduction to *From Ink Lake*, Ondaatje elaborates on what is now a common strategy of postmodern fiction,[4] the blurring of fact and fiction: "In such works the barrier between fiction and fact has been erased, creating an even more powerful form. And what *is* fact and what *is* imagining in Stegner's reconstruction of the surveying of the US-Canadian border? Where is fiction and where is memoir in Gabrielle Roy's 'The Well of Dunrea,' [...]?" (Ondaatje, 1990: xvi). However, Metcalf, for whom "memoir" and "fiction" are mutually exclusive genres that have never before met, criticizes Urquhart for "her confusion of 'story' and 'memoir,'" maintaining that Munro's story, "set in 1818, if a memoir, would make Alice Munro about two hundred years old," and insists that the excerpts from Ondaatje's *Running in the Family* are autobiography, as though the genre of "autobiography" were entirely straightforward. In fact, the apparent straightforwardness of autobiography is itself a central concern in *Running in the Family*, which repeatedly questions the boundaries

---

4 For more on examples of memoir and autobiography that draw strategic attention to their own status as fiction, see Joanne Saul. *Writing the Roaming Subject: The Biotext in Canadian Literature* (2006).

between truth and fiction, the relationship between memory and self-representation.

The resurgence of Ondaatje's editorial theory is further evident in Urquhart's construction of herself as a "canoeist [...] about to journey beyond the lakes and rivers she knew well and into unfamiliar waters bordered by beautiful and oddly shaped shores" (Urquhart, "Introduction" ix). Urquhart tells us her editorial practices are motivated by "a combination of curiosity and uncertainty." Those familiar with Ondaatje's editorial and creative discourse will immediately recognize the explorer metaphor as well as the guiding principles of curiosity. In his introduction to *The Long Poem Anthology*, Ondaatje chooses, he says, to be "governed by curiosity" (presumably his own) and so the volume becomes his "explor[ation] [of] the poets who surprise [him] with their *step*, their process" (Ondaatje, 1979: 11, original italics), at the same time as it becomes our exploration of *his* process – of "discovery, of learning about something [he's] not sure of, [doesn't] fully understand" (Ondaatje, 1979: 11). Note a further parallel here between this and Urquhart's introduction, which emphasizes both her progress as a reader and her *process* as editor beginning "[t]wo years ago, when [she] agreed to select the stories for the anthology you are now holding in your hands" (Urquhart, "Introduction" ix), and mapping her "paths into the anthology" (Urquhart, "Introduction" xi). To make a claim for the resurgence of Ondaatje's editorial principles in Urquhart's work is not to uncritically justify her practice, but simply to find a historical precedent for several of her decisions and to observe that acerbic criticism of the kind we have seen from John Metcalf was never levelled at Ondaatje. It is, moreover, to suggest that any nuanced critique of Urquhart's work as an anthologist ought to extend to Ondaatje's work as well. Only when examined in the historical context of canon-making and editing in Canada can the significance of Jane Urquhart's work on *The Penguin Book of Canadian Short Stories* be understood as one of co-existence and resurgence: co-existing in its introduction are both assumptions of transcendent literary value and attention to the material constraints of assembling an anthology; resurging in its introduction are the practices of an influential Canadian editor, Michael Ondaatje.

References

ARNOLD, M. (1936), "The Function of Criticism at the Present Time," *Representative Essays of Matthew Arnold*, Ed. E.K. BROWN, Toronto, MacMillan, 32-63.

ATWOOD, M. and WEAVER, R. Eds. (1997), *Oxford Book of Canadian Short Stories in English*, Toronto, Oxford University Press.

BOURDIEU, P. (1993), *The Field of Cultural Production: Essays on Art and Literature*, Ed. R. JOHNSON, New York, Columbia University Press.

DAVEY, F. (1994), *Canadian Literary Power*, Edmonton, NeWest Press.

GERSON, C. (1988), "'The Most Canadian of all Canadian Poets': Pauline Johnson and the Construction of a National Literature," *Canadian Literature* 158: 90-107.

GOLDING, A. (1995), *From Outlaw to Classic: Canons in American Poetry*, Madison, University of Wisconsin Press.

HERRNSTEIN SMITH, B. (1988), *Contingencies of Value: Alternative Perspectives for Critical Theory*, Cambridge, Harvard University Press.

LECKER, R. (1995) *Making it Real: The Canonization of English-Canadian Literature*, Toronto, Anansi.

METCALF, J. (summer/fall 2008), "Thinking About Penguins," *Canadian Notes and Queries* 74: 5-7.

MIKI, R. (1998), *Broken Entries: Race, Subjectivity, Writing*, Toronto, Mercury Press.

MOSS, L. (Winter 2006), "Playing the Monster Blind? The Practical Limitations of Updating the Canadian Canon," *Canadian Literature* 191: 7-11.

ONDAATJE, M. [1990] (1992), "Introduction," *From Ink Lake: Canadian Stories*, Toronto, Knopf, xiii-xviii.

ONDAATJE, M. (1979), "What is in the Pot," Introduction to *The Long Poem Anthology*, Toronto, Coach House Press, 11-18.

SAIKALI, A. "Tossed and Turned: A Literary Tempest" www.themillionsblog.com/2008/09/tossed-and-turned-literary-tempest.html (Accessed 15 December 2008).

SAUL, J. (2006), *Writing the Roaming Subject: The Biotext in Canadian Literature*, Toronto, University of Toronto Press.

TOMPKINS, J. (1985), *Sensational Designs: The Cultural Work of American Fiction 1790-1860*, New York, Oxford University Press.

URQUHART, J. (2007), "Introduction," *The Penguin Book of Canadian Short Stories*, Ed. J. URQUHART, Toronto, Penguin, ix-xv.

– (2005), "A Conversation with Jane Urquhart," *Jane Urquhart: Essays on Her Works*, Ed. L. FERRI, Toronto, Guernica, 15-41.

– (2008), "Imagination & Memory: An Interview," Kim Jernigan, *The New Quarterly* 107: 34-38.

WELLS, D. (2008), "Tweaking the Beak: An Introduction to the CNQ/TNQ Salon des Refusés," *Canadian Notes and Queries* 74: 3-4.

PART III

INTIMATE, SPECULAR, AND PERSISTENT CONFIGURATIONS

10

Intimate and Conditional

Artistic Gesture in Jane Urquhart's *False Shuffles,* *The Underpainter* and *A Map of Glass*

Neta GORDON

Brock University

David Williams's 1991 monograph, *Confessional Fictions: A Portrait of the Artist in the Canadian Novel*, remains the only sustained contemporary analysis of the artist figure in Canadian literature. It primarily takes up the genre of the *Künstlerroman* as it has manifested in fictional autobiographies, in modernist fictional portraits of the artist, and in postmodern metafictions that interrogate the crisis of the artist. In his analysis of Gabrielle Roy's *The Road Past Altamont*, he discusses how this novel's aesthetic approach mirrors the exploration of how the artist comes to terms with her familial history as "it chronicles the quest for the lost time of the generations [...] [presenting] this very tension between a linear view of time and some timeless realm where 'the dead still breathe around the living'" (176). Williams argues that in its capacity as an imagist novel which seeks to interrogate acute instances of transformation in perception, especially the perceptions of the artist, *The Road to Altamont* figures the tension between the time-bound and the timeless in spatial terms as a series of juxtapositions (of images in a photo album, of the four interconnected stories that make up the novel, of narrative lines conceived of as a material tapestry). The reader is charged with "catching up" on these juxtapositions (Williams 189). The model of "catching up," here, might be thought of as both the sudden gathering together of separate bits (of image, of time, of narrative), as well as the process of getting closer to that which has been ahead; of simultaneously drawing in and drawing forward so that the textualized artist's work, alongside the extratextual reader's, develops via a process of ever-vacillating take and give. "Catching up," further, coheres not only with the general principle of resurgence as that which has been buried becomes reconstituted – often by degrees, in fragments, with difference – but also with current theoretical considerations of the function of art as it represents history. In his introduction to the collection of critical essays, *Art and the Performance of Memory*, Richard Cándida Smith points out that one point of inquiry shared by the contributors to the collection is an exploration of how "each expressive form provides a site for memory that draws upon dispersed traces of the past that remain read only to the degree that their contents are incorporated into a repertory available to suggest options for future action" ("Introduction" 11). In other words, as the artist gives form or gesture to an historical incident and/or record, recovered via representation, he or she also invites "the dead [to] breathe around the living," to create a new sense of living progression from the "catching up" of that which has come before.

In this paper, I examine the ways the model of "catching up" manifests in Jane Urquhart's representations of the archival artist: the artist concerning himself or herself with recovering "dispersed traces of the past" and with giving spatial form to vacillations and resurgences of memory in time. I will examine the poetry collection *False Shuffles*, and the novels *The Underpainter* and *A Map of Glass*, focusing especially on how they variously depict the artist's juxtaposition of fragments to create a new, provisionally whole form, as well as how the art object, and the reception of that art object, is conceived of as a product of strategic layering. The literary "portraits" described throughout *False Shuffles* are, of course, not quite the same as the visual art objects described in *The Underpainter* and *A Map of Glass*, though in this book of poetry Urquhart begins to explore the idea of "catching up" as a sense of the past in time and space. I will argue that such representations reflect Urquhart's interest, not so much in the changes of perception that occupy Roy or the inherent untrustworthiness of representation that occupies the postmodern author, but rather in the process by which selves and others, selves and the world, are brought into open-ended, conditional dialogue through art. Further, I will suggest that Jane Urquhart's concern with the way artists become the purveyors of the past, offering aesthetic frameworks for history's resurgence, is ultimately a concern for the way the past operates as a collection of intimate moments, and that even the aesthetic gestures that are put into a public, dialogic space always retain an equally vital capacity to signify as privately meaningful. My analysis will draw upon theories of aesthetic activity articulated by Mikhail Bakhtin, which, as Deborah Haynes argues in *Bakhtin and the Visual Arts*, were sub-categories of his thinking on architectonics, "an activity that describes how relationships between self and other, self and object, self and world are structured" (Haynes 5). Urquhart's artists explore and wrestle with the way the work of art is ultimately, yet always provisionally, a spatially organized gesture towards the intersections and/or problematic collisions of lived (and yet to be lived) lives. I will also consider how the work of Jane Urquhart's husband, the artist Tony Urquhart, with whom she collaborated to produce *False Shuffles* and whose work as an artist is "caught up" in the representations of the artist figure in *The Underpainter* and *A Map of Glass*, operates as a model of the processes of creative incorporation, expression, and dialogue.

In *Problems of Dostoevsky's Poetics*, Bakhtin explains that the heroes in Dostoevsky's novels are distinctive in that their specificity of consciousness is never articulated by the author as a kind of objectivity or "finite substance" (Bakhtin 51). He writes, "The hero interests Dostoevsky not as some manifestation of reality that possesses fixed and specific socially typical or individually characteristic traits [...] What is important to Dostoevsky is not how his hero appears in the world but first and foremost how the world appears to his hero, and how the hero appears to himself" (Bakhtin 47). Bakhtin's labelling of the hero's "*all-devouring self consciousness*" (49, original emphasis), crucially hinges on the idea that although the hero's perspective is specific and involved in continuous evaluation of surroundings and events as they inhere in his self-consciousness, the hero "also knows that all these definitions, prejudiced as well as objective, rest in his hands and he cannot finalize them precisely because he perceives them; he can go beyond their limits and thus make them inadequate" (Bakhtin 53); in other words, as Bakhtin argues in relation to the hero of "Notes from the Underground," it is the hero's dedication to his own perceptions and their meaning that makes him realize their fallibility as mere perceptions. The very procedure of perceiving oneself as specifically in and of the world simultaneously reflects the instability and shortcomings of self-conscious perceptions; each shift in the self, in other selves, in the world, entails both a new moment of self-conscious specificity as well as a collapse of prior objectivities. This collapse, however, is not to be confronted with despair, but rather with laughter, as Bakhtin argues that the moment of catharsis for Dostoevsky's heroes is distinct from the Aristotelian notion of tragically conclusive purification. Rather, the fully self-conscious hero (and reader) finally perceives that

> *nothing conclusive has yet taken place in the world, the ultimate word of the world and about the world has not yet been spoken, the world is open and free, everything is still in the future and will always be in the future.* (166, original emphasis)

In her own study, Haynes points out that Bakhtin's reflections on the unfinalizability inherent to certain literary characters, as well as conceptions of readerly interactions with particular genres, also emerge in his early discussions of aesthetics in which he argued that "the aesthetic object is not a thing. It is a 'shaped content' that one enters as a participant and constituent" (Bakhtin "Content" 317 in Haynes 10). While other arts forms differ from literature, they are still subject to the principle of unfinalizability: "What we apprehend are constructions, and inevitably conflicts arise over these constructions [...] Ultimately, the unrepeatability and openendedness of the creative act makes transform-ation possible" (Haynes 19). Here, Haynes' analysis of Bakhtinian aesthetic theory reflects the idea that the creative act is resurgent, continually re-transforming by means of the dialogue among creator, art, observer; self, world, other. Jane Urquhart takes up the exploration of "the openendedness of the creative act" in order to determine the way that unfinalizability relates to tangible, though paradoxically private, manifestations of what Smith refers to as "options for future action" ("Introduction" 11).

The Bakhtinian notion of unfinalizability coheres productively with the aesthetic framework of Tony Urquhart's work, especially as it is articulated by art historian and critic Joan M. Vastokas, who introduces Bakhtinian concepts such as "performativity," "dialogue" and "intertextuality" into her analysis of his work (*Dialogues* 6, 10). Vastokas writes:

> Urquhart's works [...] are neither 'representations' [...] nor are they intended as non-verbal messages. Instead, they are more aptly described as material 'presences', as unique creations, as little worlds unto themselves. Yet, at the same time, they are not self-referential. They exist and act in relation to the wider dynamics of actual space and time, to the particular spatial, temporal, structural, and human contexts in which they are situated and in which they may be moved about. And this context includes the spectator, of whom Urquhart is constantly aware as a participant in the ongoing life of his work. (*Dialogues* 10)

Jane Urquhart's representations of artistic activity owe much to this theoretical framework which highlights, on the one hand, the site-specific particularity of "little worlds," and, on the other hand, the ongoing interaction between creative gesture and spectator. She conceives, for example, the figures "gazing out to me/like renaissance portraits [...] loose bits of paper carried by the wind/caught for a moment/on the fence around this time" ("Tales" 2-3, 24-26);[1] the *Erasure* paintings series created by Austin Fraser in *The Underpainter*, in which the little worlds vividly fashioned operate as camouflaged

---

[1] Titles of poems provided in the text are taken from *False Shuffles*. These are followed by line references.

presences meant to haunt the spectator; the art projects of Jerome McNaughton in *A Map of Glass*, which seek to "mark the moment of metamorphosis" (*Map* 11). Much as Jane Urquhart's literary representations of creative processes place emphasis on the site-specificity of "this time," as well as the way the art object is always subject to change, her ekphrastic delineations of these objects pick up on various thematic recurrences in Tony Urquhart's work. Vastokas, in both *Worlds Apart: The Symbolic Landscapes of Tony Urquhart* and *Dialogues of Reconciliation: The Imagination of Tony Urquhart*, draws attention to such motifs as lumps, enclosed landscapes, the house, and thresholds. She argues further that, "Memory [may be] the key motivating factor for Urquhart as a visual artist. Memory, it could be argued, is an ultimate expression of Reconciliation. 'Not to forget', means to tie the enduring past together with the fleeting present and to gain eternity" (*Dialogues* 19). In *Tony Urquhart, The Revenants: Long Shadows*, Joyce Zemans also notes the artist's persistent concern with "the tensions between surface and illusion, painting and narrative, remembering and imagining, and by the notion of disclosure over time" (Zemans 7). I would suggest, however, that while Vastokas reads Tony Urquhart's persistent concern with the theme of memory in relation to the transcendental signifier called "eternity," in their function as a context for Jane Urquhart's representations of transformative and transforming art, Tony Urquhart's return to particular motifs and thematics does not culminate in the stasis of transcendence. Rather, the tension that binds surface to illusion, past to future-present and self to world in Jane Urquhart's portraits of artists and artistic gestures is only provisionally resolved in intimate moments of reckoning, whereby human beings acknowledge their complex attachments to a changing world.

The four drawings by Tony Urquhart used as section headers for *False Shuffles* are a series, each representing one of the four playing card suits. The series ties in with the motif of card playing that runs through Jane Urquhart's poetry collection, ranging from its title and epigraphs that quote a guide to performing card tricks to the images of illusion that permeate the poems. Each drawing represents something like a playing card, but the images are imbued with several motifs such as those noted by critics of Tony Urquhart's œuvre. The drawing representing the "Ace of spades" (*False Shuffles* 13), for example, juxtaposes the clean line at the top of the "card" with a fraying, almost chewed upon, left edge and a bottom edge that is almost entirely unreadable as such due to the deep shadows and shading that give depth to the series of balls strewn in what look to be the hollows of a cave. At the bottom right corner of the "card" is an oddly comical lump, which signifies differently from similar such images in Tony Urquhart's work that have been read as threatening. Like other lumps, this one "has an organic quality and seems capable of growth" (Vastokas, 1988: 32), though it appears less to be a type of undifferentiated tumour than a swollen nose or foot, a possible reading enhanced by the hairs that poke out of the card/cave/creature's lower left side. The illusion Tony Urquhart presents depends on the tension between the perfections of abstract symbol such as spades, which is squared off in the middle of the drawing, and the textured, hairy mass of the rest of the card that seems to represent a creature caught in some sort of failed woodland enchantment. The "Ace of spades" drawing is of a set, along with the image of the "Six of diamonds" (*False Shuffles* 35), the "Ace of hearts" (*False Shuffles* 71) and the "Nine of clubs" (*False Shuffles* 89), in that all play with abstract, almost alchemical symbols in collision with images of decay (and/or growth), of vegetation, and of shadows, borders and thresholds.

The first poem series in Jane Urquhart's *False Shuffles* is called "The Undertaker's Bride." It is her husband's biography that is gestured toward in this series, as Tony Urquhart's maternal grandparents with whom he lived until he was 25 years old ran a funeral home in the Niagara Falls area that was attached to their house (Vastokas, 1988: 47). In "The Limit of Suspension," the second poem in the series, the speaker describes the early predilection "grandmother" (*False Shuffles* 2) has for the process of documentation, as she takes the time to record a local event that occurs one night during her childhood: "*the suspension bridge/fell down/and it did make a noise*" (23-25, original emphasis).[2] The italicization of this final remark in the poem signals Jane Urquhart's interest in the problematic insufficiency of documentation as, like the suspension bridge the time, space and framework for memory between the event itself and its formed expression are subject to limits and even collapse. As the speaker notes, what "grandmother" tersely records "On three small scraps of paper" (1) is quite different from what the speaker imagines was her self-conscious perception of the event. This slippage in perception and document is only amplified by the fact that "grandmother" was, of course, nothing like a grandmother at the time of the event, but exists rather as a site-specific conduit via which the speaker can access the process of past documentation:

---

[2]   The event the speaker obliquely refers to is the collapse of The Upper Steel Arch Bridge, which occurred in January 1938, when "a sudden wind storm on Lake Erie… [resulted in] ice pressure pushing against the bridge abutments and the hinge support of the arch," eventually causing the bridge to fall ("Bridges over Niagara Falls.")

looking at the
suspension bridge
lying
broken-backed against the ice
like an injured dragon
grandmother
must have wondered at
each of her magic crossings. (13-20)

Both the simile comparing the collapsed bridge with a dragon and the reference to the "magic crossings" the girl referred to as "grandmother" had previously made over the bridge recall the notion of a world of strange enchantments suggested in "Ace of spades": both texts emphasize the transformational moment in its wonder and horror. The dual nature of the transformational moment, in which grandmother "must" retrospectively comprehend her precarious relationship to the mysteries and dangers of the world, is further related to the poem's exploration of how we relate to events that occur in the past, how the passage to such events requires a charm of enchantment and always remains potentially menacing, vulnerable to destruction, and disappointingly limited in terms of what can actually be expressed. The grandmother, apparently, does not write all that she, in her self-consciousness, "wonders," but rather what reverberates in her world – *"it did make a noise"* – though even this unequivocal assertion is documented on "scraps of paper," the archival record seemingly as disposable as immediate perception.

"The Undertaker's Bride" series often calls attention to the process of documentation, especially after "grandmother" takes up the task of logging how many victims of drowning come under the purview of her husband's profession ("Undertaker's" 11-13). In the final poem, "Summer Dresses," the speaker culminates the interrogation of what story the document is actually capable of expressing, what the relationship is between the "memory all around her/like the river of that vein/in one thin hand/against a powdered cheek" (9-12) and an itemized register of either dresses in her wardrobe or drowning victims and "their tiny possessions" ("Undertaker's" 23-24). Despite "grandmother's" persistence in creating a "document [that] survives for years" ("Summer" 22), she is imagined by the speaker as one awash in memory, herself one of the "floaters" ("Undertaker's" 16) she has tried to account for. Further, the "surviving document" the speaker refers to is itself a type of fiction, as it is accessible solely as a highly mediated trace; this makes the question of what function the archive serves in our "catching up" with the past even more complicated.[3] A major theme of the series seems to be the importance of recognizing the unheralded, undocumented life behind the hand that kept a record of the dead, of giving shape to a particular woman's (imagined) hopes, desires, frustrations, and fears. The speaker notes that the "intricate/account of/death by water" only "looks as if/somebody/had to write it" ("Undertaker's" 11-13, 28-30), implying that the value we grant the document is not inherent, but rather a convention of perceived necessity. Tautologically, only once a document is written does what is documented signify as worthy of documentation. In the final poem series in *False Shuffles*, entitled "Tales I'm not Likely to Tell," Jane Urquhart returns to the fraught question of what responsibility we have to the past, as "fragments" of lives ("Tales" 16) turn into throwaway fodder for the reconstituting artist. The reference in "Tales I'm not Likely to Tell" to "loose bits of paper carried by the wind" (26) alludes back to the document written on "scraps of paper" ("Limit" 1), as this series of poems considers more closely the problem of defining document. It is often unclear to the speaker what can be remembered about the individuals figured in the series of "portraits," what has been imagined, what is lost, or what constitutes the archive of the past. For example, poem "V: I carry Vic's trunk" focuses on the speaker's guardianship of "Vic's trunk" (1) acknowledging in the second stanza, however, that "he is dead/his trunk is missing/we never met" (4-6). The poem goes on to delineate more clearly the entirely conceptual nature of the speaker's relationship to the trunk, describing in the meanwhile the speaker's efforts to clear away all signs of the past from a house. Later, in the final poem of the series, "XVI: My mother dismantles," the speaker describes how when her mother was nine years old, she took apart a lead tombstone and then put it back together, badly, so that "it tilts to the left /and panels of lead/groan in the wind" (11-13). The speaker describes this ill-assembled tombstone, another kind of trunk, as "one of the marks/she has left/on the landscape," before ending the poem with a *reprise* of the final line of "The Undertaker's Bride" series: "the document survives for years" ("XVI" 18). Like the lump in Tony Urquhart's "Ace of spades," the various documents described in "Tales I'm not Likely to Tell" – the faded memories, the trunks, the hoarded objects, the tombs – come to have enchanted half-lives of their own,

---

[3]   In an interview with Herb Wyile, conducted in 2002, Jane Urquhart notes that before writing *The Whirlpool*, she had discovered "a little book that [Tony's] grandmother kept, a book in which various bodies that were taken out of the Niagara River were described" (Wyile 80). *The Whirlpool*, which features a character named Maud who is an Undertaker's wife, was published in 1989, seven years after *False Shuffles*.

inspiring the speaker to "catch up" with the dead without ever really knowing them, or fully "telling" them.

Jane Urquhart's exploration of the problem of documentation, especially as that process is related to the creation of an aesthetic object or gesture that emerges out of the repertory of archival material, resumes in *The Underpainter*, her 1997 novel about how American painter Austin Fraser paints the lives of various individuals he meets on the Northern Shores of Lake Ontario. In her essay, "As Cold as Ice: *The Underpainter*," Mary Condé argues that "[t]he title of Urquhart's novel [...] [refers] to the energy which [Austin] paradoxically expends in expunging life from his existence, both in his life and in his art, so that it is only what lies beneath, beneath the ice, beneath his cold routines, beneath the layers of paint, which has any passion" (Condé 59). The meaning of Austin's practice of painstakingly painting over vividly rendered scenes with layer upon layer of pigment, however, becomes more complex when considered in light of the way Tony Urquhart's aesthetic paradigms operate as a context for Jane Urquhart's rendering of the artist. As Zemans writes, through his experiments with layering paintings into other paintings, with various types of *collage*, and with attempts to suggest the "interrupt[ion of] a painting's frame," Tony Urquhart's work has consistently been "engaged by illusion, [whereby] he is intent on problematizing the experience of painting and, in doing so, involves his viewers in the play" (Zemans 11). It is true that Austin's ostensible reason for adding layers of patina is his concern with *pentimenti* – the variations he makes to his paintings that can reveal themselves over time due to the chemical properties of the paints he uses and the potential of certain colours, and certain images, to gradually assert themselves. But this concern is represented by Jane Urquhart as both an irrational fear and an agonized yearning. Austin recalls his childhood terror regarding a painting of two dogs that hung in his house:

> I [...] was quite afraid of it, being able to discern a third dog – a dark ghost – emerging from the hill. I knew the dog wasn't meant to be there, that he was a mistake, and that I shouldn't be able to see him at all. I knew that the woman who had painted this ominous beast had been dead for a long, long time, and it seemed to me that her dead hand was attempting to change the painting before my very eyes. (*Underpainter* 182)

The "dark ghost" Austin frets over, like "the revenant" Zemans foregrounds in her analysis of Tony Urquhart's work, is an element which makes the artistic gesture unfinalizable, inviting the viewer to become both "a participant and constituent" in the aesthetic moment (Haynes 10). While Austin asserts his resistance to this dialogic association, his terrible dread of its power ironically reveals the novel's thematization of the complicated relationship between past and present, and of the ways things that are buried will, for better or worse, tend toward resurgence.

Austin himself recognizes that his attempts to control the viewer's access to the "dark ghosts" haunting his paintings reflect personal pain. He declares surprise that anyone would want to own such work: "Didn't they know they were carrying home a rectangle of sorrow? Couldn't they understand that grief itself would now be proudly displayed, hanging on their otherwise smooth living-room walls?" (*Underpainter* 184). Further on in the narrative, Austin admits that the layers of pigment operate "to protect only one being in the world. Me" (*Underpainter* 252). What is interesting to consider is which aesthetic act constitutes the gesture of "sorrow" or "grief": is it the creation of the underpaintings or the process of layering paint? While Condé suggests that "it is only what lies beneath [...] which has any passion," I would argue that Austin's aesthetic practice of "moving towards white" (*Underpainter* 252) is its own kind of invitation to the viewer to engage in a potentially painful dialogic relationship; the viewer, like "grandmother" of "The Undertaker's Bride," is invited to commune with whatever might "rise to the surface of [the] pictures like drowned corpses, bloated and obscene" (*Underpainter* 181).

I have argued previously that *The Underpainter* operates in part as a challenge to the postmodern approach to historical fiction that seeks to privilege the work of the reconstituting artist over that of the witness: "the memory of [Augusta], the witness, is thus made to struggle for attention against a narrative focus on the work of the commemorator to the point where the witness herself is almost entirely 'erased' under the layers of the artist's memory and output" (Gordon 64). My argument in "The Artist and the Witness," however, is similar to Condé's in that it neglects the issue of the *pentimenti* and what it means, notably that what has been buried within the document has the potential for a resurgence that will freshly incorporate the viewer of the aesthetic object into a dialogic experience. In this way, the artist becomes a type of ghostly mediator among past, present and future. While I still think it is the case that Jane Urquhart's representation of Austin as the self-obsessed, meddling artist reflects her critique of "postmodern pastiche [that] both signals authorial hesitancy and invites readerly scepticism regarding the stability of the historical record" (Gordon 61), it is also true that her ekphrastic descriptions of Austin's paintings, in particular the *Erasure* series which appears linked both to the aesthetic practice of Tony Urquhart and the work of contemporary archival artists, convey the power of art to "constitute a circuit through which enactive memory constantly circulates" (Smith, "Introduction" 4). In the final paragraphs of the novel, Austin offers a plan of his final painting, listing the various archived images from his memory that will be included in the work and noting that "[it] will be full of beautiful dark shorelines, this painting, full of all the possibilities that we believe exist in alternative landscapes, alternative homelands" (*Underpainter* 340). The description of "beautiful dark shorelines" recalls similar moves in Tony Urquhart's work to challenge traditional conceptions of frames, as well as Jane Urquhart's own concern with threshold spaces of memory that exist in partial shadow. Further, while *False Shuffles* primarily thematizes the exigencies and enchantments influencing the indistinctive keeper of the document, the closing references in *The Underpainter* to "alternative landscapes, alternative homelands" reflect Jane Urquhart's interest in thinking through art's "enactive" potential in responding to memory and the way, as Smith puts it, art offers "into circulation a proposition for a potentially new way of inhabiting the past" ("Introduction" 11). For Jane Urquhart's ideal spectator (or reader), the experience of "inhabiting the past" via the aesthetic experience is an exercise of "catching up," whereby what has come before is also always emergent, suggesting new ways of thinking the present or future world.

The aesthetic concept of layering suggested by the image of Austin creating his *Erasure* series is further explored in *A Map of Glass* (2005). Throughout the novel, which includes several portraits of artists and their methods, this concept of layering is most often connected with the issue of how the aesthetic gesture connects to the passage of time. Jerome's art project involves documenting the various strata of changes to a particular location with the passing of seasons, and the framework for it is Jerome's "solid knowledge of the mutability of a world that came into being and then dissolved around him before he was able to grasp what it was trying to be" (*Map* 16). Jerome's self-described role of "chronicler" (*Map* 11) of the world's mutability is made more interesting by the fact that he is unsure what phase of change is most significant, the coming-into-being or the dissolving: he explains to Sylvia that, although his favourite childhood activity was building forts, his current art projects emerge from his interest in the "idea of built things going back to nature [...] at least the beginnings of nature [...] germination" (*Map* 106-107). It is the issue of "germination" that is most intriguing for Jerome, as he tries to discover and chronicle the point at which built things stop decaying and begin reforming, growing. The artistic efforts of Branwell Woodman, great-grandfather of Andrew Woodman whose death brings together Jerome, who finds his body, and Sylvia, Andrew's lover, counteract Jerome's, as Branwell's murals painted on walls and ceilings are not meant to chronicle but to evoke "fantasy landscapes" (*Map* 285). His murals, though, are equally implicated in the passage of time which, as the narrator notes, "will always apply its patina to human effort, [as] paintings completed on walls are destined to be altered, damaged, or erased" (*Map* 291). In an almost perverse doubling of the description of the sorts of geographical layers Jerome wishes to document, the narrator describes how,

> [w]ith each change of ownership – and sometimes even without a change in ownership – a new layer of patterned wallpaper would be slapped over both the mural of Niagara Falls in the upper room and the mountain scene across the hall [...] in the end, a tenant suffering from the effects of a particularly cold winter would punch a stovepipe hole above the fireplace in the upper west room, little knowing, as he did so, that he had completely destroyed Branwell Woodman's carefully rendered moon. (*Map* 293)

What is interesting about these two descriptions of artistic gestures and their relationship to time, one self-conscious and one almost fatalistic, is that both hinge on the idea that transformative decay of human constructions is both inevitable and natural, whether the term "natural" refers to the changes of seasons or the seemingly innate desire for humans to continually reinvent their own built environments, for pleasure and/or comfort. In a text that includes stark rebukes of the ways human endeavours, particularly human capitalist endeavours of the sort engaging both Branwell's father, Joseph Woodman, and his son, Maurice, can all but destroy the natural physical properties of a place, it is a striking notion that the human desire for (sometimes destructive) renewal is also inevitable, instinctive, and often authentic.

Jane Urquhart's interest in *A Map of Glass* in the instability of the artistic gesture *as* document and/or *to* document, and the association between that instability and human desire is further developed by intermittent descriptions in the novel of both mirrors and glass. Jerome's aesthetic is informed by Robert Smithson's 1969 sculpture *Map of Broken Glass*, and the narrative explains that "Smithson had been mostly concerned with mirrors at the time and yet had chosen glass rather than mirrors, as if he had decided to exclude rather than to reflect the natural world" (18). This initial, perhaps simplistic distinction the narrative presents between the act of excluding of the world and reflecting it becomes further complicated by Jerome's fascination with "the brilliance and the feeling of danger in the piece: the shattering of experience and the sense that one cannot play with life without being cut, injured" (*Map* 18). Jane Urquhart thus provides an abrupt and paradoxical juxtaposition here between the concepts of remaining safely apart and risking being hurt by experience, which operates as a thematic anchor for the novel's exploration of how both Jerome and Sylvia interact with others. As a child, likely suffering from some form of autism, Sylvia becomes distressed during a visit to a country auction when "she [...] [passes] by a row of mirrors [...] [because] the mirrors

170

had shown her that there was no controlling what might enter the frame of experience, that the whole world might bully its way into a quiet interior" (*Map* 91). And, later in the novel, describing to Jerome her anguish at witnessing Andrew's succumbing to the effect of Alzheimer's disease, Sylvia returns to the image of the mirror:

> There was nothing beautiful about the traces of human endeavour, despite what Andrew believed, all was unravelling as quickly as it was knit. Her own strained face when she examined it in the mirror was a collection of dead cells. The love they had made was barren, had resulted in no quickening, no quickening at all except this newborn capacity of her to see things the way they really were, that and the ability to feel pain. (*Map* 135-36)

Like Sylvia, Jerome often feels "bullied" by events of the world that become part of his experience, in particular by his memories of an alcoholic, abusive father. The novel's references to glass and mirrors in this thematic context show Jane Urquhart's comparisons between the process of layering inherent to the aesthetic process, which is always subject to the vacillations of destruction and renewal, and the necessary but painful layering of interactions that occur when one embarks on a course of being fully human. Sylvia admits to being "grateful" to Andrew for her pain (136), and (Saint) Jerome can only fully emerge from his own wilderness when he shares with his lover, Mira, how he has been injured by experience. What is crucial to both depictions of layering, aesthetic and emotional, is that the changes in time that affect the artistic and/or the human gesture occur as a result of transformations in the participant of that gesture.

Close to the end of *A Map of Glass*, Jerome feverishly tries to convince Sylvia to remain in Toronto and leave her protective, paternalistic husband, Malcolm, who insists that Sylvia must be sheltered from the excitements of the world because of her disease. Jerome does not believe that Sylvia is ill at all, asking her "'Was there ever a condition?'" Sylvia responds, "'Oh Jerome [...] there is always, always a condition'" (*Map* 359). The term "condition" here is wonderfully and variously suggestive, referring all at once to an existing state, a modifying circumstance, a contingency or provision, and a state of health. Sylvia's assertion that there is "always, always a condition" connects with the fundamental Bakhtinian concept of unfinalizability, whereby the given set of material realities is always subject to transformation, always ready to be "caught up" in new and surprising ways. Significant too is Jane Urquhart's affirmation in this novel that the primary transformative agent to material reality – as artistic gesture, as human experience – is individual perspective. Sylvia recalls that when Malcolm, a physician by profession, would talk to her about the "conditions" of his patients, he would often declare: "'It presents in a very odd way'" (146). It is in this sense that the observer of the artistic gesture necessarily "enters [into it] as a participant and constituent" (Haynes 10). Whereas in *The Underpainter* Jane Urquhart considers how the artistic document may change over time and be observed differently by new observers, in her later novel she contemplates how the observer is also a conditional feature of the artistic gesture: the reason that the document is never stable is because we are not stable. In tackling the question of how the layered and conditional artistic gesture might inform an ethical responsibility to action, Jane Urquhart suggests throughout *A Map of Glass* that it is intimate acts of love, trust and hope that have the potential to break through, to locate within the process of decay the possibility of renewal.

In an interview she conducted with Jane Urquhart in November 2001, Laura Ferri questions the author on how she thinks the attacks of 9/11 will affect the place of the arts in people's lives. Jane Urquhart responds:

> There was an immediate feeling, right afterwards, that all art was irrelevant. [However, t]he role of the artist will be, once things settle down, a reflective role, as it has always been, anyway, because art comes into being as a result of reflection. But there really was a period when the arts kind of disappeared; and it was quite frightening. It was frightening in an existential way to know that a big collective traumatic event like that can destroy not only lives and architecture but also things in which we take pleasure [...] Gradually, however, I think people will begin to think more metaphorically and, at that point, the arts will come back and assume their rightful place in human experience. (Ferri 23-24).

Urquhart's emphasis in this discussion on "reflection" and "metaphor" signals her basis assumption – a not particularly radical one – that art, whether literature or visual art, allows for the expression of "alternative landscapes" (*Underpainter* 340). Her conversation with Ferri, however, seems to suggest that art can only give expression in one direction: backwards; art "comes into being" only after "things settle down." In her literary representations of artists and their works, however, the vision offered is much more multi-directional. The poems and illustrations in *False Shuffles* present a shifting portrayal of the creative act, as work of a particular purveyor in sifting through a set of documents respectively transforms the chronicler into an artist. The careful and overprotective work of an artist such as Austin Fraser to control a particular reflection of events is shown to be continually subject to the mischief of time and new participants. And, in *A Map of Glass*, the focus on the ways in which even the acknowledgement of art by participants is a matter of condition demonstrates the prevailing sense in

Jane Urquhart's work that art can never signify transcendently, but only individually. This decisive concern for the individual's role in making art readable or important is, for Jane Urquhart, a type of championing for the ways in which artistic gestures or readings, no matter how ostensibly public in terms of historical import or critical reception, are intimate acts of love and hope.

References

"Bridges over Niagara," *Niagara Falls: Thunder Alley.* http://www.niagara frontier.com/bridges.html#b11. (Accessed 21 October 2008).

BAKHTIN, M. (1990), "The Problem of Content, Material and Form in Verbal Artistic Creation," in *Art and Answerability: Early Philosophical Essays by M.M. Bakhtin*, Trans. Vadim Liapunov & Kennth Bromstrom, Eds. C. EMERSON & M. HOLQUIST, Austin, U. of Texas P.

– (1984), *Problems of Dostoevsky's Poetics*, Ed. and Trans. C. EMERSON. Minneapolis, U. of Minnesota P.

CONDÉ, M. (2005), "As Cold as Ice: *The Underpainter*," *Jane Urquhart: Essays on her Works*, Ed. L. FERRI, Toronto, Guernica, 2005, 57-64.

GORDON, N. (2003), "The Artist and the Witness: Jane Urquhart's *The Underpainter* and *The Stone Carvers*," *Studies in Canadian Literature* 28.2: 59-73.

HAYNES, D. J., *Bakhtin and the Visual Arts*, Cambridge, Cambridge UP, 1995.

SMITH, R. C., "Introduction: Performing the Archive," *Art and the Performance of Memory: Sounds and Gestures of Recollection*, Ed. R. C. SMITH, London & New York, Routledge, 2002, 1-12.

URQUHART, J. (2005), *A Map of Glass*, Toronto, McClelland & Stewart.

– (1982), *False Shuffles*, Victoria & Toronto, Press Porcépic.

–, "The Limit of Suspension," *False Shuffles*, 16.

–, "The Undertaker's Bride," *False Shuffles*, 20-21.

–, "Summer Dresses," *False Shuffles*, 29.

–, "Tales I'm Not Likely to Tell," *False Shuffles*, 91.

–, "V: I carry Vic's trunk," *False Shuffles*, 96-97.

–, "XVI: My mother dismantles," *False Shuffles*, 113.

–, *The Underpainter*, Toronto, McClelland & Stewart, 1997.

–, "A Conversation with Jane Urquhart," *Jane Urquhart: Essays on her Works*, Ed. L. FERRI, Toronto, Guernica, 15-41.

VASTOKAS, J. M. (1988), *Worlds Apart: The Symbolic Landscapes of Tony Urquhart*. Windsor, ON, Art Gallery of Windsor.

– (1991), *Dialogues of Reconciliation: The Imagination of Tony Urquhart*, Peterborough, ON, Art Gallery of Peterborough.

WILLIAMS, D. (1991), *Confessional Fictions: A Portrait of the Artist in the Canadian Novel*, Toronto, U. of Toronto P.

WYILE, H. (2007), *Speaking in the Past Tense: Canadian Novelists on Writing Historical Fiction*, Waterloo, ON, Wilfrid Laurier UP.

ZEMANS, J. (2002), *Tony Urquhart, The Revenants: Long Shadows*, Waterloo, ON, U. of Waterloo Art Gallery.

11

Maps, Icons, and Other Specular Traces of the Unconscious in Jane Urquhart's *A Map of Glass*

Georgiana M. M. COLVILE

Université de Tours

Literature is not only a mirror; it is also a map, a geography of the mind. Margaret Atwood, *Survival*.

Laura: My glass collection takes up a good deal of time. Glass is something you have to take good care of. Tennessee Williams, *The Glass Menagerie*.

Art works out of the inexplicable. Robert Smithson, *The Collected Writings*.

In her sixth novel, *A Map of Glass*, Jane Urquhart pursues her ongoing quest for the links, dislocations, and tensions between text and subtexts or intertexts, art and life, past and present, history and fiction, verbal and visual creativity, reality and myth, sanity and mental fragility, and also, in Linda Hutcheon's terms, "product and process" (Hutcheon 138-159). In Urquhart's five previous novels, other art forms reflect, enhance, underlie or challenge the medium of fiction. One finds poetry in *The Whirlpool* (1986); painting as well as other palimpsestic variations of the form in point – interpolated fiction and meta-fiction – in *Changing Heaven* (1990); dancing and oral story-telling in *Away* (1991); painting and porcelain-painting in *The Underpainter* (1997), and sculpture in *The Stone Carvers* (2000). Similarly, *A Map of Glass* inscribes map-making, painting, conceptual art, performance art, journal writing, and historical chronicles.

In *A Map of Glass*, three stories of three interconnected protagonists come together in a tight diegetic braid, and the text unfolds in three very long titled chapters, dividing into untitled subchapters. The first story, concerning the historical geographer Andrew Woodman, begins with the five-page prologue and opens as follows: "He is an older man walking in winter," the winter not only of his discontent but also of his demise. His story ironically starts with his last hours on earth, as he

175

trudges painfully through the snow to his death, while simultaneously struggling with an escalating loss of language. Not until the end of the novel is he (posthumously) referred to as "the Alzheimer's patient..." (*Map* 353).[1] He is searching for an island, ironically unaware that he is actually there, and groping for the word *island*, instead of which "He has a map of the shoreline in his brain; its docks and rundown wooden buildings, a few trees grown in the last century [...]" (1) and later "an image of an enormous raft made of timber floats through his imagination" (3). The prologue is written in a timeless present, and the confused old man appears to be in a state of eternal beginning: "He knows the island was the beginning [...] He begins once again to move forward" (3). Various words flash through his mind, mainly geographical terms, but also fragments of the past such as *glass* and *ballroom.* Finally Andrew falls asleep in the snow and wakes to utter "his first full sentence in more than a month" (5): "I have lost everything," which turns out to be his last. Andrew next appears in the story of the second protagonist, Jerome Mc Naughton, a young conceptual artist, who discovers the old man's corpse, later that same winter, on "an island that a hundred years ago was busy with ships and lumber," but that is now a "difficult to reach" retreat for visual artists (9).

A year after the newspapers had reported Jerome's discovery, Sylvia Bradley, a middle-aged woman, who had been Andrew's secret lover for many years, sets out, without telling her husband, from the small lakeshore town where they live, to find the last person to have seen Andrew, i.e. Jerome, at his studio in Toronto, thirty miles away. The rest of the first chapter, "The Revelations," takes place in Toronto, in Sylvia's hotel room and mainly at the studio flat where Jerome lives with his Indian girlfriend Mira, a performance artist. The sign on their door significantly reads: *Conceptual Fragments.* Long conversations ensue between Jerome and Sylvia, interspersed with flashbacks to their respective pasts, triggering strong emotional responses and psychological breakthroughs, as in an analysis. At the end of this section, Sylvia's husband Malcolm turns up, wanting to take his wife home.

The notebooks written by Andrew, left to Sylvia when he disappeared for good and later lent to Jerome and Mira, contain the story of Andrew's ancestors on Timber Island and constitute the interpolated 19th century narrative of the second chapter "The Bog Commissioners," thus providing the floating character of Andrew with a background. The third, shorter chapter "A Map of Glass" picks up the thread of the first, with more intense conversations in pairs, partly about the notebooks.

---

[1]   Further unspecified page references concern the novel under scrutiny and are provided in the main text.

These essentially involve Sylvia and either Jerome or Malcolm, and Jerome and Mira, and occasionally the two women or the two men. Before returning home, Sylvia hands Jerome an envelope containing "a kind of final chapter" she has written as a sequel to the story of Andrew's ancestors.

The three main characters' stories are also structured from a triple angle. The first angle involves their difficulties with communication, intimacy and love, which lead them to invest in or fetishise inanimate objects, architecture or landscapes as substitutes for people. The second involves their varying degrees of mental frailty or illness, while the third angle brings into play interconnected verbal and visual forms of creativity, combining an extension of the symptom with a form of therapy, which readers are incited to hope will lead to an at least partial cure. Jane Urquhart's fragmented postmodern writing, ranging from gaps and blanks to entropic proliferation, layered with multi-disciplinary subtexts and inter-texts and interspersed with specular devices and mimetic visual descriptive strategies such as *ekphrasis* (Louvel 32-34), proves to be the perfect process to convey the complexity of her product.

The three protagonists, from three different generations, are all depicted consciously turned toward their past, attempting to create something in the present and unconsciously trying to recognize their selves or identities in the mirror of memory and through their work. Even in his advanced stage of aphasia, Andrew has nevertheless retained visual memories of his quest for his origins and the former Timber Island, before the trees were felled and the buildings buried by a fatal sandstorm, as well as of a mysterious kind of love that cannot be put into words:

> The whole unnamed world is so beautiful to him now that he is aware that he has left behind vast, unremembered territories, certain faces and a full orchestra of sounds that he has loved. (4)

More of a scientist than an artist, Andrew had thoroughly researched the history of his family[2] and subsequently recorded the facts, using the scrapbook of his great-great aunt Annabelle and the journals of his great-grandfather Branwell, her brother. The drawings and paintings produced by the brother and sister, as well as the ornate maps crafted in secret by their father Joseph Woodman, enabled Andrew to visualise the Island as it was in the prosperous days of the Woodman timber business. He communicated that vision to Sylvia, who was his last link with the

---

[2] Andrew's great-great-grandfather Joseph Woodman, an engineer with a repressed artist's talent, had immigrated to Timber Island in the early 19th century.

world during his dark Alzheimer days, and she passed it on to Jerome, with the notebooks.

In the narrative set in the present, Jerome appears as the main artist figure, yet the detailed passage relating his lonely but productive retreat on Timber Island minimizes the differences between his quest as a conceptual artist and Andrew's more intellectual cum scientific research. This section (9-31) of the initial chapter "The Revelations" is the most informative passage concerning Jerome and is followed up at the very end, when most of the tormented young man's psychological tangles finally come undone. Interestingly, during Andrew's trek through the snow, "the word *tangle* slips into his mind" (2). At this point, Jerome's "tangle" is expressed in fragmented flashbacks to his traumatic childhood and love-hate relationship with his angry, alcoholic father and clammed-up, destroyed mother. Like Andrew, Jerome is obsessed with the past, and the wreckage of his early family life becomes a metaphor within his artwork, in which he inscribes traces of destruction and neglect, in both urban landscapes and deserted natural spots, with a special fascination for fences:

> He quickly became obsessed by the ruined fences [...] and [had] begun to search out remnants of rails, boulders and stumps, sometimes tramping for hours through swamps and scrub bush following a line of decaying posts or a path defined by rusting, broken wire. He began to think of fences as situations rather than structures. (17)

Jerome also maintains a paradoxical relationship with language. When alone, he toys with words, expressions and titles for his works and yet, "Made uncomfortable by any kind of verbal explanation," he exhibits them without any anchoring text at all. From his own point of view: "He himself would never be a painter, considered himself instead a sort of chronicler" (17), again like Andrew. Later, Jerome tells Sylvia: "I've never been a painter, really. What I do is more sculptural [...] involv[ing] three-dimensional space" (77).

Jerome projects cultural codes onto nature. When looking at the ice he thinks of Robert Smithson's *Map of Broken Glass* (18), referring the reader back to Urquhart's title *A Map of Glass*. The American artist Robert Smithson (1938-1973) provides an important subtext for Urquhart's novel as well as a model for Jerome. Killed in a plane crash at thirty-five, Smithson remains suspended in time as a young artist and a revolutionary for his period. According to Jack Flam, the editor of his collected writings:

> In recent years, the iconoclastic Smithson has himself become part of the art-historical canon that he fought against so vigorously. He has now come to symbolize the expansive, anti-formalist movements that emerged in the

mid-1960s and early 1970s, and he is acknowledged as an early and influential advocate of cultural and historical relativism. (Flam ix)

Smithson broke down the barriers between established art categories, as well as between art and non-art forms, such as mapmaking. In 1969, he built an outdoor conceptual piece in New Jersey, entitled *The Map of Glass*, defined by Flam as "one of thousands of hypothetical arguments in favour of Atlantis," to be followed by a series of *Maps of Broken Glass*. The main idea was to create a fragmented evocation of the lost Atlantis, just as Urquhart's Andrew and Jerome will each try to revive a vanished Timber Island from the present-day wreckage. For Smithson, "The map is a series of 'upheavals' and 'collapses' – a strata of unstable fragments is arrested by the friction of stability" (Flam 133). He liked to study the play of light on and through the glass fragments of his maps and used them for an "abstract geology" (133), consisting in determining wasteland sites and then collecting samples and fragments of raw materials, which he structured into the patterns and grids he called "non-sites". On the island, Jerome replaces glass with ice and uses black and white photography to capture both the light effects on the ice and the entropic sense of loss and decay in that deserted location, as concretized by broken fences and other rubble, such as "remnants of abandoned architecture" (13). Similarly, Sylvia recalls: "All that sad refuse, Andrew used to say. And that island of course [...] abandoned by those ancestors a century before" (97). The Smithson subtext, echoed in Jerome's work, can be read as a vast extended metaphor for Urquhart's postmodern, open-ended, fragmentary fiction-writing process.

A specific painting from the early Flemish Renaissance is evoked in the episode of Jerome's island retreat: "Joachim Patinir's 16th century *Saint Jerome in the Wilderness*" (25), of which Mira had slipped a reproduction into Jerome's pack. It represents St. Jerome with a devoted lion from whose paw, according to the legend, the saint had removed a thorn. Similarly Jerome, in his grey surroundings, meets a large orange tomcat: "It's feral, I think, growls a lot" (24), he tells Mira on the phone and she immediately connects it with St Jerome's lion. Accordingly, the young artist feeds and combs the animal, disinfects a wound, names the cat Swimmer "Because of the soundless fluidity of the animal's movements" (27), talks to it constantly and brings it home tamed. The cat provides life, colour, communication and everything Jerome had meant to leave behind when on the island. The cat extends Jerome's pattern of cultural projection onto their island surroundings, and together they embody a *tableau-vivant* of the Patinir painting. The cat presents a mirror image of a scruffy male, angry and hurt by past traumas, yet it comes to trust Jerome, just as the latter uncharacteristically trusts Mira, in spite of "the disturbing truth of his own feelings, the pleasure he felt when thinking of her" (11). He also loves looking at her. Her name means "look" in Spanish, "Almost like mirror," as Sylvia later suggests (73). Furthermore, Mira's exotic Hindu background, vital performance art and the colourful materials she uses both enhance and counter the puritan starkness of Jerome's creations.

Finally, the cat leads Jerome to Andrew's dead body on the island, a morbid discovery which, being a reminder of the "horror of his father's death" (14), shocks him out of his indifference. At the end of the novel, by reading the notebooks to Jerome, Mira ultimately enables him to retrieve the repressed facts and unearth his buried love for his father.

A sort of *ekphrasis* occurs in the form of a flashback staged in Jerome's mind on the island, calling up his and Mira's joint reading of certain details in their fetish painting:

> [...] they had eventually come to understand that the several tiny lions in the vivid blue- and-green Patinir landscape they were so fond of – each lion engaged in a particular activity: chasing wolves, curled at the saint's feet, chumming around with a donkey, or standing in a field filled with sheep – represented only one lion and that the painting was episodic in nature, depicting a number of events from the saint's life [...]. (25)

The sequential narrative aspect of the painting thus described creates an unexpected link with Jerome's conceptual art.

Sylvia's first name seems as significant as Jerome's, Mira's or Andrew's, which simply means "man," from the Greek *andros*. A mysterious character, Sylvia echoes Shakespeare's song in *Two Gentlemen of Verona*: "Who is Silvia, what is she?" She herself recalls Andrew's rather contrived view of her as a dryad: "...he had run his hands through her hair, had looked at her and said: 'Sylvaculture, the encouragement of trees'" (104), linking her first name with his own surname Woodman, his ancestors and "Timber" Island.

Sylvia's description of her younger self to Jerome represents an intertextual emulation of Tennessee Williams's Laura in *The Glass Menagerie*, with deliberate differences. Both young women are handicapped and generally fragile. According to Williams's stage directions, Laura is "crippled, one leg slightly shorter than the other, and held in a brace," as well as "exquisitely fragile" (228), like her glass collection. In *A Map of Glass*, the limp is displaced onto Andrew's tough ancestress Annabelle, while the beautiful Sylvia suffers from an indeterminate, equally crippling mental frailty: her behaviour ranges from normality to the verge of psychosis. The reader becomes an analyst struggling to form a diagnosis. As the internal focalizer of the framing narrative, Sylvia provides most of the information herself. She recalls "the bubble-like world of her childhood, a world whose skin had not yet been pierced, broken by the shock of connection, of feeling" (56), an image which expresses a back-to-the-womb death instinct. She was bright but shunned the pressure of institutions or people in general and so never left the family house, remaining overprotected, introverted and distant from her rigid, puritanical parents (80-81). She tells Jerome: "I was content, unless I was interfered with, unless I was interrupted, unless someone else stood in my path and blocked my view of my private world" (133), a world of buildings, landscapes, household and other inanimate objects, books and artefacts, which Sylvia found reassuring.

As in *The Glass Menagerie*, a young man comes to dinner, but here the situation is reversed: Sylvia allows Malcolm Bradley, her doctor father's locum, to tame her by talking exclusively about her china horses for six months, yet he arouses only curiosity in her. A wedding is arranged but the marriage remains unconsummated and the doctor/ patient couple live in the golden cage of her parents' house. Later, Sylvia expresses pity for her husband: "a feeling that she experienced only in relation to his faithful attachment to her disability, if that's what it was, a disability" (116). Sylvia wonders: "had he in fact married his conclusion?" (96). The main symptoms of her so-called "condition" were a touch of phobia, a tendency to fetishise objects and an obsession with death, until Andrew became her lover and "opened the door of the world for her" (117). He also brought her anxiety and suffering: "he had broken into my calm like a burglar" (127). Those in her circle then divided into two groups: those who believed in her "condition" and wished to maintain it – i.e. her parents and Malcolm; and those whom she could touch and love in various ways, and who did not believe in the "condition". Consequently, Sylvia related to Andrew sexually, to Jerome more maternally, to Julia and later Mira through female bonding.

The bond between Sylvia and Jerome intensifies as their conversations turn into a mutual *talking cure* and the release of repressed experiences emerges in symmetrical, specular patterns. Both retrieve fragments of a lost past, for Jerome "the disappeared world of his childhood, the place he couldn't stop visiting," inhabited by his "handsome, laughing father, architect of the underground, a singer, a dancer"(321), until the latter's involvement in a terrible mining accident drove him to drink and (self)-destruction. Sylvia needs to talk about her passionate but painful affair with Andrew, that she had always kept secret: "We remained utterly unrecorded, unmarked" (338-339). By sharing her own story and Andrew's notebooks with Jerome, Sylvia saves her relationship from oblivion, just as Andrew had preserved the historiographic fragments he had gathered by transmitting them to Sylvia. In each case, links are established between past memories, present narratives and artistic creativity. All three protagonists suffer from grief and guilt, as in Jerome's case, "[T]he inexplicable guilt he had felt after his father's death" (65).

Following Sylvia's final departure, Jerome is at last able to tell Mira how his drunken father fell off a balcony to his death, after a quarrel between the two of them. Just as Jerome had shouldered his father's guilt, Sylvia had both absorbed and visualized Andrew's grief, increased by age and illness: "He could never let go of the picture of a raped landscape" and even with Alzheimer's, "that inherited memory of destruction was still in Andrew's mind" (99). As Andrew deteriorated, Sylvia's grief emulated his: "everything was in a state of decay" (135), her face in the mirror "was a collection of dead cells," like a reflection of his.

Urquhart's usual fascination with wild weather, Emily Brontë, and *Wuthering Heights* permeates the whole novel. It is structured by a kind of simplified chaos theory, a palimpsestic minefield, geologically layered with fragments, generations after an apocalyptic explosion. The two sibling protagonists of the meta-historical 19th century part emulate the Brontës: Branwell, like his namesake, rejects the conventional working world and in the face of adversity, paints angry allegorical frescoes. Annabelle, like Emily Brontë, loves only her brother; she also only paints romantic shipwrecks. Her name condenses the "e" of Emily, Anne and Bell, the Brontës' masculine pseudonym. Stormy, bereaved Heathcliff figures prowl this wasteland: Branwell, Andrew, Jerome's father and finally Jerome himself. They are all lovers and, except for Andrew, artists. Annabelle is to Turner what Jerome is to Smithson, and the text moves achronologically between the explosion of Modernism and the open sluices of Postmodernism. Synesthesia, fragmentation and mirroring structure and deconstruct the form and content of the text. Time remains horizontal, the time of memory and obsession as in Deleuze's "sheets of time" (Deleuze in translation 98-125). Space is that of a lost island, like Smithson's Atlantis, here the fictional Timberland. The island is the embodiment of history for Andrew, who "was walking toward the past" (326), an eternally present *locus amoenus* for love for Sylvia, and inspiration for future creativity in Smithson's wake for Jerome. It reflects the *I-land* or identity they all seek and constitutes the ideal vision or *eye-land* for Jerome's art as it had for Annabelle's.

As the story progresses, art as process becomes entropic as well as instrumental in the postmodern characters' ongoing therapy. Sylvia says of Andrew: "I loved that fragment of him that I was given" (332). She herself works with fragments in her map-making. Both she and Jerome leave blank spaces in their lives as well as in their art. Sylvia considers her "ability to be absent" (124) a skill, while Jerome admits to frequent daydreaming and mentions the often "blank slate" (127) of his mind.

Biblical undertones emerge, ironical and subversive. The apocalyptic sandstorm which destroys Branwell's greedy son and daughter-in-law's Sodom and Gomorrah-like mansion, smashes "the opaque glass ceiling that was also a ballroom floor" (364), propelling its shards into Andrew's and Sylvia's writing and Jerome's conceptual art. Contrary to Lot's wife, Sylvia is told by Andrew to look back at the disaster, and instead of turning into a pillar of salt, she later carries a salt shaker from her home around with her for protection. Similarly, literary fragments are made to surface out of Sylvia's and Jerome's unconscious to become mirrors for their psychological problems. Sylvia treasures an old edition of the morbid nursery rhyme "Who killed Cock Robin,"[3] and after Andrew's death, identifies with the 9th verse: "Who'll be chief mourner?/'I', said the Dove/'I mourn for my love'". In Jerome's case, a fragment of Felicia Hemans's poem *Casabianca* (1849) oneirically fuses his adolescent loneliness faced with his parents' wrecked marriage with Annabelle's shipwreck paintings and the Timber Island disaster: "The boy stood on the burning deck/Whence all but he had fled/The flame that lit the battle's wreck/shone round him o'er the dead". These childhood poems also relate to voice, the phatic memory that returns with oral story-telling, or the impact of a loved one reading aloud. When Mira reads Sylvia's conclusion to Andrew's notebooks out loud to Jerome, he can at last retrieve his beloved younger father's voice reading to him as a child. Similarly, hearing Sylvia's candid confession had brought back his lost mother. Jerome also visualizes things from the sound of Sylvia's voice: "I can almost see everything you say. Everything you're talking about" (132).

According to Liliane Louvel, maps are different from other images, because they attempt to put the world in order (Louvel 117). Thus Sylvia, being neurotically obsessed with order, "had been an expert map-reader since childhood" (41); she made Braille maps as a hobby and consulted library maps of Timber island. Likewise, Andrew's job as a geographer had been "mapping the County" (344) and Jerome's father had "worked for a while making geological maps for a metallurgical company" (335). Not so for Jerome, his master Smithson or Urquhart: their oxymoronic "Maps of Glass" transgress the idea of order by emulating the world's chaos.

Finally, the talking cure within the *Conceptual Fragments* studio where Mira presents Sylvia with a wealth of colourful scraps for her maps, together with the novel's signifying discourse, conjure up three

---

[3] Probably the earliest version, in *Tommy Thumb's Pretty Songbook* (c.1944)

variants of an imaginary, subversive, neo-religious painting, in a different version for each protagonist. The weeping man cradled by a female partner icon resembles a Madonna and child configuration in a *pieta* mode. First Sylvia remembers being with the terminally sick Andrew: "often he wept when we made love" (340). Secondly, Jerome recalls a sad scene during his father's drinking days: "his mother was holding the sobbing broken man his father had become in her arms" (356). Finally a third scene, described by the external narrator, shows Jerome and Mira in the same position but with an opposite connotation: "Mira was holding Jerome as he wept, shaking in her arms like the child he had never permitted himself to be" (361). Andrew's tears express pain and grief, Jerome's father's shame and humiliation, Jerome's release and redemption. Urquhart's diffuse weeping-man image proves as powerful as Picasso's *Weeping Woman* (1937, Tate Gallery) and subtly challenges traditional gender roles as it resurrects canonical configurations.

References

ATWOOD, M. (1972), *Survival*, Toronto, Anansi.

DELEUZE, G. (1985), *L'Image-temps*, Paris, Éditions de Minuit. (1989), *The Time-Image*, Trans. Hugh TOMLINSON & Robert GALETA, Minneapolis, University of Minnesota Press.

FLAM, J. (1996), *"Introduction"* and *"Notes"*, in Robert Smithson, *The Collected Writings*, Berkeley, University of California Press.

HEMANS, F.D. [1849] (1912), "Casabianca," in *Historic Poems and Ballad*, Ed. R. S. HOLLAND, Philadelphia, George W. Jacobs & Co.

HUTCHEON, L. (1988), *The Canadian Postmodern*, Don Mills, ON, OUP.

LOUVEL, L. (2002), *Texte Image/Images à lire, textes à voir*, Presses universitaires de Rennes, Collection « Interférences ».

SMITHSON, R. (1996), *The Collected Writings*, Ed. J. FLAM, Berkeley, University of California Press.

URQUHART, J. (2006), *A Map of Glass*, San Francisco, MacAdam/Cage Publishing.

WILLIAMS, T. [1945] (2000), *The Glass Menagerie*, in *A Streetcar Named Desire & Other Plays*, Harmondsworth, Penguin.

12

Reconstructing the Past Through Objects
in *A Map of Glass*

Christine LORRE

Université Sorbonne Nouvelle – Paris 3

Jane Urquhart's work reflects her fascination with landscape, history, and objects from the past, as well as her interest in other arts and in the links between various art forms.[1] *A Map of Glass*, her 2005 novel, offers a fresh look at all these themes and concerns and how they are related. The main narrative relates the encounter between Sylvia Bradley, an autistic woman, and Jerome McNaughton, a Toronto-based land artist whom Sylvia tells about her love story with Andrew Woodman, a man whose body Jerome found during an artist's residence in the Kingston area, where Sylvia is from. Parallel to this encounter, Jerome and his partner Mira carry on their conversations about artistic creation. The central section of the novel, "The Bog Commissioners," has an ambiguous narrative status. Although the omniscient narratorial voice of the framing story confers the authorship of this framed narrative upon Andrew and locates it within the diary form that fuses scriptor and receptor, Urquhart at times superscribes an omniscient voice upon Andrew's first person stance. The narratological blurring produces a certain ontological confusion. This embedded narrative entails a *mise-en-abyme* of the whole metafictional question of how to deal with history in fiction, and how to locate the subject, or the artist, in this process, while the frame narrative allows for an exchange between various art forms, mainly fiction and land art. It raises anew questions about truth, memory and authenticity, as opposed to imagination, in the process of reconstruction of the past. The aim of this article is to examine how Urquhart reasserts the role of the past in her fiction, giving central place to objects in the creation process. Victorian objects play a

---

[1] Jane Urquhart's husband, Tony Urquhart, is an artist, and they have done collaborative work – for example he illustrated *False Shuffles*, her 1982 poetry collection.

key role in the reconstruction of a late 19th century timber industry saga in the Kingston area, and of its decline at the turn of the century. The embedded narrative provides a degree of self-reflexivity to this position. The article will thus expose how *A Map of Glass* challenges the role of objects in artistic creation, examining the narrative role of some of the omnipresent Victoriana, and focusing on three tropes that function as locations of artistic questioning – namely maps, mirrors, and museums.

"I thought you said that the art object itself was finished." (300)

The first section of the novel, "The Revelations," alludes to an artistic project Jerome undertook on Timber Island during his residency in an old sail loft dating from the days when timber was the main industrial activity of the area. Jerome's creative mind works conceptually: he is intrigued by the idea of the memory of nature, and works with snow, for its wonderful ability to be "marked on its surface, like memory, for a brief season" (23).[2] He then takes photographic records of his installations, the meaning of which is left to the viewer's interpretation. Jerome is a tormented artist figure, ill-at-ease with his family history and his personal past, in the process of defining his artistic principles. Although it is not stated explicitly, loss and longing are what his work is really about, particularly the early loss of childhood innocence underlying his *Fence Line Series*, the work that launched him as a promising young artist, and the loss of the tall trees, and then of the schooners of the industrial age on Timber Island in his emerging new conception, *Nine Revelations of Navigation*.

Jerome's intellectual source of inspiration is Robert Smithson, an American land artist active in the late 1960s and 1970s who has had a huge influence on abstract art. He is recurrently mentioned in the quiet but intense conversations about art that go on between Jerome and his partner Mira, who works at a gallery and experiments with artistic creation. Jerome sees many parallels between his own work with snow and one of Smithson's famous installations, *A Map of Broken Glass* (1969), an abstract piece dealing with displacement and landmarks, and which gives its title to the novel. Abstract art, "also called nonobjective art or nonrepresentational art, [is] painting, sculpture, or graphic art in which the portrayal of things from the visible world plays no part" (*Encyclopedia Britannica Online*). Art is thus conceived not as a mimetic representation of the world, including objects, but as being based on concepts, which means that objects play no central part in the

---

2   Quotations from *A Map of Glass* will be followed by the page number in parentheses, referring to the edition given in "References".

artistic process. When it developed as an artistic movement in the United States in the postwar period, abstraction, did trigger a rejection of objects among artists, certain objects in particular, and sometimes quite vehemently, as in this 1948 statement by Barnett Newman, an artist emblematic of the current:

> It is interesting that when the Greek dream prevails in our time, the European artist is nostalgic for the ancient forms, hoping to achieve tragedy by depicting his self-pity over the loss of the elegant column and the beautiful profile. This tortured emotion, however, agonizing over the Greek objects, is always refined. Everything is so highly civilized.
>
> The artist in America is, by comparison, like a barbarian. He does not have the superfine sensibility toward the object that dominates European feeling. He does not even have the objects.
>
> This is, then our opportunity, free of the ancient paraphernalia, to come closer to the sources of the tragic emotion. Shall we not, as artists, search out the new objects for its image? (Newman 170)

Newman and others argued for "new objects" – and by this he meant abstract ones, as opposed to "classical ones" – to render the tragic emotion. A literary precursor of this search for "new objects" is T.S. Eliot in his famous 1919 statement on the "objective correlative,"[3] which epitomizes the Modernist search for new ways to express emotion that rely on obliqueness, and signals a major aesthetic rupture through the arts, shifting the focus from what is perceived to the process of perception and the perceiving subject.

Sylvia's aesthetics seem totally opposed to Modernity. She pathologically hates change, disruption and rupture. When she first meets Malcolm, her husband-to-be, he shows her he understands her by quoting from Keats's "Ode on a Grecian Urn": "And, little town [...], thy streets for evermore will silent be." (88) Keats's poem praises the eternal quality of art, in contrast with the ephemeral nature of human love and happiness, and epitomizes the Romantic understanding of art and beauty, with due respect to the Classical tradition. Yet this view, along with the famous last line of Keats's poem, "'Beauty is truth, truth beauty, – that is all/Ye know on earth, and all ye need to know'" (Keats 346), takes a morbid turn in Sylvia's world, which is a veritable mausoleum in which her tormented inner life is repressed. It eventually finds an outlet in story-telling.

---

[3] "The only way of expressing emotion in the form of art is by finding an 'objective correlative'; in other words, a set of objects, a situation, a chain of events which shall be the formula of that *particular* emotion; such that when the external facts, which must terminate in sensory experience, are given, the emotion is immediately evoked" (Eliot 102).

Jerome's stance as a conceptual artist, and a follower of Smithson's abstract land art, does contain contradictions or ambiguities, just as Smithson's did. When he mentions the Chianti bottle in relation to Smithson, Jerome looks on it as "an artifact [...] that Robert Smithson would have been familiar with in the 1960s" (299), that is to say a historical and lyrical object, now a symbol of bohemia. So Mira points out to him: "I thought you said that the art object itself was finished" (300). This statement of Jerome's is contradicted by fact and calls for re-examination. The semiotic role of the Chianti bottle is proof that objects still have the power to signify meaning and convey or trigger emotion, even for him. This anecdote points to the question of historical emplacement in abstract art: where does the subject, the artist stand? This is a question Jerome is forced to reconsider when he finds Andrew's body and then meets Sylvia; both act as intruders in his new conception.

In the contrast evoked by Barnett Newman between Europe and America, and in the 1950s and 1960s, European sensibility (including European abstraction) was considered as "effeminate" by American critics, who viewed themselves as the possessors of all the "masculine" virtues (Leclerc 39). This lingering contrast between a masculine and a feminine view of art is enacted in the novel by Jerome and Mira. Jerome identifies with Smithson intellectually and emotionally, taking after the masculine artist figure who refuses to display his own emotions and has little patience for other people's – "Any sign of male adult tears caused [him] to close down completely" (356). By contrast, Mira, whose Indian origins link her to a subcontinent associated with femininity and sensuality, has an eclectic and syncretic approach to art, which reflects her situation as a migrant solidly moored to the city and its mix of influences. She is equally appreciative of Christian saints and Hindu gods for their symbolism – as demonstrates her attraction to Patinir's *St. Jerome in the Wilderness*. Her work combines sensuality and conceptualization, as in the performance she works on, using fabric and sand. It also blends referentiality and abstraction, as in her "cosies," or "swaddles," "soft protective coverings for a variety of solid objects: toasters, books, bicycle pumps, even, eventually, and much to her parents' bafflement as she always delighted in telling [Jerome], for her father's lawn mower" (62). Mira's work is feminine, but includes the masculine sphere too: the word "cosy" evokes the beauty of ordinary objects, ranging from the convivial teapot to more trivial appliances, while "swaddles," which perform a similar role, recall motherly (and Christian) love and protection. Together they reflect Mira's ability to wonder at ordinary objects, and the love and care that are put into daily gestures.

What emerges from the artist figures of Jerome and Mira, in their interaction with Sylvia, is the tension between a Romantic understanding of art and culture that is an extension of the Classical European tradition, and a Modernist view that turns its back on Europe, and leans towards abstraction and conceptualization. Yet the incongruous meeting between Sylvia and Jerome, with her knocking at his door one day to tell him about the man whose body he found, leads to a dialogue between these two traditions. Urquhart had previously examined this problematic of the rupture with Europe's past and history in her fiction. In *The Underpainter* the narration by Austin Fraser, an American modern artist, of his friendship with George Kearns, a Canadian ceramic painter who becomes a soldier, reveals the difference in their relationship to Europe, history, the war, and to art as a means of expressing emotion. Similarly, in *A Map of Glass*, Sylvia's world seems enclosed and stuck in the past, in contrast with Jerome's life, which seems free of such burdens. However, there is more to it than meets the eye.

"You are at home in museums." (298)

At the end of the novel, Malcolm tells Jerome and Mira that the love story Sylvia has been telling them about over several days is totally invented, and results from her condition which causes her "a kind of hallucinogenic imagination" (354). Malcolm's diagnosis reveals symptoms of Bovary-ism[4]: "[Sylvia] has trouble, you see, separating reality from what happens in books" (354), and according to him, Andrew Woodman, her "lover," is merely a man she bumped into on the street one day. These words of Malcolm's in direct speech are never confirmed by the narrator, and Mira and Jerome do not seem to give his revelation full credence. This reinforces the ambivalence at the core of the narrative – whether Sylvia made up Andrew or not – an ambivalence which is never lifted.[5] For instance, when Sylvia is talking about Andrew (338-339), direct speech alternates with the narrator's voice, which may be either an omniscient narrator's voice, or a narrative voice focalized through Sylvia, thus not giving narratorial veracity to the summed-up love story. That the character of Andrew may have been the result of Sylvia's fancy is arguably suggested in her *postscriptum* to "The Bog Commissioners," in which she insists on "the *miracle*" of their meeting, and "the *idea* of him, and *the arm of that idea* resting on

---

4   This cannot fail to call up Fleda in *The Whirlpool*.

5   Asked in an email about the status of the narrative, Urquhart replied that she "wanted the ambiguity [… and] kind of liked the fact that in this novel, as is often the case in life, the reliability of the narrators (i.e. the author, Sylvia, her husband, Andrew himself) is called into question." Personal email, 3 July 2009.

my shoulder" (369, emphasis added). Urquhart thus implies that "truth" is unreliable, and that imagination and art are what make life bearable.

The house Sylvia lives in, which is her parents' house, is full of family objects and Victoriana that seem to hold her back in the past and to keep her from communicating with other people. These objects are connected to a certain Victorian mind-frame, to the heritage Sylvia is left with, but eventually they also act as devices that help her deal with this heritage. With Sylvia, objects act simultaneously in the narrative as symptoms of her condition, which is visible in her various obsessions and phobias, and the cure for that condition, which consists in telling a story. If one takes into account the often-made distinction between object and thing, the former being functional, particular, immediate, lyrical, and the latter being opaque and impossible for the human senses to grasp totally (Lemardeley and Topia 7-9), then one could say that Sylvia seems to perceive her environment as one full of objects that she can describe, and which she keeps describing in order to prove to herself that she is in control of that environment. This compulsive need is partly linked to the fact that she feels threatened by the outside world. Yet she actually has a rich inner life, and these objects become more than a simple extension of herself: they act as things whose mystery inspires her with stories. Thanks to them, she manages to master her fears and to define her relationship to the world.

Sylvia's house is full of objects that have been in the family for a long time: plates and cutlery, china, children's toys, books, Bibles, family photo albums, maps, mirrors, and more. Many such lists sprinkle the narrative, as Sylvia goes through mental reviews of objects in her house, especially in times of stress, for example when she is on her own at the hotel: "Soon she began to go through the inventory of the house she had left behind, an inventory she had made in early childhood and had never forgotten" (117). By denominating these objects and occasionally briefly describing them, Sylvia restricts them to a name and a physical appearance, and feels comforted by the feeling that she is in control of her world. However, all these things have a signification well beyond that of simple objects, because Sylvia also "knew the histories of the old settlers as well as she knew her own body" (37). This intimate knowledge of personal histories is what brings the objects, and Sylvia, to life.

Certain items are particularly important in Sylvia's world, and speak for her condition. The group of china horses and the Staffordshire piece representing the girl, the dog, the bird and the tree, "these were the kind of things she liked to think about at the time that Malcolm first came into her life" (87). She believed a connection "existed between her and the shape such a thing [as the Staffordshire figure] would hold on to unchangingly, forever" (87). Even though Sylvia's story about these objects is one of permanence and timelessness, the objects tell the reader another story. The horse figures are reminiscent of Tennessee Williams's *Glass Menagerie* and its atmosphere of maladjustment and sexual repression. The Staffordshire piece has eloquent historicity. Staffordshires were very popular in Victorian times (Briggs 47), and somehow epitomize the aesthetics and spirit of that period. As a decorative object, they were part of a common Victorian frame, a claim to aesthetics and beauty, a sign of a certain civilisation, perhaps a sign of nostalgia for arts and crafts, as well as the demise of agrarian society in times that saw the birth of mass production. The fact that they are made in a region of England gives them a certain authenticity deemed consubstantial with that culture, and they are a way of claiming attachment to England. They are small and easy to export, which means that they can stand as so many pieces or fragments of England in any far-flung colony. In the narrative, the Staffordshire figure crystallizes the impact of all this Victorian history on Sylvia.

The stories of the settlers that Sylvia is so familiar with, both from hearing or reading about them, and through the objects in her house, appear in a different form in "The Bog Commissioners," the account of the Woodman family. In this narrative, Annabelle mirrors Sylvia's emotional and psychological condition – for example Sylvia turns from quasi-autistic woman to storyteller, after the shock of physical contact with a complete stranger, not unlike the shock caused by Gilderson's hand on Annabelle's shoulder. Patriarchy is omnipresent, and Annabelle feels entrapped by it. Her world is dominated by her tyrannical father, the timber businessman, for whom she keeps house after her mother's death. When her father's rival of old, Gilderson, proposes to her because the property she inherited, after years of decay, is on the verge of collapse, she realizes that something important is missing from her life and becomes insane. Her madness manifests itself in obsessive inventories and accounting of all the objects in the house she is now the sole ruler of. The pathological aspect of this listing and counting echoes the darker side of the Victorians' obsession with lists and accounts[6] (Briggs 13), a practice which developed as the Empire expanded, and Victorians felt the need to implement the "fictive thought of imperial control" (Richards 2). The fantasy of one's control over objects, through lists, as a sign of control over the course of things is echoed in Annabelle's crazy few days following Gilderson's visit.

Annabelle's other response to the existential questioning that imposes itself on her is focusing intensely on things: "Not since she had

---

[6] See also *The Whirlpool*.

been young had Annabelle looked at objects with such intensity: the hairbrush on her dresser, the leather of her boots," etc. (269-270). This intense attention to objects raises yet more questions, increasing Annabelle's dizziness instead of soothing it. She sees familiar objects in a new, defamiliarizing light, as if her world had been toppled by Gilderson's masculine touch. The obsessively recurring image is that of the details of Gilderson's hand: "the man's fingers on her shoulder, the Masonic ring, the grey and black hairs that grew just above the knuckles" (275). Annabelle instantly knows that she has not been able to live her life as a woman because of the oppressive patriarchal environment she lives in, but is unable to confront the thought. Only when she hears of Marie's death does she come to her senses and conclude: "What would any of their lives have been without the quickening that an orphan had caused in the only world that Annabelle had ever known?" (276)

Much as Marie is Annabelle's "better, more beautiful self" (276), her opposite and best friend at the same time, Annabelle appears as Sylvia's double, as a projection of herself in the past, which emphasizes what appears as Sylvia's inheritance from Victorian times. Apart from an instinctive estrangement from men, and a fear of childbearing, this includes a feeling of guilt. Again, this can be read in the accumulative effect of some of the lists that appear in the narrative. As Annabelle is having dinner with Gilderson,

> an absurd list of all the goods Gilderson had trafficked up and down the lakes was building itself in her mind: barley, cabbages, weather vanes, sets of china, hacksaws, buggies, furniture, whisky, horses, human beings. What a lot of *things* there are in the world, she thought, and more all the time. (264)

The list illustrates Canada's mercantilist past, the stunning scale of mass production, and the parallel development of unbridled consumerism, caused by the greed of capitalists like Gilderson. The very rafts that leave Timber Island participate in this economy, as "the wood that made up their construction might re-emerge in the shape of furniture in a multitude of Victorian parlours or, if the timbers were oak – and large and long enough – as masts on the decks of the pugnacious vessels of the Admiralty" (199). The critique of what Gilderson embodies is also present in Branwell's mind after he visits the Invalides in Paris and its records of international wars. Back on Timber Island, he sees it not as a pastoral and bucolic environment, but as a place "in a state of complete destruction [...], and the ships themselves too attached to greed and commerce" (161). The timber industry left behind itself a heritage of guilt for the key role it played in wars and commerce both guided by greed for profit, a heritage which the national literature has not yet fully dealt with.

Intertextuality is prominent in "The Bog Commissioners," in a way that further blurs the lines of narrative authority. Biblical overtones are omnipresent. Joseph Woodman is said to resemble "certain powerful Old Testament leaders" (168); Branwell calls his son "a creator of deserts," and after his hotel has been buried by sand, fears "a plague of sawdust, or of iron filings to appear in his future" (285, 288), in an industrial-era reinterpretation of the Exodus. Intertextuality is also at work with the novels of the Brontë sisters (who are mentioned as writers Joseph Woodman would not have read, 156), in particular *Jane Eyre*, whose eponymous character Marie is modelled after. Like Jane Eyre, she is an orphan, she finds comfort in her friendship with Annabelle, as Jane does with Helen Burns, and later, finds love with Branwell, the young master of the house where Marie is taken in, even though their first contact was unpromising – and this recalls the first contact between Jane and Rochester. The characterization of Annabelle, not as a romantic soul, despite appearances, but as someone who "read no novels and brooked no nonsense, and was an astute and unsentimental judge of character" (166), has echoes of Jane Austen.[7] Denial that Annabelle is a romantic soul is found again in the mention of Tennyson, whom she deems "a pretentious romantic" (232), but nonetheless quotes. The Bible, the Brontës, Jane Austen and Tennyson are all part of the Victorian culture Sylvia knows so well, allowing one to wonder, yet never acting as sufficient proof, whether she may be the author of "The Bog Commissioners." Above all, this central section reads as a parody of an epic narrative of love and doom through which Urquhart mocks, but also claims her own fondness for, this same literature.[8]

When Malcolm says to Sylvia, suggesting a visit to a museum in Toronto, "You are at home in museums" (298), he continues to see her as someone who looks for reassurance in objects from the past. He does not realize that these objects are also mysterious things that can summon all her daemons at once, that fire her imagination and enable her to come to terms with her fears and to reveal her passionate inner life. They can perform this because they are not units that tell an existing narrative, but fragments that are part of a story that waits to be told.

---

[7] See for example Emma's description and praise of one of her friends' "unsentimental disposition" (*Emma*, chapter 26, 228). Warm thanks to Ariane Hudelet for helping me locate this passage.

[8] For instance, see Urquhart's *The Whirlpool*, as well as *Changing Heaven*, which stages an encounter with the ghost, or the memory, of Emily Brontë.

"I loved that fragment of his that I was given." (332)

What Jerome and Sylvia have in common is a sense of loss, and of the fragmentation of a world they once knew or imagined. For Sylvia, certain objects or places act as liminal spaces in this experience of fragmentation – this is the case with mirrors, maps, and museums. These are tropes that favour the ontological quest in terms of perception of the outside world, space and time, the environment, the landscape, history. They will be examined here as an extension of the overall questioning about the artist's relation to and place in nature and history.

As a young girl, Sylvia is shocked when she sees the reflections in a row of mirrors at an auction, because "the mirrors had shown her that there was no controlling what might enter the frame of experience, that the whole world might bully its way into a quiet interior, and that there would be no way of keeping it out" (91). In her house, mirrors are strategically placed so as to reflect non-moving things only. But even so, this cannot conceal entirely her own inner moods, which are projected onto the frame of the mirror, not the reflective part of it: "The two round mirrors with the child, and then the girl, and now the mature woman in them, always with the same carved eagle on the frame hovering over her head, benignly some days, and on others hunting, about to unfurl its talons, wanting to carry off her brain" (118-119). Sylvia is apparently unmoved by the physical changes of her body, but the sight of the all-powerful force that threatens her brain is disturbing. For all of her efforts to protect herself from the outside world, the perceived threat comes from the interior, from herself, and then the very familiar objects that surround her turn into haunting things that seem beyond her control.

A mirror acts as a medium between the subject and the world: it reflects the world mimetically, faithfully duplicating an image, but because it is a reversed image, and a reflection, not the actual thing, it may appear differently. Mirrors, which have the power of revealing self-awareness and existential anxieties, thus stand for the Modernist concerns with perception and subjectivity (Lepaludier 82, 88). As Jerome recalls while looking at the ice breaking, Robert Smithson used mirrors in his work, "to reflect the natural world" (18). Smithson explained that his work with outdoor mirrors "deal[s] with the raw materials," with the land, with natural light, and "spill[s] out to peripheral zones [to] the area of surd[9] possibilities, the other side of the rational" (Smithson 235, 240). The parallel between Sylvia's experience of mirrors and Jerome's interest in Smithson's work with them to probe

---

[9] In mathematics (of a number), irrational.

in the direction of the irrational eventually leads to questioning the subject's relationship to the world.

Like mirrors, maps act as objects that reveal an unknown, hidden side of life. Here again, Sylvia has contradictory experiences. Her 1878 County atlas feels safe to her, because it belongs to the past and the pictures in it will never change (88). It reflects the world she imaginatively inhabits. Much more creative are the tactile maps that Sylvia makes for her blind friend Julia, to whom "the whole world is a kind of Braille" (68). By having to describe sensually the world around her, Sylvia opens herself up to it. This finds an echo in the embedded narrative, "The Bog Commissioners," as Annabelle discovers another side of her father when she finds the twelve beautiful maps he drew before he emigrated to Canada, of bogs in Ireland that he planned to drain, but eventually was not allowed to. "How was it possible that her father could render the very landscape that had been the source of his humiliation with such meticulous affection?" (228) Through this work of art, Annabelle discovers a different man from the tyrant she always knew, an artist who was able to express his love and intimate knowledge of the land. The maps turn into a poetic, sensuous object that reveals Joseph Woodman's sensitivity. As objects, these maps have as much power as Robert Smithson's *Map of Broken Glass*, which to Jerome conveys a warning: "the shattering of experience and the sense that one cannot play with life without being cut, injured" (18). The old object and the abstract installation, for all the differences that separate them, converge towards expressing a comparable fragility of the subject.

Museums are a third liminal space of fragmentation, and again Sylvia has opposite experiences of them. Her house, which is full of objects inherited from the Victorian period, the time of the settlers, is like a museum in which nothing is to be touched. The village museum Sylvia does part-time volunteer work for, trying to put her obsessions to good use, has a curious effect on her. For one thing, she started "amassing [her] own peculiar collection" (129):

> a rendering of a family tomb made from human hair, a painting of a dog mourning the recently drowned body of a young child, cumbersome pieces of machinery that resembled instruments of torture, stuffed and boxed birds and animals, and all those ominous-looking porcelain dolls that she honestly believed had survived for a century or so because no child really wanted to touch them. (130)

Sylvia's personal choice of such odd things reflects her morbid and tortured spirit, her inhibition towards the senses, especially touch, her recurrent association of childhood and death, her fear of loss. In itself, it is representative not so much of a period, as of Sylvia's personal interpretation and view of that period. Unlike ordinary objects, these things are also mysterious, and conducive to the making of stories. By contrast, the current type of objects that the museum holds is listed in the donations received in great quantities as the old families were leaving the County: "parasols and baby buggies and high button boots and silver tea sets and crochet work and coal oil lamps and strange pioneers' tools: planes, clamps, lathes, all the things Gilderson's ships would have brought into the County" (330). The second effect of Sylvia's work at the village museum, at a time when it was literally overflowing with such everyday objects that had to be catalogued, is to make her aware of the passing of time, entailing a kind of crystallization in her mind of that period of settlement – which may correspond to the time when Andrew reappears in her life, after an unexplained seven-year absence. As a character, he enables her to explore her feeling of guilt, which she calls "responsibility," and which reappears in "The Bog Commissioner," through the character of Gilderson – his name hints at wealth (gilder), but also, less distinctly phonetically, at guilt.

Sylvia is uncomfortable in the large museum she visits with Malcolm. The scale of it intimidates her, the journey in time back to prehistory and geological times frightens her, the rapid succession of historical periods does not make her feel at home. The Victorian age she identifies with is displayed in a room the sign for which reads: "*A Victorian Parlour.* [...] *Do not enter. Do not touch*" (305). The sign epitomizes not only the period it refers to, a time of clearly defined boundaries, in which feelings and sensuality were kept in check. It also epitomizes traditional museums in general, which display objects as if "periods" could be contained in these objects. Urquhart's irony about such displays calls to mind Robert Smithson's commentary about museums: "The museum undermines one's confidence in sense-data and erodes the impression of textures upon which our sensations exist. [...] Visiting a museum is a matter of going from void to void" (Smithson 41). But conversely, Urquhart also sees museums as sites that have the potential to create new meaning, as with Sylvia's "peculiar collection". She has expressed this view in a poem entitled "Museum," in which objects from the past are "loose fragments drawn into new configurations" (Urquhart, 1990: 7). Through Sylvia's idiosyncratic choices, Urquhart revitalizes the concept of the museum as a valuable place to stimulate the imagination, as opposed to a place where objects are displayed in a set way, calling for univocal interpretation.

This method for reconstructing the past, of drawing loose fragments into new configurations, is epitomized in Annabelle's scrapbook, or "book of relics, her splinter book, [which contained] samples from any number of wooden constructions [...] – all dated, identified, and catalogued" (205). The scrapbook also contained other fragments, of fabric, maps, or used matches, which are as so many fragments that served to ignite the narrative. The reader here recognizes a metafictional conceit for Urquhart's technique and her relationship to objects, which are like so many fragments of stories, or traces of the past, in the creative process.[10] The key to reconstruction is the flicker of life, a quickening of passion, which Sylvia receives when she bumps into Andrew on the street in a brief moment, and which she alludes to when she says: "I loved that fragment of him that I was given" (332). Sylvia then becomes a veritable artist figure, a conjurer, a performer, even though Malcolm thinks her incapable of such a feat.

For Jerome, a quickening takes place when he sees Andrew's frozen body, caught in ice, floating by. This traumatic moment reappears, transformed, in a dream in which Jerome sees his father's face in place of Andrew's. When he tries to touch his father's cheek,

> the whole head fragmented, collapsing into a confusion of thin transparent pieces on a flat surface, and suddenly [Jerome] was looking at Smithson's *Map of Broken Glass*. Each shard reflected something he remembered about his father: a signet ring, a belt buckle, a dark green package of cigarettes, an eye, a cufflink, the back of his hand, and Jerome knew his father was broken, smashed. The toe of a shoe, a plaid sleeve, the seam of a pair of pants, an Adam's apple. (144-145)

Jerome's dream is striking for its clarity of details, and the way body parts of the father, or objects that were in contact with his body, come together as so many fragments to reconstruct an image of the father. The familiar objects that belonged to Jerome's father, along with memories of what he looked like, are crucial elements in triggering the reconstruction of a vivid memory of him in Jerome's mind. This vision is juxtaposed with that of a completely abstract work of art, that is somehow at the other end of the artistic spectrum that goes from mimesis to abstraction, as if these two opposite forms of representation had become reconcilable, and even complementary.

By giving objects and things a prominent role in her novel, Urquhart contends the aesthetic position that art and imagination are powerful forces to reconstruct the past, and claims the freedom to do so. This is achieved through the unlikely encounter between two very different, almost antagonistic, art forms. The central romantic fiction, depicting

---

[10] See Urquhart's interview with Laura Ferri: "Think of saints and relics and little tiny bits and pieces of something: there is always a great deal of narrative associated with relics; this has fascinated me for years – the idea that if you have a fragment of bone in a reliquary, you have a fragment of narrative, because each Saint has his or her own story" (Ferri 27). In *Away*, objects are similarly viewed as synecdoches of a greater narrative whole.

and criticizing a bourgeois world, relies on objects that trigger the narrator's imagination and that of the characters, leading to prophetic scenes, but leading also, eventually, to the symbolic demise of the Romantic, pastoral ideal of harmony between man and nature in modern industrial times. Jerome's land art, in the wake of Robert Smithson's, relies on abstraction to explore the changing relationship between man and his environment during and after industrial times. Yet abstraction may depersonify a situation, to the point where the artist loses his own bearings in history and represses his own past, or ignores the human aspect of a situation. The apparition of Andrew's body, frozen in ice, comes to unsettle abstraction by introducing flesh and blood human beings into the landscape Jerome is working on. The true revelation of Jerome's work and of his conversations with Sylvia is not so much about the past as about the impact of the past on the present, and how people in the present relate to the past. The encounter between Sylvia, Jerome and Mira allows for a form of artistic reconciliation to take place, in which Sylvia and Jerome, in their respective approach to creation, reconnect themselves to a certain reality – the reality of history for Jerome, and the reality of the disappearance of the old families for Sylvia. By reconstructing the past through objects, Urquhart defines for herself a middle ground between Romanticism on the one hand, and Modernism and subsequent abstraction on the other, in which fiction is driven by imagery (Urquhart in Ferri 32). The art object is not finished; it is bound to be subject to fresh imaginings and interpretations.

References

"Abstract art," *Encyclopedia Britannica Online*, (Accessed 30 March 2009).

AUSTEN, J. [1816] (1966), *Emma*, Harmondsworth, Penguin.

BRIGGS, A. (1988), *Victorian Things*, Harmondsworth, Penguin.

BRONTË, C. [1847] (1966), *Jane Eyre*, Harmondsworth, Penguin.

ELIOT, T.S. [1919] (1953), *"Hamlet,"* in *Selected Prose*, Harmondsworth, Penguin.

FERRI, L., Ed. (2005), *Jane Urquhart: Essays on Her Works*, Toronto, Guernica.

KEATS, J. [1819] (1977), "Ode on a Grecian Urn," *The Complete Poems*, Harmondsworth, Penguin.

LECLERC, D. (1992), *The Crisis of Abstraction in Canada: The 1950s*, Ottawa, National Gallery of Canada.

LEMARDELEY, M.-C. and TOPIA, A. (2007), "Préface," in M.-C. LEMARDELEY and A. TOPIA, *L'empreinte des choses*, Paris, Presses Sorbonne Nouvelle.

LEPALUDIER, L. (2004), *L'objet et le récit de fiction*, Rennes, Presses universitaires de Rennes.

NEWMAN, B. [1948] (1990), "The Object and the Image," in *Barnett Newman: Selected Writings and Interviews*, New York, Alfred A. Knopf.

RICHARDS, T. (1993), *The Imperial Archive: Knowledge and the Fantasy of Empire*, London, Verso.

SMITHSON, R. (1996), *Robert Smithson: The Collected Writings*, Berkeley, Los Angeles, London, University of California Press.

URQUHART, J. (1982), *False Shuffles*, Victoria, Toronto, Porcépic.

– (1983), "Museum," in *The Little Flowers of Madame de Montespan*, in (2000), *Some Other Garden*, Toronto, McClelland & Stewart.

– (1990), *Changing Heaven*, Toronto, McClelland & Stewart.

– (1997), *The Underpainter*, Toronto, McClelland & Stewart.

– (2005), *A Map of Glass*, London, Bloomsbury.

WILLIAMS, T. [1945] (1962), *The Glass Menagerie*, in *The Glass Menagerie, A Streetcar Named Desire and Other Plays*, Harmondsworth, Penguin.

13

A Biography of Stones: Mourning and Mutability in Jane Urquhart's *A Map of Glass* and Michael Redhill's *Consolation*

Pilar CUDER-DOMÍNGUEZ

University of Huelva

A poet, short story writer, and novelist, Jane Urquhart is well known for her "soaring lyrical style" (Ferri 32). *A Map of Glass* (2005), her sixth novel, consolidates some of her most recurrent concerns, namely the multifarious ways of seeing and of representing past and present in art. By now it has become a commonplace of Urquhart criticism to say that she is a masterful writer of the Ontario landscapes, and that in her fiction, the landscape is "articulate with stories" (Compton 135). Yet, those landscapes are cut down to human size by virtue of the human eye that takes them in, and imbued with meaning by the human lives that unfold among them, often experiencing much hardship. In looking at the Prince Edward County lands where she lives, the protagonist of *A Map of Glass* ponders that "The old settlers [...] had left behind nothing but a statement of labour, nothing but *a biography of stones*" (*Map* 37, my italics). In this image Urquhart has concisely brought together the human being and the land in a momentous symbiosis. The term "biography" conveys the notions of life story as well as of human history, while the fact that it is built on stones rather than on words signals the imprint humankind makes on the land they inhabit. In addition, the fact that a biography is written at all hints at the memorability of the settlers' presence, or at the very least, at the tension between time's erasure of all things and beings and people's conscious efforts to fight its effects by remembering.

The essential mutability of the world and of human life has worried artists of all times, but it was probably best expressed by the English Romantic poets, as in William Wordsworth's sonnet "Mutability," describing how "the tower sublime of yesterday [...] could not even sustain [...] the unimaginable touch of Time" (Feldman and Robinson

131, lines 10-14). Much the same spirit pervades John Keats's celebrated "Ode on a Grecian Urn," that is explicitly quoted in Urquhart's novel: "And, little town, thy streets for evermore/Will silent be," murmurs Malcolm in an odd moment of communion with his estranged wife Sylvia (*Map* 88). In these poets, mutability is intrinsically connected to feelings of loss and therefore to mourning over what is gone forever, whether it be something tangible or intangible, a house, a person or a smell. Mourning over the departure of a loved one is at the heart of the main plot in *A Map of Glass*. It also featured prominently in Urquhart's previous novel *The Stone Carvers*, in which Klara Becker's loved ones kept disappearing on her, whether due to wanderlust (Tilman), war (Eamon), or old age and death (Joseph Becker).

Interestingly, Urquhart's novels are not the only ones engaging with the interrelated concepts of mourning and mutability in Canadian writing of the last few years. Published only one year after *A Map of Glass* but apparently written over a much longer period,[1] Michael Redhill's second novel, *Consolation* (2006), displays striking commonalities in subject matter, plot, narrative structure and underlying sensibility. Both novels construct two time frames and narratives, one set in the 19th century, another one in our present time (the late 20th and early 21st centuries). Both feature the death of remarkable men mourned by lovers or family who, in their grief, try to understand these lost ones better by considering the lessons on history and the land that their lives imparted. A consolation of sorts is achieved through the interaction between the dead man's lover and a young man with only a peripheral relation to him. Finally, in both novels there are fictional intertexts recreating the 19th century. As we will see, mourning and mutability are explored through the narrative dynamics of the confession and intertextuality in order to offer complex accounts of humankind's relation to their habitat, although this habitat is a rural one in Urquhart's novel and urban in Redhill's.

Mourning

The two novels open with the poignant accounts of the death of a man that for a while remains unnamed. Andrew Woodman, who suffers from Alzheimer's, dies an accidental death as, disoriented, he makes his way on foot to Timber Island, which he dimly remembers as the land of his forebears, and his body is slowly covered by a blanket of snow (*Map* 1-5). On the contrary, David Hollis chooses the time and place of his own death. After two years of suffering Lou Gehrig's disease, he

---

[1] Redhill's acknowledgements at the end of the novel mention that the book was written in Toronto between 1999 and 2006.

decides to take his own life by jumping off the ferry going to the Toronto Islands (*Consolation* 1-4). In both cases, bodily decay brought about by a degenerative disease is the prelude to death as well as its explanation.[2] What's more, the landscape is an integral part of the death itself, even to the point of providing the weapon: cold and snow in one, water in the other. Quite literally, these men encounter "death by landscape," evoking Margaret Atwood's short story in the collection *Wilderness Tips* (1991).

Overwhelmed by grief over their sudden loss, the life partners of the two men undergo a breakdown that drives them away from their home and families. Sylvia Bradley is a doctor's wife in a small town in Prince Edward County, whose life has been shaped by an undiagnosed "condition" that might be Asperger's syndrome or another form of autism. Her social skills have remained underdeveloped, and she is easily upset by any change of routine. Her life to this point has been one of complete stasis and repetition. Conversing with her only friend Julia, she explains that she likes "to count on things being the same way they were the last time [she] saw them," feeling that the world is just too crowded, too full of people rearranging things, touching each other, making changes" (*Map* 70).

Sylvia finds comfort in stability and permanence. Yet she has apparently maintained a secret affair with Andrew Woodman for many years. Her husband Malcolm, to whom she confessed the affair on learning of Andrew's death, believes this is quite impossible for a woman whom he has always thought of as "disabled," and that the affair has always been an imaginary one (*Map* 354). Many segments of third person omniscient narration (such as the next off-set quotation) indicate that the intimate relationship did exist, but readers may wonder whether they should believe Sylvia or Malcolm. Asked whether there was ever a condition, Sylvia replies that "there is always a condition" (*Map* 359), that is, perception is so subjective that the very notion of normality is, at best, an approximate construction. When her blind friend Julia asks "how do you know for certain [...] that what you see is what other sighted people see," Sylvia replies that she does not know for certain and she never has (*Map* 315).

Grief, however, upsets her world to such an extent that she decides to travel to Toronto and search for the man who discovered Andrew's body. She embarks on a conscious attempt to (re-)remember him, because "she was losing the shape of his face, the look of his legs and

---

[2]   Alzheimer's is a form of dementia involving progressive memory loss and language breakdown. Lou Gehrig's is a neuromuscular disease that brings on increasing paralysis.

arms and hands, the way his body occupied a chair" (*Map* 38), and this is a final act of disappearance that she is not capable of accepting after enduring those caused by the ravages of his disease:

> There were few words between them by then, and no laughter. His silences were huge, mystical almost, and, to her mind, full of portent. Everything about him, even when they were inches apart, suggested disappearance. When she said that she loved him, he appeared to be confused by the phrase, then embarrassed, then fearful – a man locked in a room with a stranger who was being inappropriately intimate. She loved him harder then for everything that they had said and done together. [...] For everything she knew they were, again, going to lose. (*Map* 55)

Sylvia's breaking away from all that feels safe and familiar to her is a brave struggle against the very forgetfulness and oblivion that destroyed her lover. In Toronto she finds Jerome McNaughton, a young up-and-coming artist who happened to find Andrew's body during a residency in Timber Island. He is less than welcoming to this strange middle-aged woman who wants to talk to him about a man he never met except as a frozen corpse "with a sad and puzzled expression on the face" (*Map* 60). Yet, he cannot refuse Sylvia's request, and so he becomes the somewhat unwilling recipient of her confession. The act of talking about Andrew and their relationship is completely unprecedented for Sylvia. Silence has always been an act of resistance against any upsetting circumstances, whether casual probing from strangers or insistent questions from her husband. Talking to Jerome becomes, first of all, a liberation and a way to cope with her grief. Secondly, it allows her to act as Andrew's biographer and to memorialise his life and his history:

> "I am now, you see, his memory." She sat forward in her chair. "Andrew thought he was the history that his forebears created, he felt responsible for that history, I think, and for those people. They are my responsibility now." (*Map* 75)

The theme of making a memorial for someone's death, which had notably shaped Urquhart's *The Stone Carvers*, runs through this section of the novel in recurrent intertextual references to the English nursery rhyme "Who killed Cock Robin," which, in the form of questions and answers, lists how animals feel such grief over his passing that they all offer to help in his funeral, whether it is by digging a grave, carrying the coffin, or singing a psalm. In the end, "all the birds of the air fell a-sighing and a-sobbing,/When they heard the bell toll for poor Cock Robin." Similarly, all of Sylvia's world (and perhaps, one can assume, all the landscape of rural Ontario he comes from) is rocked by grief over the loss of him who meant so much.

Like Sylvia, Marianne Hollis in Michael Redhill's *Consolation* has had a safe, rooted life. She met her husband when she was a student and he was a teacher at the University of Toronto in the early 1960s; they married and raised two children together. Well into middle age, Marianne's carefully constructed world suddenly breaks down when her husband is diagnosed with Lou Gehrig's disease and she becomes a powerless witness to his increasing bodily decay. Later she regrets having treated her husband too protectively in his final months. During an argument, David had challenged this excessive care:

> "You do not get to tell me how to spend my time on earth," he said. [...] If you're planning on ditching me at home with nothing but a television and a pill-holder to mark the time, then you're damn well right I'll be making my own fun." (*Consolation* 149)

His suicide, and the fact that he did not choose to share either the decision or its actual execution with her after so many years of living together, feels to Marianne like a betrayal, and she is unable to cope with her grief. Like Sylvia, she then leaves her safe environment, holing up in a hotel room in downtown Toronto for months, surrounding herself with her husband's writings and books, without giving her two children any explanation of what she is doing or why. Too angry or too overwhelmed by grief themselves, Marianne's two daughters fail to reach out to her, but she starts receiving visits from her older daughter's fiancé, a young man called John Lewis. It is on him that she vents much of her anger and grief, eventually opening up and confessing her feelings of inadequacy and guilt.

Although the young men in the two novels are relatively external to the traumatic deaths at their heart (one a mere passer-by, the other not yet a full family member), their role in triggering and receiving the women's confessions is essential, as it brings about a much needed catharsis. For the young men themselves, the dialogues with Sylvia and Marianne also have liberating side-effects, helping them face their own traumas. After years of living with his partner Mira, Jerome McNaughton in *A Map of Glass* is still unable to talk to hereabout the dysfunctional family he grew up in. However, after Sylvia's visits, Jerome finally feels up to telling Mira about his traumatized childhood. He also discloses the extent to which he resents his father's addiction, which erased his family's past:

> "There was never any past for her," he said. "It was all eaten away by my father's addiction, which was so huge a part of her life that everything else paled in comparison. She never told me about the farm where she grew up, she never told me who her people were, where they had immigrated from, why we were sort of Catholics, why she had called me Jerome. There were some old dishes around for a while that she said had belonged to her

grandmother, but he destroyed them [...] he destroyed them on purpose. I think he broke them to smash up her past, to shatter anything that didn't relate specifically to him. There were no photo albums, no pictures of anything at all." (*Map* 362)

Therefore, Jerome is Sylvia's perfect balancing opposite. He lacks a past while she has too much of it. He has lived in constant change and transience, whereas she keeps in her head the full records of her family's and her county's history. As an artist, Jerome records metamorphosis and change. He made a reputation with his first installation, "Fence Line Series," which featured fence lines and black and white photographs in which he tried to represent "the solid knowledge of the mutability of a world that came into being and then dissolved around him before he was able to fully grasp what it was trying to be, what it had been" (*Map* 17). On Timber Island he was working on a second project related to his fascination with winter landscapes, and particularly the traces he found on the snow: "How wonderful the snow was; every change of direction, each whim, even the compulsion of hunger was marked on its surface, like memory, for a brief season" (*Map* 23). Here the snow is like a blank paper, a surface that can be written on and then erased, very much as Austin Fraser does with his canvases in Urquhart's earlier novel *The Underpainter*. The whiteness hides signs under its surface, and so it is a kind of palimpsest as well, since one can make out the underlying structures if one pays attention.

John Lewis in *Consolation* is also haunted by his own ghosts. Like Jerome, his early life has been touched by impermanence, and he is in search of stability and rootedness. He lost his parents at a young age and was raised by an aunt to whom he does not feel a deep attachment. While Jerome is still exploring artistic forms, John successfully completed a degree in accountancy only to decide that he did not like it. He now works as a part-time research assistant to a playwright suffering from writer's block, a job that pays little but that affords him a lot of freedom. His relationship with Bridget Hollis granted him a new family: "An unexpected boon to be loved, after a childhood of dutiful care under his Aunt Cecilia's roof. Her family had done their best to enfold him in their lives, but he was an only child with dead parents, a cursed child, and he knew he was a raw wound in their home. He'd never dreamed of another family" (*Consolation* 147). This newly acquired stability came to an end with the news of David Hollis's terminal disease and his suicide. He lost then "the only true father of his life" (*Consolation* 147), and like the other members of the family he is still in mourning. Deeply hidden under this surface of suffering is his guilt at the part he secretly played in David's suicide, for he drove him to the ferry on that fateful morning. As in the case of Jerome and Sylvia, it is only through conversation with Marianne that John eventually manages to find the strength to make that important revelation and to face his own anger and grief.

Consequently, both narrative pieces are built on strong dialogical structures. The interlocutors have been defined in terms of oppositional features that allow Urquhart and Redhill to confront stability and change, playing stasis and aimless drifting against each other. Conversation becomes the vehicle to negotiate a balance between opposites that necessarily feed one other, and thus to bring to the surface the powerful interaction of past and present, human beings and landscape. Dialogue is also the key to overcoming grief's paralyzing effects, as the speakers ultimately find the strength to put their trauma into words. Thus, the contemporary plots in these two novels display the traits of confessional discourse, not understood as admitting to past crimes (although there is some occasional guilt involved), but rather as a true account of the self as, in Foucault's terms, it involves a deep self-examination "that yields, through a multitude of fleeting impressions, the basic certainties of consciousness" (Foucault 60).

Mutability

Human reaction towards mutability is a pervasive topic in *A Map of Glass* and *Consolation*. Both novelists have stressed the passage of time through case studies of its effects. These are twofold, as its traces can be detected on the landscape (rural or urban) as well as on human beings. Connecting both sets of evidence is the concept of decay, that can be used productively for one as for the other. In turn, decay is the term most clearly associated with the dead men, Andrew Woodman and David Hollis, due to the terminal diseases they suffer from. As described above, Andrew's deterioration due to Alzheimer's slowly becomes evident to his lover, just as she starts noticing the progressive decline of the cottage they use for their trysts:

> "It wasn't until then," Sylvia told him, "that I fully realized that not only had the inside of the cottage deteriorated but the gate that I remembered at the top of the lane was gone altogether and the cows were gone as well. What had been pasture was now scrub bush, almost impassable except for one narrow, winding path. The surviving orchard trees were choked and twisted and the view was visible only in certain empty spots. I barely knew where I was." (*Map* 341)

The cottage and its surrounding land is deployed by Urquhart as an objective correlative that transmits the successive "disappearing acts" and the increasing neglect and confusion within Andrew's formerly bright mind, as Alzheimer's symptoms spread. Thus, his final disappearance is suggested by the cottage being covered by snow, "the last vestiges of the old house were finally being folded into the white landscape" (*Map* 346). Snow, as pointed out above, also becomes Andrew's tomb, and its whiteness suggests silence and oblivion, even while retaining within it the traces of former life. Urquhart reinforces the symbolic strength of the palimpsest with recurrent allusions, both in the contemporary plot and in the intertext, to the Woodman family hotel that lies buried under sand dunes.

It seems oddly fair that Andrew should "die by landscape" after having been a historical geographer, "a man whose profession allowed him to explore not only geological phenomena but also the traces of human activity that were left behind on the textured surface of the earth" (68), as Sylvia puts it. Unlike her husband Malcolm, Andrew was a man who had a gift for seeing beyond surfaces. He appreciated Sylvia's mind and connected with her despite her "condition" just as he managed to see the past as a landscape held in the present. From the landscape, he conjured up "unobserved histories" (*Map* 104) that he defined as "a physical memory" (*Map* 103). In a way, he made change seem much more bearable for someone like Sylvia, for he constructed permanence out of what was in continual flux. As Sylvia worriedly muses over the tactile map she is making for her friend Julia: "Landscapes are unreliable [...] Landscapes are subject to change" (*Map* 46), Andrew's lessons also provide consolation for loss, since he made the point that everyone always leaves a mark on the landscape they inhabit (*Map* 326). Therefore, absence and presence should not be regarded as true opposites. Instead, they are conflated in just one unbroken line of presences, that is, human history.

Michael Redhill's novel also carefully records the ravages of Lou Gehrig's disease on David Hollis. Increasing paralysis affects all aspects of his life, making the easiest and most quotidian actions a feat of sheer will and patience:

> These days, his body felt both light and deaden at the same time: his muscles had wasted, but despite the loss of body mass he still felt like he was carting around an increasingly inert weight. He'd learned, in the past eight months, to balance momentum with muscle control: he could get himself moving and then continue by using the natural forces of walking or turning. His arms had become pendulums. [...] Gripping was one of the chief problems: he could not hold a fork anymore, and to stir a cup of tea he had to put his shoulder into it and transfer the rotation down his arm and into his hand. (*Consolation* 43)

The painful progress of the terminal disease, that turns each living day into a slow agony, is symbolically portrayed in the image of a dying sparrow whose "hollow chest suddenly expanded in panic" (*Consolation*

310). John notices it on the pavement near Toronto City Hall, and returning that way later, he spots it still in agony, "its eye roving round and it spread its clawed feet and gaped silently. How could something be this nearly dead for – what was it? – half an hour, and in all that time it hadn't worked out this simple thing, this dying" (*Consolation* 316-317). Unable to stand as passive witness to it suffering, John helps it die just as he had done with David, and then, racked by guilt, "his eyes stinging, [he] vomited onto the clean surface of the white plaza" (*Consolation* 317).

Toronto's cityscape is indeed David's last sight, and he is as intimately tied to it as Andrew himself is to the countryside of Timber Island and Prince Edward County. Unlike Alzheimer's, however, David's disease does not affect his mind, so he stays lucid and cogent, imparting his lessons until the very end. He created his own field, "forensic geology," combining "landforms with sleuthing" (*Consolation* 10). He would take his students on trips to local fields, caves, abandoned cemeteries, neglected heritage houses, and so on. Like Andrew, he too believes that the city is full of submerged stories: "There is a vast part of this city with mouths buried in it, John. Mouths capable of speaking to us. But we stop them up with concrete and build over them and whatever it is they wanted to say gets whispered down empty alleys and turns into wind" (*Consolation* 263).

After being diagnosed with Lou Gehrig's disease, David worked obsessively on a monograph, published shortly before his death and received with scepticism and derision by academics. In it, he claimed to have discovered the diary of an Englishman that had photographed the whole city of Toronto in 1856.[3] Travelling back to Toronto with the original plates, his steamship had foundered in Lake Ontario. David believed that the ship still lay buried underneath downtown Toronto, since part of the city had been constructed on landfill, and he had even triangulated its possible location. After David's death, his widow Marianne chose a room in a hotel that overlooked the construction site of a sports arena, over which she kept constant watch. For Marianne, if the ship was uncovered during the foundation dig, her husband's theories and with them, his academic prestige and his whole life, would be vindicated. As a result, like the interred hotel in *A Map of Glass*, here the ship buried under the city becomes a powerful symbol conveying the permanence of the past within the present, while the city itself becomes a palimpsest, endlessly erasing and rewriting its own core self. As John

---

[3] Redhill has revealed to *The Toronto Star* that he was inspired by his discovery (in a book entitled *Lost Toronto*) of a series of thirteen photographs of Toronto taken in 1856 (Peverell 2008).

reminds his fiancée: "This whole place erases itself every day, it kills itself, Bridget [...] do you understand? It gets wiped clean like a hotel room" (*Consolation* 436). Yet, as the novel's title hints, Redhill concurs with Urquhart in that the permanence of history and the conscious effort at holding on to memory can bring consolation for those grieving at a loss.

Both writers' most scathing critiques are reserved for those uninterested in learning the lessons of the past. David's lesson was, in Marianne's words, that "neglect of the past is a form of despair" (*Consolation* 173). Even though the outline of the steamship is identified by sonar, it is never recovered due to the greed of the city authorities, who decide to proceed and pour in the cement for the foundations of the new building. A sympathetic journalist wonders:

"I don't know why heritage is such a hard sell here," said Lowinger. "It just is."

"You know what David said?" The reporter waited. "No one wants to hear the story of a whore's childhood." (*Consolation* 446)

It was just such greed that caused Andrew's family's hotel to be buried by sand in *A Map of Glass*. The soil was depleted when the farmers stopped rotating their crops, trying to get rich by growing only barley for the American market (*Map* 249).

Through the figures of Andrew Woodman and David Hollis, the two novelists stress the connections between history and space, and meditate on decay, concerning both its impact on landscape and on the human body. Nevertheless, these multifarious links are also powerfully conveyed through the juxtaposition of the framing text conveying the contemporary plot and an embedded text that delves into the buried 19th century past. In *A Map of Glass*, the intertext is clearly identified as a separate section entitled "The Bog Commissioners," which lies within the frame story just as the past is contained within the present, and the human being within a landscape. It is a long family memoir written by Andrew, salvaged by Sylvia from the decrepit cottage, and passed on to Jerome, who reads it along with Mira with an occasional comment. Andrew describes the arrival in Canada of his ancestor Joseph Woodman, an English engineer who worked for some time in Ireland. He bought a little island in the area where Lake Ontario and the St. Lawrence River meet, and became involved in the brisk trade of timber sent upriver for export to Britain. Andrew's multi-generational narrative enhances many of the main motifs of the framing story. Thus, for instance, the father-son conflict between Joseph and Branwell mirrors Jerome's troubled memories of his own father. Though not an alcoholic, Joseph too, is bent on destruction, and his family suffers: his wife languishes while she dreams of far-away England, his homebound daughter dreams of escape, and his son would like to pursue a career as a painter but is forced to help out in the family business, for which he has neither the inclination nor the talent. Art is another major topic, for both Branwell and his sister Annabelle are landscape painters. Branwell goes on to make a living later as a painter of *trompe l'oeil* murals, while Anabelle produces endless renditions of the ships passing by her island:

> Annabelle had been left behind in the silent, empty house. This echoing, vacant region, she had concluded, was to be her territory, her prison. She would bang up against its walls as long as she breathed while, mere steps from her window, all those wonderful cathedral-like ships moved soundlessly, like floating works of art, away from the shore. It is sometimes difficult to believe in Annabelle's fondness for all the schooners and sloops and privateers that were moored at the docks of Timber Island, or which cut through the waves of the lake, or whose sails dipped and flashed on the horizon, and yet, despite all the paintings she made of the demise of such vessels, she couldn't help but be affected by their beauty. (*Map* 174)

Characters can mark the passing of time by their sightings of ships in both directions. In time, the sailboats are replaced by steamships, and later their traffic stops altogether with the demise of the timber trade. Indeed, their absence is received with a sense of loss quite as deep as grief over a human death (*Map* 254). Yet the most tragic feeling in this section is certainly associated with the thoughtless exploitation of the land and its cruel effects. The lumber industry leads to the area's deforestation, just as failure to rotate the crops depletes the soil. As discussed above, Andrew's family memoir attests to the changes brought about by greed, as well as to the decline of a whole way of living, and in fact, the end of a whole era. As Branach-Kallas has pointed out for Urquhart's earlier novels, this novel suggests that:

> [J]ust as the past should not be forgotten nature must not be destroyed, because both nature and the past represent essential elements of a holistic vision of the world. Only when alive the past and nature can help individuals define themselves as autonomous and sane human beings in the chaos of the modern world. (Branach-Kallas 66)

Consolation also makes use of an intertext describing 19th century society, but it is placed in alternative chapters and its origin is unclear. Readers may at first believe that this is the Englishman's diary found by David Hollis in a library, but towards the end of the novel it is revealed that John himself penned this recreation of Toronto, inspired by David's life work. Rather than a multi-generational story, it describes the hard beginnings in Toronto of J.G. Hallam, a young London apothecary who has left behind a wife and two young daughters. Thus, the novel shifts from the late 1990s to the mid-1850s and back again, connecting both periods and amplifying their resonating concerns. Jem Hallam is adrift in a new world whose rules he fails to understand. Charged by his father with the task of opening another shop like the ones they already have in Camden Town, Hallam finds that Toronto is too small a settlement to provide him with a living, particularly since there are already several shops like his and competition is fierce. Like John himself, Hallam is undergoing a deep crisis, cut loose from the old and safe rules. An accidental meeting with an Irish photographer, Sam Ennis, and an English widow, Claudia Rowe, puts him on a new career path. As he establishes a new set of relationships and learns a new trade, Hallam ends up reinventing himself.

The city of Toronto itself is an important factor in this reinvention. At times disgusted by its roughness, by its provincialism, Hallam's sense of his emerging new self strongly relies on his appropriation of this new space. Walking its many streets and paths, he experiences the city's globality. And yet, by virtue of his new trade in photography, he is not only a walker, but also a *voyeur* in Michel de Certeau's sense (de Certeau 92-3). His photographer's eye produces an imaginary totalization of the city space, making it readable by means of the series of photos, taken from the tallest building in town, that David Hollis became so obsessed with.

Rather than the linear time of the multi-generational story in *A Map of Glass*, Redhill's novel highlights the excavation of the past, the layers of history as they lie physically underneath the current inhabitants. While linear time goes forward and back, "up and down was organic, it was growth and decay, it was time as experienced by vegetation. It was history itself" (*Consolation* 175). The organic quality of this historical time is emphasised by references to parts of the city having been built on debris and garbage: "All through the end of the previous century, they'd trucked soil and stone and unwanted building materials down past Front Street and dumped it into the lake, and the city had pushed forward onto it, as if it were walking onto a bridge as it was being built" (*Consolation* 261). This organic dimension of urban growth belies strict separations of nature and artifice and once more suggests their interrelatedness. While the contemporary plots set out to convey a "hermeneutics of the self" (Tell 1), as Foucault would have it, the embedded texts in *A Map of Glass* and *Consolation* contribute to the heteroglossia of the novels, enlarging the already substantial cross-referential network of the framing narratives. They open up ever newer interactions between people, spaces, and chronologies, and encompass a wide range of voices and stories that lie interred in the rural and urban landscapes of Ontario.

References

ATWOOD, M. (1991), *Wilderness Tips*, London, Bloomsbury.

BRANACH-KALLAS, A. (2003), *In the Whirlpool of the Past: Memory, Intertextuality and History in the Fiction of Jane Urquhart*, Torun, Wydawnictwo Uniwersytetu Mikolaja Kopernika.

CERTEAU de, M. (1984), *The Practice of Everyday Life*, Trans. Steven Rendall, Berkeley, U. of California P.

COMPTON, A. (2005), "Romancing the Landscape," *Jane Urquhart: Essays on Her Works*, Ed. L. FERRI, Toronto, Guernica, 115-143.

FELDMAN, P. and ROBINSON, D. Eds. (2003), *A century of Poems: The Romantic Era Revival 1750-1850*, Oxford, Oxford University Press.

FERRI, L. Ed. (2005), *Jane Urquhart: Essays on Her Works*, Toronto, Guernica.

FOUCAULT, M. (1990), *The History of Sexuality, Vol. 1: An Introduction*, Trans. Robert Hurley, New York, Vintage.

PEVERE, G., "Old Photos Inspire 'One Book' Michael Redhill's Consolation" http://www.thestar.com/entertainment/Books/article/299870. The Toronto Star, Feb 03, 2008. (Accessed 26 April 2009).

REDHILL, M. (2006), *Consolation*, Toronto, Anchor Canada.

TELL, D. "Michel Foucault and the Politics of Confession" Paper presented at the annual meeting of the NCA 93rd Annual Convention, TBA, Chicago, IL. Nov 15, 2007. Online <PDF>. (Accessed 25 April 2009). http://www.allacademic.com/meta/p187824_index.html>

URQUHART, J. (1997), *The Underpainter*, Toronto, McClelland & Stewart.

– [2001] (2003), *The Stone Carvers*, Harmondsworth, Penguin.

– (2005), *A Map of Glass*, Toronto, McClelland & Stewart.

– , "A Conversation with Jane Urquhart," Interview conducted by Laura Ferri, *Jane Urquhart: Essays on Her Works*, Ed. L. FERRI, Toronto, Guernica, 115-141.

14

The Persistence of Facts

A Discussion with Jane Urquhart[1]

This discussion with Jane Urquhart took place at the University of Orléans on 17 May 2008 at the outcome of a panel devoted to her work organized by Marta Dvořák and Christine Lorre, hosted by Héliane Daziron-Ventura within the framework of the 48th Congress of the Association of French University Professors of English which she organized. Jane Urquhart attended the panel, consisting of two papers which were subsequently fleshed out and included in this volume: a joint paper by French academics Catherine Lanone and Claire Omhovère entitled "Mourning/Mocking Browning: The Resurgence of a Romantic Aesthetics in Jane Urquhart's *The Whirlpool*," and Marta Dvořák's paper entitled "When the Underpainting Shows Through: Jane Urquhart's Resurgent Transmutations." The ensuing discussion between Jane Urquhart and the panel participants and public, in which her husband, artist Tony Urquhart, also intervened, was triggered by the writer's response to the analyses of her work.

Jane Urquhart:

I was intrigued when I listened to those wonderful papers. Both of them were just fascinating for me. Since the subject of them is myself, and my work, my interest, of course, increased. (laughs) I am a bit startled to be reminded how much of my work is inspired by facts, how it has had its source – in some way or another – in reality. Let's take for example the brooch made out of human hair which I describe in *The Whirlpool* and which the first paper brought to our attention.[2] It is actually one of our household heirlooms – the person that should be up here talking to you about that brooch is my husband, because that particular piece came from his family. It was made for his great-grandmother from the hair of his great-grandfather, Michael Kick, after

---

[1]   The editors are grateful to Marc Morlat, who originally transcribed the discussion from audio tapes. The transcription was subsequently edited with the help of contributors C. Omhovère and C. Lanone to whom the editors are also particularly grateful. The papers to which the discussion recurrently alludes are included in this volume.

[2]   See C. Lanone & C. Omhovère's contribution at the beginning of Part I in this volume.

the latter's death. It is exactly as described in the book: there is a little willow tree, there is a little tomb on which the initials of the deceased appear. An entire landscape made from human hair! It is really quite an amazing little work of art in itself. Almost everything described here today has its roots somewhere in the real world, bizarre as those roots may be.

I'll leave the path to questions. Someone always has to ask the first question….

Catherine Lanone:

How interesting that you should say that almost everything has its roots somewhere in the real world. Does this apply to spiders too, those spiders Claire Omhovère and I referred to in our paper which the character Maud in *The Whirlpool* is never supposed to kill?

JU:

At the time I was writing *The Whirlpool* I was interested in how the upper class people of Victorian England became amateur naturalists, how that obsession rampaged through 19th century. Spiders interested me in particular because – this is again rooted in fact – in my family's summer house on Loughbreeze Beach, the place where I have spent every summer of my life since I was a child, there were and are an enormous number of spiders, inside and out. I do a lot of writing at that location and while I was writing *The Whirlpool* I was looking at spiders a lot, watching what they did. I was fascinated by how persistent they were – I suppose this is something – the only thing – I share with Robert the Bruce, in his Scottish caves: every time he took the web down it would reappear the next morning, as legend has it. So, yes, the spiders are rooted in fact in the sense that the spiders were catching my attention at the time when I was writing. But the amateur naturalist craze that was so popular in Victorian Britain fascinated me as well. In order for many of those naturalists, or amateur naturalists, to be able to collect the things that they were looking for, they also had to kill them. Apparently, at one point, there was such an interest in tide pools in England that the ecology of tide pools was being destroyed by the very naturalists who were collecting specimens from them. The person who explained this to me felt that the tide pools had never fully recovered from the great number of Victorians who went to the beaches and basically destroyed the very things that they loved. This process fascinated me.

Question from the audience:

I am intrigued by your use of the documentary. Reading your fiction, one often has the impression that the emphasis you put on facts is also a way for you of stimulating your readers' imagination and encouraging them to bring into the picture whatever is missing.

JU:

In Canada, in particular, this use of historical facts as an inspiration for fiction has been very important. Unlike the United States, since we were, and still are part of the British Commonwealth, we don't really have an official history. Therefore in school, people of my age studied British history and US history – we didn't study Canadian history. Those countries were referred to by students of my era as Mother England and Father USA. We Canadians do not have rigid or permanently set way of looking at ourselves, which in fact creates two things. First of all, it allows fiction to flourish, I think, allows it to enter the country's narrative in a very free way because there is no official history to run up against. At the same time, once that entrance has been made, the writers of fiction are permitted to explore an unofficial history which involves varying points of view. This is terribly important in our country, because we have so many different settlers from so many different parts of the world. I believe that a settler is a person who is either the *descendant* of someone who arrived, in the sixteenth, seventeenth, eighteenth, nineteenth and even early 20th century, and also someone who is a new Canadian, arriving as recently as two weeks ago. There are an enormous number of points of view contained in this settlement and these can be, and are, I believe, being explored at this time. In terms of stimulating the imagination I agree with you that attention to visual reality can make the world more resonant in several ways. When suddenly the object becomes more than the object, for example. When this bottle of water becomes the bottle of water that was on the table when Marta Dvořák gave her paper, it has a story, it is no longer just a bottle of water.

I remember coming to an understanding of this when I began to write seriously... poetry initially. Part of the reason why this realisation occurred was that, because I was at home with two stepchildren and a baby, and often four stepchildren and a baby, everyone, or almost everyone, would leave me alone in the morning when they departed for school. The table in the kitchen would be a complete mess after breakfast, and of course it was my job to clean it up. I started to realise that every single one of the objects I put away or washed was pregnant with meaning: you could follow the hand that held the glass right back through its history. It was that realization that made me want to take my writing more seriously.

Claire Omhovère:

You belong to this rare category of writers who are read and appreciated by a wide spectrum of readers. One does not need to have a university degree to buy a book by Jane Urquhart.

JU:

Thankfully, that's why I am able to travel.

CO:

Do you write with a particular audience in mind?

JU:

No. But I do feel that writing is a collaborative act. Or at least, once you have finished writing, it becomes an act of collaboration between the reader and the writer, with each reader reading a different book. In Canada we really were starved for books that in any way reflected our own lives, whatever form those lives might have taken. So that I find that I have readers who will read my books simply because they speak of home. I was interested in your mentioning my use of the names of places in *The Stone Carvers*, Marta.[3] For Canadians it is a new and very important experience to see the name of their village or their street mentioned in a book. One word will bring a flock of Canadian readers to a book of mine simply because they never before experienced that wonderful feeling of having your life made larger by the fact that someone else is telling a story about some aspect of it. If the name of one's village appears in a story written and then disseminated elsewhere, if it comes from outside back in, the people in that village will all suddenly want to be readers. I had no idea that was the case before I began to write my novels, and of course I do not consciously put in names of villages. If I did put in names, I'd put the names of major cities, because everybody knows the names of major cities, while some place like Castleton, Ontario, Canada has, at the moment, a population of only two hundred souls, I think. I found it interesting that people who were not necessarily readers were reading my books because of known landscapes, known places.

That is also true in a historical sense, as we can see with something like the Vimy monument which Marta brought up in her discussion of *The Stone Carvers*. I received so many letters about that book, because as children we Canadians had been taught the history of the British Empire, rather than Canada specifically, and no one, apart from novelists such as Timothy and certain academic historians, had written about Canada's participation in the First World War. Those of my

---

[3]   See M. Dvořák's contribution at the beginning of Part II in this volume.

generation were truly not taught about our participation in the First World War, though, of course, we knew the Canadians had gone overseas to participate. Now whether one approves of war or disapproves of war, it's a fact that everyone close to me had grandparents or great-grandparents or at least knew someone who had parents or great-grandparents who had experienced that terrible world war first hand.

Even more moving, I had a number of letters from newer Canadians to say thank you for telling us about the past. Some claimed that they had been trying to find something about the history of this country ever since they arrived and no one would tell them: perhaps because of that lack of education I spoke about. So newer Canadians from a number of different cultures had entered that world through the novel, as well, and in fact, in many cases, had gone to Vimy Ridge to see the memorial and the battlefields. So, while I am extremely gratified by any intellectual attention to my work, I think that it is magical when someone who otherwise might not have become connected to the world of literature does so as a result of some details that they find in my work that are meaningful to them.

Question from the audience:

What you said about people recognizing themselves in your characters made me think of Margaret Laurence for whom this also mattered. Have you been influenced by the writings of Margaret Laurence?

JU:

She was a generation or two ahead of me, and so she would have been doing her work in a world that would have had even less context of a literary nature for the people who were alive and reading at that point. But, yes, Margaret Laurence's writing was extremely important to me and to other Canadian women writers, and to Canadian writers more generally, if only because there were so few women writers at the time. Writers like Margaret Laurence operated as a kind of mother for those of us who were women, in particular, because they gave us permission in a sense, perhaps quite literally. When I was growing up in the Canada of my childhood, it was considered laughable to aspire to be a writer. People would really laugh at you if you said you wanted to be a writer: it was like saying you wanted to be a movie star: it was not even considered to be possible. So the fact that women like Margaret Laurence – or, earlier, like Lucy Maud Montgomery, – existed, was tremendously important to me and also to other women writers that I know living in Canada. They inspired us with their work, and gave us courage with the example of their lives. Personally, I responded to Laurence's books, which I read as a teenager, because they were concerned with landscapes and characters defined by landscapes; they unfolded in a world that I recognized. Added to this, of course, was the fact that she was a wonderful writer.

Question from the audience:

I understood that your grandmother has inspired some of your characters. She appears in your poetry and in some of your fiction where she is linked to the past and the objects that haunt your characters. Would you like to comment on your recurrent use of this motif?

JU:

My grandmother's name was Fleda, and she does come to light in my work: once in a short story called "Forbidden Dances," which was based on a story that my grandmother had told me about her own girlhood, and later, when I used her name for the main character in *The Whirlpool*. My grandmother – a wonderful woman – was already dead when I used this material, so that gave me another form of freedom.[4] Once the person who has inspired you is dead, you feel more comfortable about altering the narrative. Otherwise, not surprisingly, you get objections when you stray from the factual truth. I therefore pushed the story, "Forbidden Dances" a little further than I would have, had my grandmother still been alive. What's perhaps more interesting is the fact that – and, once again, you should probably be asking my husband this question – *his* grandmother was the first person to enter my work[5] even though I had never met her. Her name was Mamie Morse, and she was indeed a woman who owned and managed a funeral parlour in Niagara Falls, and she did indeed keep a record of the bodies that were fished out of the Niagara River by a man called Red Hill. (Red Hill is referred to as the Old River Man in *The Whirlpool*.) She was in a sense my introduction to narrative in that my first narrative poems were about her. I suppose this was because Tony-- you remember I mentioned my stepchildren, – each night Tony was telling his children stories about people like the Old River Man pulling bodies out of the river, pleasant bedtime stories, you'll agree. The stories, of course, made reference to the hair brooch and to Tony, himself, at a much younger age: in school, or at university.

---

[4] See the story called "Forbidden Dances" in Jane Urquhart, *Storm Glass*, Erin, Ontario, The Porcupine' Quill, 1987. This story has been analyzed by the late Simone Vauthier in "The Mirror and the Window: Jane Urquhart's 'Forbidden Dances'," Cross/Cultures (47), *Telling Stories: Postcolonial Short Fiction in English*, Rodopi, 2002. The editors would like to draw attention to the outstanding quality of this analysis, and pay homage to a most revered pioneer in the field of Canadian Criticism in France.

[5] Notably *The Whirlpool*.

Tony, was it in high school that you wrote your little essay called "Granny's little floater book"?

Tony Urquhart:

No, I discovered my grandmother's book a bit later than that. It was a little black book with incredible descriptions in it, so incredible that I, a visual artist, could not make any drawings out of them. So I did little essays.

JU:

And I found the essays and said, "where is this wonderful book?" Tony's brother then sent it to us. It was really quite remarkable, because it was a very practical listing of what was left of someone who had gone over Niagara Falls, or drowned in the Niagara River. In some cases all that remained was a leg or an arm. I seem to remember that one of the pages described an arm that the Old River Man had found in the whirlpool. Astonishingly, on that arm there was a tattoo. Tony's grandmother had drawn the tattoo in her little notebook, because the purpose of this book was to enable the relatives of disappeared members of the family to identify the bodies of their loved ones, which had been buried very quickly. We won't ask for the technical details.

TU:

The one that first got my attention, the first time, was a very careful description of fingernails. I don't remember if the nails were those of a man or a woman, but, listed under the fingernails, she wrote that they were those of a working man. She then went on to detail what kind of shoes the person was wearing, the colour of his shirt, his tie. This kind of description went on and on for a whole page, and then it ended with the words... "head missing".

JU:

So you can see that that would be enough to make somebody want to start to write fiction. At approximately the same time I came across a diary by Julia Cruikshank, who was married to the founder of the Ontario historical society. The wonderful fact about fiction is that you can do whatever you want as long as you can make the reader believe in some way that what you are doing is true, in some definition of truth, perhaps emotional truth. So I was able to bring those two women together (Tony's grandmother and Julia Cruikshank), even though, in fact, Tony's grandmother kept her record of the bodies from the river much later than the 1880s in which *The Whirlpool* is set. Even Julia Cruikshank's diary was written a couple of decades after the 1880s. It was the inclusion of Robert Browning that determined when the book should be set. Actually, I did not know that I was writing a novel. That's another act of freedom. When you don't know that you are writing a novel you can do whatever you want, because you know that you are not writing a novel and that novel that you are not writing will never be published, and therefore you are very very free.

Marta Dvořák:

You do know, now, that you are writing a novel.

JU:

Unfortunately, not knowing you are writing a novel is only a one-time experience, because after the novel you are not writing does get published, you have to confess that, yes, indeed, you have written a novel. I have tried to be as relaxed about the experience as I can, however, because by the time you get to the second, third, fourth and fifth novel there are certain expectations circulating in the real world, and I think that it is necessary to ignore these expectations in order to get on with the work. I am lucky in that I have an editor and a publisher who don't put any demands on me in that regard. I am not forced to finish anything by a particular date, and nobody suggests that I repeat the subjects of my previous books. If they had been of that mind, I think they would probably have encouraged me to write *Away* over and over again. But that hasn't happened, and I am very fortunate in that I can allow my imagination to take me wherever it wants to go.

Question from the audience:

You emphasized the freedom of the fiction writer, but on the other hand, you also stressed that you always start from something tangible, something historical, a document or an object. This reminded me of "re-memory," a concept that Toni Morrison uses. She may also start from a rag rhythm, or something fished out of the river, and then she uses her imagination to bring it back to life. Would this be similar to your own experience of creation?

JU:

Yes, very similar. Something that catches my attention will be the starting point. Sometimes it is a piece of architecture, as happened in *The Stone Carvers*-- When something does catch my attention, it can, of course, cease to catch my attention, so I have to be sure it deserves to be pursued. The only way that I can know this is if I become semi-obsessed by the thing that has caught my attention. This is what happened with the Vimy memorial. At the same time I became intrigued by the history of a very large church in Canada that had been built by a German priest, or had been imagined and then brought into being by an itinerant

German priest in the mid 19th century. I knew there had to be a connection between those two works of architecture, otherwise they would not both be obsessing me at the same time. I needed to write *The Stone Carvers* in order to discover what the connection was. Either that or I should be hospitalised in a psychiatric institution – I suppose it is not *that* crazy, but it is almost that crazy. But I like that notion of how one is sometimes caught by something in the perceived world. Afterwards, one just has to let the narrative unfold before one, because one cannot really force these things. I cannot, anyway-- if I try to control it, it slips out of my hand, so… I don't try.

MD:

So when did you find out that it was the mad Bavarian king Ludwig who had financed that church?

JU:

Oh, that was part of my interest, of course. I found out about that very early on. I discovered a little pamphlet in the local library, in Stratford, Ontario, where I live. By pamphlet, I mean something like a chapbook. This one was a publication on the history of a Canadian village called Formosa, and I began to read it just out of curiosity. I read a letter sent by the Ludwig Mission to the priest who was trying to build the church in what was then essentially the wilderness. The letter said that Ludwig himself was quite interested in the location of the church and that he wanted to know more about the wilderness in which it might be situated. He eventually sent money for the building of the church. Everyone says that Canadian history is boring, but it's not. I changed the name of the village from Formosa to Shoneval, however, because I realised that the name Formosa carried with it too many other connotations. The reason why the priest had called the village Formosa was because it meant, in the Latin sense, beautiful, so I changed it to something else which meant "beautiful valley," in German.

MD:

Yes, you chose to call it Shoneval, which in German signifies a beautiful place in an analogous way. Thank you ever so much, Jane, for generously sharing your views and providing us with this informal and immensely stimulating discussion.

Notes on Contributors

Barbara Bruce completed her Ph.D. at the University of Western Ontario in 2007. She teaches in the English and Film Studies departments at Carleton University in Ottawa, Canada. She has published on the trope of collection in works by John Richardson and Thomas King and has an article forthcoming on race in George Romero's *Night of the Living Dead*. Her current research focuses on representations of disaster in Canadian and American literature and film.

Georgiana M. M. Colvile is Professor Emeritus in Anglo-American Studies at the University of Tours, France, and in French Literature, Film and Language, as well as Comparative Literature at the University of Colorado, Boulder, USA. She has published a dozen books and over a hundred articles in her three main fields of research: a) Modern and Avant-garde French Literature, with emphasis on Surrealism and women's contribution to that movement; b) Film (mainly French, American and Irish); and c) Contemporary North American Literature, mainly both English Canadian and Québécois women's writing. In the Canadian field she is the editor of *Contemporary Women Writing in Canada and Quebec*, Lewiston/Queenston/Lampeter, The Edwin Mellen Press, 1996, and the author of numerous articles and book chapters in French and English, on writers such as Sheila Watson, Anne Hébert, Mavis Gallant, Margaret Atwood, Alice Munro, Audrey Thomas, Carol Shields, Francine Noël, Madeleine Monette, Aritha van Herk and Jane Urqhhart. Georgiana Colvile has also given many lectures and conference papers, as well as taught seminars on both sides of the Atlantic, on Canlit and Québécois women's fiction.

Pilar Cuder-Domínguez is Associate Professor at the University of Huelva (Spain), where she teaches British and English-Canadian Literature. Her research interests are the intersections of gender, genre, nation, and race. She is the author of *Margaret Atwood: A Beginner's Guide* (2003), and the (co)editor of five collections of essays (*La mujer del texto al contexto*, 1996; *Exilios femeninos*, 2000; *Sederi XI*, 2002; *Espacios de Género*, 2005; and *The Female Wits*, 2006). She has been visiting scholar at universities in Canada, the US and the UK: McGill (1997), Dalhousie (1999), Northwestern (2002), Toronto (2004 & 2007), and Cambridge (2006). Her latest publications have discussed the works of writers of Black and Asian ancestry in the UK and Canada.

Héliane Daziron-Ventura is Professor of Contemporary Literature in English at the University of Orléans where she directed the research group "Intertrad" from 2003 to 2007, organizing research around the concept of cultural transfer. She directed the Center for Canadian Studies at the University of Strasbourg from 1990 to 1998. She has published a monograph on Atwood's *The Handmaid's Tale* and co-directed eight volumes of essays on Canadian literature. She has published mainly on Alice Munro but also on Kroetsch, Findley, Hodgins, Lemire Tostevin, Brand, Shields, Robinson, Watson or A.S. Byatt and Elizabeth Spencer. Her research interests are focused on the relationship between words and images, the resurgence of myths from Antiquity, and more particularly on theoretical close readings of the contemporary short story in the English speaking world. She has been awarded a Visiting Fellowship at the Institute for Advanced Studies in the Humanities at the University of Edinburgh for the first semester of 2010 in order to carry out research on Transatlantic Relationships, working on the filiation between James Hogg's ballads and memoirs and Alice Munro's short stories.

Marta Dvořák is Professor of Canadian and Commonwealth Literatures at the Sorbonne Nouvelle, Former Associate Editor of *The International Journal of Canadian Studies*, and Editor of *Commonwealth Essays and Studies*. Focussing her research on cross-culturalism via rhetoric and narratology, she has authored and edited numerous books on Canadian writers from Margaret Atwood to Nancy Huston. These include *Ernest Buckler: Rediscovery and Reassessment* (Wilfrid Laurier UP, 2001) and *Carol Shields and the Extra-Ordinary* (co-ed. Manina Jones, McGill-Queen's UP, 2007). She has contributed chapters to *The Literary History of Canada* (Cambridge UP), *The Cambridge Companion to Canadian Literature*, *The Cambridge Companion to Margaret Atwood*, and *The History of Canadian Literature: English-Canadian and French-Canadian* (Camden House, 2009). Her most recent books, *The Faces of Carnival in Anita Desai's* In Custody (PU de France 2008) and *Tropes and Territories: Short Fiction, Postcolonial Readings, and Canadian Writings in Context* (co-ed. with W.H. New, McGill-Queen's UP, 2007) investigate the concomitant spaces of territory and writing, and study writing and reading practices across cultural divides. Visiting Fellow at Jawaharlal Nehru University's Institute of Advanced Study (2009-2010), she has been working on a critical edition of Buckler's *The Mountain and The Valley* and has co-edited a book with Diana Brydon (*Crosstalk: Canadian and Global Imaginaries in Dialogue*, Wilfrid Laurier UP, 2010).

Marlene Goldman is an Associate Professor at the University of Toronto where she teaches Canadian literature. She is the author of

Paths of Desire (1997) and *Rewriting Apocalypse in Canadian Fiction* (2005). Her most recent book *DisPossession: Haunting in Canadian Fiction* is under consideration by McGill-Queen's Press. Recently, she co-edited three special issues of *The University of Toronto Quarterly* on "Models of Mind and Consciousness," "Ethics and Canadian Literature," and "Haunting in Canadian Culture." She has also published numerous scholarly articles on Canadian writers such as Dionne Brand, Timothy Findley, Thomas King, Joy Kogawa, Daphne Marlatt, Alice Munro, Michael Ondaatje, Jane Urquhart, and Aritha van Herk.

Neta Gordon is Associate Professor at Brock University, where she teaches Canadian literature and literary theory. Her work on such authors as Ann-Marie MacDonald, Barbara Gowdy, Sky Lee and Jane Urquhart has been published in such journals as *Studies in Canadian Literature, Canadian Literature, Descant, Narrative*, and the *Canadian Review of American Studies.*

Catherine Lanone is Professor at the University of Toulouse II. She has written a book on E.M. Forster and a book on Emily Brontë, and articles on 19th and 20th century British literature. She is currently working on representations of the Arctic in British and Canadian literature, including Jane Urquhart's *Changing Heaven.*

Georges Letissier, Professor of Victorian and Contemporary British fiction at the University of Nantes (France), has published on neo-Victorian writings (Ackroyd, Byatt, Gray, Swift and Urquhart) and on Victorian literature (Brontë, Dickens, Eliot, Rossetti). His main field of study is rewriting, or "second degree" fiction writing.

Christine Lorre is Senior lecturer in the English Department at Université Sorbonne Nouvelle. After a doctorate on Canadian fiction, she expanded her area of research to fiction from the United States, New Zealand, Australia, and India. Her publications include a co-edited book entitled *Comment comparer le Canada avec les États-Unis aujourd'hui : enjeux et pratiques* (Presses Sorbonne Nouvelle, 2009), book chapters on Nancy Huston, Carol Shields, Janet Frame, and Ying Chen, and journal articles in *Commonwealth Essays and Studies* and *Revue française d'études américaines*. In 2007, she was Visiting Scholar at the Stout Research Centre for New Zealand Studies.

Claire Omhovère is Professor of English and Commonwealth Literature at University Paul Valéry Montpellier 3 (France). She has published articles in French and Canadian journals and contributed book chapters on the novels of Robert Kroetsch, Aritha van Herk, Thomas Wharton, Rudy Wiebe and Jane Urquhart (notably in *Tropes and Territories*, McGill-Queens UP, 2007; *History, Literature, and the Writing of the Canadian Prairies*, U. of Manitoba Press, 2005). She is the author of *Sensing Space: The Poetics of Geography in Contemporary English-Canadian Fiction* (PIE Peter Lang, 2007). She is currently engaged in a research project on representations of the void in Canadian literature and iconography.

Ian Rae received a Ph.D. in English Literature from the University of British Columbia in 2002. He held postdoctoral fellowships at McGill University until 2005 and then joined the North American Studies Program at the University of Bonn, Germany, as Visiting Assistant Professor. In 2006, he returned to McGill as Visiting Assistant Professor and as the Acting Program Director of the Institute for the Study of Canada. He is currently Assistant Professor in the Department of Modern Languages at King's University College at the University of Western Ontario. Rae is a specialist in Canadian literature and he published *From Cohen to Carson: The Poet's Novel in Canada* in 2008 (McGill-Queen's University Press). He is presently writing a monograph on Anne Carson, as well as papers on Al Purdy, Alice Munro, and the creative economy in Canada.

Karis Shearer teaches Canadian literature at McGill University, where she is a SSHRC postdoctoral fellow. She completed her Ph.D. in 2008 at The University of Western Ontario and is currently working on an edition of correspondence between Canadian poet Louis Dudek and the American modernist Ezra Pound, and a book manuscript titled "Postmodern Cultural Workers and the Canadian long poem."

"Canadian Studies" Series titles

No.21 – Héliane DAZIRON-VENTURA & Marta DVOŘÁK (eds.), *Resurgence in Jane Urquhart's Œuvre*, 2010, ISBN 978-90-5201-634-4

No.20 – Pierre ANCTIL, André LOISELLE & Christopher ROLFE (eds./dir.), *Canada Exposed / Le Canada à découvert*, 2009, ISBN 978-90-5201-548-4

No.19 – Gunilla FLORBY, Mark SHACKLETON & Katri SUHONEN (eds.), *Canada: Images of a Post/National Society*, 2009, ISBN 978-90-5201-485-2

No.18 – André MAGORD, *The Quest for Autonomy in Acadia*, 2009, ISBN 978-90-5201-476-0

No.17 – Carmen CONCILIO & Richard J. LANE (eds.), *Image Technologies in Canadian Literature. Narrative, Film, and Photography*, 2009, ISBN 978-90-5201-474-6

No.16 – John-Erik FOSSUM, Johanne POIRIER & Paul MAGNETTE (eds.), *The Ties that Bind. Accommodating Diversity in Canada and the European Union*, 2009, ISBN 978-90-5201-475-3

N° 15 – Pascale VISART DE BOCARMÉ & Pierre PETIT (dir./eds.), *Le « Canada inuit ». Pour une approche réflexive de la recherche anthropologique autochtone / "Inuit Canada". Reflexive Approaches to Native Anthropological Research*, 2008, ISBN 978-90-5201-427-2

N° 14 – Serge JAUMAIN et Nathalie LEMARCHAND (dir.), *Vivre en banlieue. Une comparaison France/Canada*, 2008, ISBN 978-90-5201-415-9

N° 13 – Nick NOVAKOWSKI & Rémy TREMBLAY (eds.), *Perspectives on Ottawa's High-tech Sector*, 2007, ISBN 978-90-5201-370-1

N° 12 – Jean-François DE RAYMOND, *Diplomates écrivains du Canada. Des voix nouvelles*, 2007, ISBN 978-90-5201-346-6

N° 11 – Claire OMHOVÈRE, *Sensing Space. The Poetics of Geography in Contemporary English-Canadian Writing*, 2007, ISBN 978-90-5201-053-3

N° 10 – Caroline ZÉAU, *L'Office national du film et le cinéma canadien (1939-2003). Éloge de la frugalité*, 2006, ISBN 978-90-5201-338-1

N° 9 – Serge JAUMAIN et Paul-André LINTEAU (dir.), *Vivre en ville. Bruxelles et Montréal (XIXᵉ-XXᵉ siècles)*, 2006, ISBN 978-90-5201-334-3

N° 8 – Madeleine FRÉDÉRIC et Serge JAUMAIN (dir.), *Regards croisés sur l'histoire et la littérature acadiennes*, 2006, ISBN 978-90-5201-333-6

N° 7 – Pierre ANCTIL & Zilá BERND (eds./dir.), *Canada from the Outside In. New Trends in Canadian Studies / Le Canada vu d'ailleurs. Nouvelles tendances en études canadiennes*, 2006, ISBN 978-90-5201-041-0

N° 6 – Anne MORELLI et José GOTOVITCH (dir.), *Contester dans un pays prospère. L'extrême gauche en Belgique et au Canada*, 2007, ISBN 978-90-5201-309-1

N° 5 – Britta OLINDER (ed.), *Literary Environments. Canada and the Old World*, 2006, ISBN 978-90-5201-296-4

N° 4 – Madeleine FRÉDÉRIC, *Polyptyque québécois. Découvrir le roman contemporain (1945-2001)*, 2005, ISBN 978-90-5201-096-0

N° 3 – André MAGORD (dir.), *Adaptation et innovation. Expériences acadiennes contemporaines*, 2006, ISBN 978-90-5201-072-4

N° 2 – Robert C. THOMSEN and Nanette L. HALE (eds.), *Canadian Environments. Essays in Culture, Politics and History*, 2005, ISBN 978-90-5201-295-7

N° 1 – Serge JAUMAIN & Éric REMACLE (dir.), *Mémoire de guerre et construction de la paix. Mentalités et choix politiques. Belgique – Europe – Canada*, 2006, ISBN 978-90-5201-266-7

Discover the general website of the Peter Lang publishing group
Visitez le groupe éditorial Peter Lang sur son site Internet commun

www.peterlang.com